FOR I HAVE SINNED

For I Have Sinned

THE RISE AND FALL OF CATHOLIC
CONFESSION IN AMERICA

James M. O'Toole

HARVARD UNIVERSITY PRESS

*Cambridge, Massachusetts,
and London, England*

2025

First printing

Publication of this book has been supported through the generous provisions
of the Maurice and Lula Bradley Smith Memorial Fund.

Library of Congress Cataloging-in-Publication Data

Names: O'Toole, James M., 1950– author.

Title: For I have sinned : the rise and fall of Catholic confession in
America / James M. O'Toole.

Description: Cambridge, Massachusetts ; London, England : Harvard
University Press, 2025. | Includes bibliographical references and index.

Identifiers: LCCN 2024018115 | ISBN 9780674294523 (cloth)

Subjects: LCSH: Catholic Church—United States—History. |
Confession—Catholic Church—History. | Catholics—Religious
life—United States—History. | Child sexual abuse by clergy—United
States—History.

Classification: LCC BX2263.U6 O86 2025 | DDC 282/.73—dc23/eng/20240513

LC record available at https://lccn.loc.gov/2024018115

For Paul Ginnetty

Think where man's glory most begins and ends,
And say my glory was I had such friends.

— W. B. YEATS

structural issues — not chronological, skips around in time + place

little contextual information about the US + its regions

Contents

FOR I HAVE SINNED

Introduction

THE CHURCH ALWAYS SEEMED different when the boy went to
confession. To begin with, most of the lights were off, a shad-
owy contrast to the brightness of Sunday mornings. A soli-
tary red sanctuary lamp flickered in a corner, and just inside
the altar rail there were several racks of small votive candles,
only about half of them lit at any one time. The natural light
of the afternoon sun came through the stained glass windows
from outside, and he could stare at the radiant scenes, imagin-
ing himself in the stories they depicted: the adolescent Jesus
instructing the astonished elders in the Temple, the hesitant
Peter sinking into the sea while Jesus stood serenely on the
waves, extending his hand. The smells of Sunday were gone,
too, the pungent incense and the sweetness of flowers having
grown faint after a week's time. Now, his nose detected only
the varnish that made the wooden pews shine, particularly on
the ends, each one topped by an ornate carved fleur-de-lis.
Above all, the place was quiet. No matter how many people,
young and old, were there—as few as a dozen, as many as
fifty—they all kept silent, absorbed in their own thoughts and
averting their eyes from one another. It was a curious sensa-
tion: somehow, he was alone in public.

He took his place in a pew on a side aisle, kneeling to say
some silent prayers. Periodically, he would get up and move

to the pew ahead of him once that one had been vacated by its previous occupant, everyone successively inching closer to the small enclosure, like an oversize box, that stood out from the side wall. There was a door in the middle of it, and on either side an open archway, covered by a curtain, into which the waiting parishioners would disappear, one after another, reemerging a few minutes later. By the time he got to the head of the line, the boy's random thoughts had begun to focus. He had decided—rehearsed, really—what he was going to say to the priest who, he knew, occupied the center compartment. Just as important, he had decided what he was not going to say. When it came his turn, he walked purposefully, went in behind the curtain, and knelt down. He could hear the little click of the electrical switch in the kneeling pad that turned on the light above his entryway outside, alerting others to his presence so they would not burst in unexpectedly. He waited in silence, aware of indistinct murmurs as the priest talked with the person in the opposite stall. He knew he was not supposed to make out what they were saying, and he was seldom tempted to try, more concerned with last thoughts of what was about to happen. Then, at once, the wooden panel covering the window that separated him from the priest slid open, sometimes with a soft bang. The window was covered with an opaque plastic shield, making it possible for him and the priest to hear but not to see one another. They were both in darkness.

The boy began by crossing himself and reciting the words he had first learned in the second grade: "Bless me, Father, for I have sinned. It has been two weeks since my last confession, and these are my sins." Then he launched into his brief catalog, specifying the things he had done wrong and the number of times, according to his best recollection, he had done each of them. They were pretty much the same from month to month, year to year. He didn't snitch money from his mother's pocketbook, and he mostly followed his father's good example in not cursing, but there were always squabbles with siblings and schoolmates to report. Over time, he had developed some lawyerly skills, consolidating a number of miscellaneous offenses into the single category of disobedience. His reasoning, he thought, was ironclad. His parents may not have known that he was doing these things, but they would have forbidden them if they had; this constituted a form of implicit disobedience. Better to confess that than to recount potentially more graphic details. When he had finished his list, again following the formula, he concluded by saying that he was sorry "for these and all the sins of my past life." The priest might then ask a clarifying question or two—the boy's later memory was that this did not happen very often—and he would usually give a word of advice or encouragement to do better in the future. After that, the priest assigned what was called a penance, a kind of punishment, far from onerous but necessary for forgiveness to be complete. Finally, as the boy recited aloud the prayer known as the Act of Contrition, the priest whispered the words of absolution in hasty, mumbled Latin, which the boy could not really hear and would not have understood if he could. He also vaguely discerned the priest's silhouette making the sign of the cross in his general direction. With that, it was over. The slide closed again, and the boy went back outside, his place taken by the next person who had been waiting, setting off another chain reaction in the pews.

Not looking around, he walked up to the altar rail at the front of the church, knelt there, and silently performed his penance. Usually this consisted of some combination of the fundamental Catholic prayers, the Our Father and the Hail Mary, repeated for perhaps three to five times each, depending on the priest's instructions. If he had a dime in his pocket, he might slip it into the slot and then light one of the votive candles; there was always a little thrill that came from this permissible playing with fire. Then he was done. He went back outside to wait for those others in the family who had come along that day. They did not speak about what they had just done, simply going home to Saturday night supper. But without dwelling on the idea or even quite understanding how, they nevertheless believed that something important had just happened to them, that they were different now from what they had been earlier in the day, that they were reconciled with God in spite of their human failings. It was a remarkable thing.

It was also a completely common and ordinary thing. This particular scene may have played out in one place and time (Saint Leo's Church in Leominster, Massachusetts; the late 1950s and early 1960s), but it was replicated millions of times by American Catholics—and those of other nations too, of course—in the nineteenth and twentieth centuries. From the time they were small children and extending through adulthood, Catholics made this ritual of confession as much a part of their religious practice as going to Mass. Known officially as the sacrament of Penance, it was one of the seven central rites of Catholicism, and it was one that they could repeat as often as they wanted to. A person could be baptized, confirmed, ordained, or married only once. But, like receiving the Eucharist and being anointed when ill, Penance was something they could do again and again, and confession thus became both regular and frequent. Even those who did not think of themselves as exceptionally devout might confess ten or a dozen times a year, and many made a particular point of doing so before special occasions like Christmas and Easter, or even their birthday. If we measure a religion by the faithfulness with which its adherents practice it, by what they actually do with the beliefs they profess, confession stands at the center of what it meant to be an American Catholic.

Going to confession was a distinguishing marker for Catholics amid the diversity of churches and denominations in America. It was something they did which their Protestant and other non-Catholic neighbors did not do. The Protestant reformers of the sixteenth century had abolished confession (reluctantly, in Luther's case), thinking it ungrounded in authentic Christian tradition and too prone to misinterpretation and misuse, but Catholics insisted on its importance. They did not particularly like to do it. They were grateful that at least it was done privately, but the anonymity of the process never fully dispelled either the lingering fear that the priest might recognize a voice or the simple embarrassment of having to declare their failings aloud to another person. But these difficulties came to be seen as essential to the whole business. The believer could derive a redoubled spiritual benefit from the sacrament precisely because it was difficult. "But, sir," a rigorous Catholic serviceman once told a Jesuit chaplain (who years later recounted the episode to me), "religion ought to be hard." For many Catholics, almost nothing about their religion was harder than going to confession. That they submitted themselves to it as a matter of course confirmed the sense that theirs was a demanding but ultimately redeeming faith.

More important, because it concentrated such attention on personal behavior, on the easily identifiable and just as easily describable things that individuals had done (or not done when they should have), confession reinforced in Catholics a clear moral vision. When their conduct was not what it should have been, going to confession demanded that they own up. It required candid reflection on their own thoughts and actions. However fully or perfunctorily they may have done this, they were admitting that they had fallen short of ideals they otherwise embraced—sometimes by a little, sometimes by a lot. Either way, they knew that there were standards against which they ought to measure themselves. Theirs was a world of well-defined right and wrong, a world in which they could not duck their responsibility, make excuses, or blame someone or something else. Their faults were *their* faults. Yes, a few cases might be difficult and complicated, but these could be resolved, and an authoritative source was available from the church to settle any doubts. The littlest of things, the most ordinary of actions, the habits born of inattention or laziness, were all freighted with significance. At almost any hour of the day they might face moral choices, and if they made the wrong choice the consequences could be serious indeed—in the afterlife if not in this one. Confession was designed to get them to acknowledge what they had done, to accept the consequences, to try to do better, and finally to let them know that God himself had forgiven them. Not a bad exchange, in the end.

As with many other practices of their church, American Catholics, no less than Catholics in other parts of the world, thought that this sacrament existed somehow outside of time, that the pardoning of sins had always been accomplished in this way. But, as with church architecture, music, and even belief itself, confession had a history, one marked by change as well as continuity. In ancient times, it had been a public event, fully exposing the wrongs that had been committed and requiring the sinner to be temporarily separated from the rest of the community. Private confession took hold in Europe centuries later, and the practice came to America with the first missionaries, who hoped to instill regular religious habits in their parishioners, including the habit of going to confession. For their part, sincere laypeople wanted to be able to fulfill the obligations their religion placed on them. But at first, the church infrastructure needed to make this possible, everywhere present in the Old World, was lacking in the New World. Of necessity, early circuit-riding

American priests sometimes said Mass in private homes in scattered settlements, and they often heard confessions in the open air, standing with each individual apart from the crowd. Only slowly were they able to build up the institutions that would make routine churchgoing possible. By the time of the Civil War, the structures (physical and otherwise) of church life had emerged in many places, and by the beginning of the twentieth century, particularly in dense urban neighborhoods, churches with confessional boxes inside them filled the landscape. Stricter standards of practice could now be presented as ideals to which even the most average parishioner might aspire. Monthly confession was not too high an expectation, pastors insisted, and Catholics—by no means all of them, but many of them—responded. Priests could now report sitting in their confessional boxes for hours at a time every week, anonymously encountering a steady stream of sinning people.

Sin lay at the heart of it all, and the church had an elaborate system for classifying sins. There was original sin, and there were actual sins; there were mortal sins and venial sins; there were sins of omission and sins of commission; there were even occasions of sin, not offenses in themselves but circumstances that might well lead the unwary into sin. The church taught these categories to Catholics at an early age, and lay people learned to speak this language almost as fluently as the clergy. It gave them the words to talk about their sins in confession, and they did so in impressive numbers. In the pages that follow, for example, we will meet a priest who noted in his diary that, on one occasion, he heard seventy-one confessions at a single sitting, a tally he characterized as "few"; another time, 169 was only "a fair number." Such a pace was not uncommon as parishioners learned the proper form of the sacrament and increasingly put it into practice. Their personal experiences of the encounter were varied, depending on their age, sex, social condition, and other factors. Some of them found comfort, just as the church intended; after all, the burden of their sins had been lifted. Others had an unhappier time of it, with the priest scolding them or questioning them too closely. Still others merely went through the motions. Even so, virtually all of them appreciated that nothing they said in confession could ever be revealed, and that they did not have to look their priest in the eye (or he them) as they were going about it.

And then, with a speed that may fairly be described as breathtaking, confession all but disappeared in the last quarter of the twentieth century. The hundreds who had once lined up for confession in their local church, especially on Saturday afternoons and evenings, dwindled to a mere handful. Even those who identified themselves as active, faithful members of the church went to confession seldom or never. Many causes contributed to this collapse. Some Catholics seemed suddenly to notice that the things they confessed were often trivial, that they continued to confess as adults the little sins of childhood. Others began to question some of the church's doctrines and to make their own decisions about right and wrong. Married couples in particular increasingly doubted the church's clearly articulated (and re-articulated) teaching on the sinfulness of contraception. More generally, a spreading acceptance of the concepts of modern psychology challenged the idea that sins were freely chosen, that Catholics could always unambiguously know what to do and that, when they deliberately decided to do the wrong thing, they had to accept the consequences. Was human behavior really that simple? At the same time, the church itself began to talk about sin in new ways, with less emphasis on individual actions and more on broader collective or social sins. To be sure, children who lied were still committing a sin, and so were adults who cheated on their taxes or their spouse. But weren't racism, sexism, and unjust economic structures sinful, too? In fact, weren't these more serious sins? Such insights represented a sophisticated kind of moral and ethical thinking, but how could individual Catholics recognize and regret their own personal share in these larger and more intractable wrongs? The failings for which they were now urged to seek forgiveness no longer fit into the traditional sacramental practice. Confession as they had done it for years came to seem inadequate to the task, and they voted with their feet, feet that did not take them to confession very often any more.

Throughout its history, one dimension of confession in America had remained hidden from public knowledge, but a flood of revelations has now brought it into the bright light. This is the role that confession played in the sexual abuse of minors and adults by Catholic priests, abuse that had been going on for a very long time, even if most parishioners were unaware of it. The extent of the problem began to emerge in the last decades of the twentieth century, and it was unavoidable by the early years of the twenty-first. Its full impact is still being played out. While abuse is always and everywhere horrific, there was something particularly loathsome when confession became its own occasion for this sin. Abusive priests took advantage of the personal intimacy of the encounter and the power of their role in confession to identify victims in advance. Worse, some of them even used the confessional itself as a site of their crimes. The potential for misuse of the sacrament had always been present; that this potential had been realized so often and so widely helped mitigate any regret that the practice, so long established, had become rare.

The historian writing about all this faces many obstacles. Confession is a private, entirely oral transaction between two individuals, the priest (the confessor) and the parishioner (the penitent). All direct evidence of the content of any confession vanishes with the sound of the spoken words, leaving no records of the kind that historians normally study when investigating the past. Thus, there are many things we cannot know about confession; many of our questions simply cannot be answered. What did penitents actually say to the priest? What did he say to them? What offenses were common, and what punishments did he assign for them? How did he decide on penances? What broader counseling was sought, and what was given? The seal of confession barred the priest from speaking later about anything he had heard and, so far as we can tell, priests scrupulously adhered to this requirement, even under pressure. Penitents themselves of course had every reason not to talk about their own confessions. They did not have to tell their family or friends what they had said in the box, and they did not have to worry about what the priest might think of them when they encountered him in another setting. Given this confidentiality, it would seem impossible to reconstruct what confession was really like and what it meant for generations of Catholics.

Still, a start can be made by looking at apparently mundane church sources. Aggregate statistics of the confessions heard in local parishes survive in some places, and a few—alas, only a few—priests kept their own counts. Such statistics can be viewed comparatively, helping to gauge varying rates of confession in parishes with different ethnic populations. Revealing, too, is information about the times that churches regularly set aside for hearing confessions. Parish clergy had many duties, and they would not have sat in their confessional boxes for long hours if their parishioners were not coming. Confessional "supply," in other words, is a rough measure of confessional "demand."

Getting at the actual experiences of laypeople is particularly difficult, but we can learn something if we know where and how to look. Interviews by scholars and journalists are helpful, particularly in charting the decline of practice, and so are deliberately assembled survey data. The pages of Catholic newspapers and magazines reveal how penitents who were uncertain about their sins sought the advice of priestly experts, and we can study the answers to their questions as well. Instructional materials—not merely textbooks for school children, but also pamphlets and other publications designed as tools of continuing adult education—seem at first glance to present only an idealized picture of how confession was supposed to proceed. But between the lines, we can find what laypeople worried about as they tried to put into practice the requirements and rules of the church in which they claimed membership. Class lectures and texts for seminarians are also informative, allowing us to see how the clergy were prepared to perform this service for parishioners, how they were trained to convey the church's expectations to its members. By putting all these pieces (and others) together, we can begin to understand how confession helped shape the moral universe of Catholics, a moral vision that affected other Americans too.

Unfortunately, there are gaps in the story these sources tell. In particular, they do not shed light evenly on how American Catholics of different ethnic and racial groups experienced confession. For decades, the heartland of the American church was concentrated in the East and upper Midwest, and the attention of bishops, priests, and sisters was focused on the European immigrants and their descendants, who had been flooding into the country since the 1840s. The evidence of that work is reflected more fully here than work among populations of African American and Latino Catholics. Information about distinctive confessional concerns or practices, if any, among those groups is frustratingly rare; despite looking for it everywhere I could think of, not much turned up. Even church organizations and journals devoted to work among them had virtually nothing to say about the practice

of confession. Wherever possible, however, this book will
seek to clarify the issues particular to various communities of
parishioners—not only by ethnicity and race, but also by age,
gender, geography, and special circumstances.

Some readers may find all this familiar; some not. Catholics of a certain age will perhaps be reminded of their own
experiences of confession, and they may also recognize the
reasons why they stopped going. Other Catholics will wish
that the habit of regular confessing would return on a wide
scale, an eventuality that frankly seems unlikely. Younger
members of the church and those who identify themselves as
having been "raised Catholic" (with the implication that they
no longer define themselves as such) may remember the sacrament from their early religious education. But both groups
will acknowledge that their own recourse to confession was
always occasional at best and usually done at the insistence
of teachers or parents. As adults, they never made it part of
a personal religious identity, never submitted themselves to it
voluntarily. Non-Catholics, who have always been at least a
little curious about what went on in the dark private enclosure, may be surprised to discover here just how ordinary
confession was for so long. More broadly, they may come to
understand the thinking, the mental dispositions, that provided the foundation for the confessions of their Catholic
neighbors. While, for the most part, other faith traditions had
nothing like it, most traditions have had their own ways of
thinking about good and evil, about the problem of connecting belief on the one hand with the implications of belief on
the other, implications for how we should act in the world.

Sooner or later, moral and ethical dilemmas present themselves to everyone, regardless of religious affiliation or the
absence of it; how to address and to resolve such dilemmas is a
universal human problem. The ways in which American Catholics confronted those dilemmas in the past may prompt useful

reflections about the present. Confession did not decline, as a friend once jokingly suggested to me, because people are just better now than they used to be; no one does anything wrong anymore. He did not really believe this any more than I do. The Catholic practice of confession presents us with an opportunity to see how one community came to terms with the recognition that we are not always as good as we think we are or hope to be. Wrestling with that realization is a task for the present and future, but one that will be enlightened by understanding the past.

1

Habit

Saint Louis, Missouri, 1807. A new town, not quite fifty years old, and situated in an obvious place, near the spot where two great rivers meet. The surrounding territory, once home to Native peoples and then claimed by a succession of European empires, had now belonged to the United States for four years. Almost every institution of settled society—government, business, schools, churches—had to be created from scratch. Religious fervor was sweeping other parts of the country; upstate New York at the time was described as a "burned over district," with religious enthusiasm spreading as far and as fast as a wild prairie fire. But in Saint Louis, people seemed more intent on the things of this world than those of the next one. A French priest, hoping to bring some spiritual leaven to the rough and tumble, came up the Mississippi River from New Orleans to see what he could do. Father Joseph Dunand had fled the revolution in his native country and come to America, but he was not impressed with what he found. "Ignorance of religion was so general," he recalled later, that even those who had been baptized as children "scarcely recognized the name Catholic." Even worse, "debaucheries" were everywhere. The most serious of these in his estimation was dancing, a "corruption," he thought, introduced by "foreigners," by which he probably meant the

American settlers from the East who were crowding out the older French population from down river. He tried mightily to discourage such behavior (or worse), urging moral reformation, and he even got a little divine assistance in making his point. A violent lightning storm swept through one day, killing three animals at a stroke. Quickly reasoning that "nothing is more appropriate to give a vivid idea of the majesty of God than the clap of His thunder," Dunand drew the obvious lesson as he preached to an assembled group: God was "incensed at the sins which they committed on earth." The priest "pointed out the evil of their ways and the horror of the crimes by which they had provoked the wrath of this avenging God. This," he concluded on an oddly cheery note, "produced good effect." Soon, he found himself "overloaded with confessions." Not everyone got the message: there was one "hardened sinner who repulsed all my entreaties" to confess and another whom "nothing could move." But enough people confessed that he pleaded for a second priest from New Orleans to come and help him.[1]

NEW YORK CITY, 1897. A bustling metropolis, full of churches. The Catholic population had been swelling with new immigrants for decades, with little sign of slowing down. All over, new parishes were opening in an effort to keep up, and two of them were staffed by priests of the Jesuit order. The larger one was Saint Francis Xavier, downtown on West Sixteenth Street, and its companion, smaller but still busy, was Saint Ignatius, farther up on Park Avenue. Unlike the earlier Catholics of Missouri, the people in these congregations did not have to be scared into confession by thunder and lightning. Encouraged by their priests, they had developed the habit of confessing regularly. It was one of the distinctive practices, together with weekly Mass attendance and not eating meat on Fridays, that marked them as Catholics. With a discipline perhaps suitable for priests in a religious order that had been founded three hundred years before by a former soldier, the Jesuits in these parishes kept track of how many confessions they were hearing. Between July of 1896 and June of 1897 — perhaps they possessed the spirit of accountants as well, calculating on the fiscal year—the ten priests at Francis Xavier reported that they had heard 173,394 confessions; their seven confreres at Ignatius were less precise, rounding off their count to an even 78,000. There were, of course, not that many parishioners in these two churches, and not every parishioner confessed. But many of them (though names were never recorded) did so several times over the course of the year, and they were counted anew every time. Hearing confessions was at the heart of the ministry of these priests. At Francis Xavier that year, by contrast, there had been just seventy-two marriages, and at Ignatius 253 baptisms—not insubstantial figures, by any means, but dwarfed by the number of confessions.[2] Parishioners and pastors encountered one another, however anonymously, most often in the confessional.

One of the priests at Saint Ignatius was meticulous in recording what he was doing. Father Patrick Healy was in all respects an unusual man. His father was an Irish immigrant to Georgia; his mother was one of his father's slaves, who was also his common law wife. Educated in the North before the Civil War, Patrick joined the Jesuits in 1850. Light-skinned enough to "pass" as white, he went on to a remarkable career. From 1873 to 1882, he had served in the nation's capital as the president of Georgetown University, where he reformed the curriculum, expanded the student body, developed the law and medical schools, and rebuilt the campus. His academic career over, he spent the last thirty years of his life in parish work in Philadelphia, Providence, and New York City; once, he even accompanied a Coast Guard ship to Alaska.

By 1897, he was one of the priests regularly hearing confessions, and he kept his own running tally, probably by making a hashmark on a scrap of paper every time a parishioner
entered his confessional box. Later, he added up the number
every week, "brought forward" each sum into a monthly total
(accountancy again), and then in the pages of his diary he
computed his semiannual and annual "score." His share of
the 78,000 for 1896–1897 was 9,047, about 11 percent of the
parish total. The numbers might vary with the season. His
slow month was August, when he heard just 253 penitents,
but that was because he was on vacation with his brother in
Maine for two weeks. Busiest was October, when he counted
1,188. This level of activity came to seem normal to him. Saturday, May 30, 1896, for example, had been just another day:
seventy-three confessions during unspecified hours in the
afternoon, 102 more between 7:45 and 11:00 that night. A
couple of weeks later, on Thursday, June 11, he thought the
pace was "slack" because he heard "only 88." Another time,
seventy-one at a sitting counted as "few," and yet again 107
he considered "not numerous."[3] Whatever else Father Healy
did for the people of his parish in Manhattan, he was there to
listen to their confessions.

✠

MILWAUKEE, 1944. A CITY of neighborhoods, defined largely
by ethnicity. Like the other urban centers in what had become
the American Catholic heartland of the Northeast and upper
Midwest, its population of immigrants, mostly from Europe,
had been steadily on the rise, placing demands on their church
that never seemed to end. In particular, the desire of many
to hold onto their mother tongue had practical implications.
Parishes often had to be organized along ethnic and linguistic
lines so that Poles, for instance, could attend a Polish church,
even if they had to walk past the church of another ethnicity to

get there. Such a parish, regardless of the particular national-
ity, had many attractions. It could preserve traditional devotions that were meaningful to one group but not to another.
It often had a school in which the mother tongue was taught
to younger generations, though this was usually a losing battle, as children and grandchildren increasingly spoke English
at home as well as in public. Sermons in the vernacular language were likely to have more impact than those delivered
in English. But above all, it was in confession that language
mattered. This was the only ritual of the church that was not
conducted primarily in Latin, a language that was foreign to
everybody. And since confession might deal with personal,
intimate matters, it was crucial that priest and people be able
to understand one another in the verbal exchange; if they
could not, many Catholics would stay away from confession
out of frustration, as some surely did. Parishioners who spoke
only German—or French or Italian or whatever—wanted to
and needed to use that language in confession.

Reports that the pastors of these parishes filed annually
with their bishop's office give us a window into how the practice of confession varied from group to group. Priests were
usually only estimating the numbers they reported—none of
them counted as scrupulously as Patrick Healy did—but the
figures were probably not very far wrong. Milwaukee's Irish
and German Catholics were generally more regular than
some of their neighbors in seeking forgiveness of their sins.
In Irish parishes, where English was the common language,
large numbers of congregants were in the habit of going to
confession monthly. In 1944, about 40 percent of the 2,500
Irish parishioners of Saint Helen's were there every month
and, the pastor estimated, another 10 percent of them came
every week. German Catholics were similarly, or maybe even
more, consistent. At their Saint Augustine's Church on the
city's south side, also numbering 2,500 "souls," about 1,300

were identified as adhering to a monthly schedule; almost
400 came weekly. Polish parishioners, by contrast, were less
regular. At Saint Adalbert's, just over the city line in South
Milwaukee, only 20 percent confessed monthly, and it was
about the same at Saint Josephat's, the largest Polish church
in the city. Among other ethnic groups, the rates were lower
yet. Just 13 percent of the Slovaks at Saint Stephen's went as
often as monthly, though the pastor assured the bishop that
all of his parishioners confessed at least once a year, the minimal expectation. Moreover, the shifting composition of ethnic
neighborhoods over time might bring on an abrupt change in
practice. Holy Trinity, a German parish in the 1940s, had a
monthly confession rate of 45 percent; by the early 1960s, the
neighborhood would become predominantly Spanish-speak-
ing, with the pastor lamenting that only 12 percent of his people were coming that often.[4] Catholics of every ethnicity were
used to hearing their priests recommend confessing regularly;
depending on ethnic traditions, some did, some did not.

✠

NEW ORLEANS, 1951. MATER Dolorosa (Mother of Sor-
rows) parish in the East Carrollton neighborhood, roughly
equidistant from Tulane University in one direction and
Loyola University in the other. As the priests and parishioners there went about their normal devotions and worship
services, they were being observed closely by a professor
from Loyola and his ten student research assistants. Joseph
Fichter was not a local, originally from New Jersey. He had
dropped out of high school to take a job as a bricklayer, but as
a young man he went back to school, became a Jesuit priest,
and earned a PhD in sociology from Harvard, later moving
to New Orleans to teach. An ambitious and prolific scholar,
he had originally hoped to produce a multivolume study that
would examine the parish as a complete, self-contained social

system. Once underway, however, he had to scale back and, after an argument with the pastor (who was unhappy with many of the findings), had to publish the results by identifying the parish anonymously as "St. Mary's" and renaming the neighborhood "Riverside." Fichter and his team looked at everything. The parish population (6,436) was predominantly white. There was a separate parish for Black Catholics nearby in the strictly segregated city; he had thought about studying it, too, but in the end did not, even though he himself was active in helping to desegregate the local parochial schools. Attendance at the half dozen masses on Sunday mornings averaged 3,465 per week, hitting almost 4,500 on Easter. Fichter counted the number of students in the parish grammar school (647) and even the number of households that had a telephone (just under 75 percent), at the time a rough measure of economic and social standing.[5]

His data on the practice of confession was characteristically thorough. Of the entire parish population, he determined that 5,281 of them (82 percent) were subject to the church law that they confess at least once a year; this number excluded children younger than seven and non-Catholic spouses. "Even the least-informed parishioner," Fichter wrote, knew about the annual requirement, and for the most part these Catholics were meeting that standard. One third of the people at Mater Dolorosa confessed annually, and another third did so twice a year, probably at Christmas and Easter. A noticeable number (21 percent) apparently never went to confession at all, and this may have been one of the things that the pastor did not want publicized. Applying his calculations to all these numbers and adding in those who confessed weekly or monthly (about 12 percent together), Fichter computed an average of 3.4 confessions per person per year, the equivalent of one every 105 days—the kind of statistics, perhaps, that only a sociologist can love. As expected, the busiest day of the week for priests in the confessional was usually Saturday; a little less than half of the nearly 18,000 total confessions in the parish for the year came then. But people might confess at other times too—1,786 had done so while Sunday Mass was being said—and not all Saturdays were created equal, with some drawing bigger crowds than others. The two busiest months were March and May, which included the day before Easter and the day before Mother's Day, respectively. Parishioners who wanted to receive communion at Mass on those special occasions made a point of going to confession the day before in preparation. A parish mission, two weeks of intense nightly preaching designed to promote increased fervor even among regular churchgoers, also boosted attendance. Fichter rightly noted that "the number of confessions heard during these two weeks may be used as a partial criterion of the success of the mission," and the visiting priests in charge of it had reason to be happy: 1,001 more confessions (237 men, 379 women, 385 children).[6]

But Fichter's study produced more than just raw data. Supplementing his numbers with extensive interviews, he also gained insights into the attitudes that governed the parishioners' practice. In particular, he could see something of the personal dynamic between priests and people. There were four confessional boxes in the corners of the church, and they were staffed by the three priests of the parish, each occupying the same one from week to week, with the fourth left available for any visitor. This allowed those who came to confession to choose which of the priests they would speak to. Sometimes, the decision depended merely on which line was shortest—there was almost always a line—but clerical personality and style could also figure in the determination. The longtime pastor, given the pseudonym "Father Urban," heard confessions only occasionally, leaving most of this work to his curates, and for many parishioners that was just as well.

He tended to be stern, though at least one man said that he "like[d] a priest to 'bawl them out' for their sins, and Father Urban was not 'always making excuses for sinners.'" A newly ordained assistant, "Father Paul," by contrast, was "serious, patient, understanding, and given to pious counseling." This attracted some parishioners, and beyond that his French was the best on the parish staff, bringing him a subset of older penitents who felt most comfortable in that language. "Father Dominic" was even more popular, particularly with men, in part because he seemed like such a regular guy—"a card," one interviewee called him. At other times, he would stand on the church steps, smoking and chatting with passersby, and in the summers he treated the kids to ice cream. Moreover, in the confessional box, he "didn't take all day to give the absolution," another man said appreciatively.[7]

By adding these personal anecdotes to his dry numbers, percentages, and charts, Fichter was able to work backward from what the parishioners were doing to what they were thinking. Some came to confession largely to fulfill the obligation the church put on them; Father Dominic was their man, getting them in and out efficiently. Others wanted more personalized attention and advice; they knew they could get it from Father Paul. Some apparently even wanted the spiritual equivalent of a kick in the pants, and they knew that Father Urban was ready to administer it. Whatever their motives, these New Orleans Catholics were living out a commitment to their church through confession.

☩

FOUR SNAPSHOTS OF AMERICAN Catholics going to confession. Remember these people; we shall meet some of them again. Thousands of scenes like these were replicated across the landscape and across the decades. As the Catholic Church grew in the United States throughout the nineteenth and early twentieth centuries—it was probably the largest single religious denomination in the country by the time of the Civil War and has remained so since—countless ordinary parishioners built confession into their understanding of what it meant to be Catholics. From the time they were small children and for the rest of their lives, they made this ritual an essential part of their religious practice. It was one of the seven sacraments recognized by Catholic theology, and for decades parishioners were probably more familiar with it than with any of the others. Even reception of the Eucharist in communion at Mass, though always possible, was for a long time rare among the laity. Committed, "practicing" Catholics knew that confession was something they should be doing, as serious an obligation as Sunday Mass, and so many of them did it regularly. Even if, as in Saint Louis, fear of God's punishment was more of a motivator than desire for God's consolation; even if, as in New York, they had to wait in long lines (imagine being number fifty-three on the day Patrick Healy heard the seventy-one confessions he counted as "few"); even if, as in Milwaukee, they had to seek out a priest who spoke their native language or had to struggle with one who didn't; even if, as in New Orleans, they confessed only the 3.4 times per year that Joseph Fichter calculated; even if the whole procedure might be a difficult and humbling thing that could include getting "bawled out" for what they had done—even with all that, they made a point of doing so anyway.

The forgiveness of sins had, of course, been a part of the Christian tradition from the very beginning. The necessity for believers to repent of their transgressions and to reconcile themselves with God and with one another traced its foundations to the words of Jesus himself as recorded in the scriptures. "Whose sins you shall forgive," he told his disciples as he sent them out into the world, "they are forgiven them; whose sins you shall retain, they are retained" (John 20:23).

This text was interpreted to mean that, even though it was God who did the actual forgiving, clemency was imparted to individuals in this life through the agency of the church, and from the outset the early church made this a crucial part of its message. "You must repent," Saint Peter had told the people of Jerusalem in one of the earliest recorded sermons (Acts 2:38), and many of his hearers were convinced and joined the nascent Christian movement. A few years later, Saint Paul reinforced the same theme for the citizens of Athens: "God now calls upon all people everywhere to repent" (Acts 17:30). But how to give ritual expression to the process of repenting and forgiving? At first, simple baptism into the faith was understood to wipe away the offenses of one's life, and potential converts often delayed their formal initiation into the church as long as possible for just this reason. Baptism at the point of death cleared the believer's entire slate immediately before encountering God at the judgment seat of heaven; baptism too soon in life practically guaranteed that there would be subsequent offenses to be answered for and punished.[8]

But putting off repentance and baptism until death involved risks. Death was, after all, unpredictable and might not afford the chance. Moreover, wasn't it better for converts to join the church through baptism as soon as possible in order to embrace the Christian message? If so, the problem would be how to handle the sins that Christians might commit after baptism—indeed, inevitably would commit, given the deficiencies of human nature. In that context, practices of penance for the living had to develop. By the end of antiquity, these took the form of public shaming, in which individual sinners acknowledged their guilt and begged forgiveness from the community. The rituals varied from place to place, but common elements included temporary denial of the other sacraments, particularly the Eucharist, and such humiliations as donning the biblical sackcloth and ashes, a tradition that gave rise to the cliché that still endures. These punishments were rigorous, perhaps required of the contrite sinner for years at a time, and many believers understandably resisted submitting themselves to them. In consequence, public penance was becoming rare by the end of the sixth century, and by 800 CE it had largely disappeared. A new means of expressing the church's understanding of forgiveness emerged first in the monasteries of Ireland, marking it sometimes as Celtic penance. Individuals—at first other monks, eventually laypeople too—could speak personally to a priest, recounting their sins against God and neighbor and asking for pardon. The priest could both counsel them on improving their behavior in the future and assign them various good works, performance of which demonstrated the sincerity of their sorrow while also atoning for the wrong that had been done. These penances might be severe or not, though in comparison to the earlier public punishments they were far milder, and the believer could go away from the encounter confident that the pardoning power entrusted by Jesus to his first followers had been conveyed through their successors in the church. Moreover, here was a private practice, absent public observation and humiliation, repeatable whenever the sinner's spiritual welfare called for it, and not so onerous as to discourage its use.[9]

By the early Middle Ages, these procedures had coalesced into the practice of auricular confession. The adjective is telling: confession was an oral transaction, and it went literally into the ear of the priest. The penitent enumerated specific sins and asked forgiveness for them. The priest listened, judged the gravity of the offenses, and formally imparted absolution; he also assigned an appropriate penance (such as prayer or almsgiving) as a means of atonement, and he might offer a word of reassurance. Bishops mandated specific rules for their own territories, addressing such matters as how frequently one should confess and whether confession was necessary before receiving communion. There was enough consensus of opinion and practice, however, that a general council of the church, held at the Lateran Basilica in Rome in 1215, adopted rules to be applied universally. All Christians were now required to confess their sins and to receive communion at least once a year, and this expectation remained the standard thereafter. With the Protestant Reformation at the beginning of the sixteenth century, however, some Christians were beginning to question both the form which confession had taken and its underlying theology. The principal reformers, Martin Luther and John Calvin, certainly never doubted the innate corruption of human nature; both possessed a strong sense of the power and effects of sin. But to them, auricular confession seemed more a human invention than a divine mandate. They could find no specific biblical warrant for it: Jesus's general command to forgive sins (or to retain them) prescribed no particular procedure. Moreover, the practice tended to convey the impression that it was the priest rather than God who absolved from sin, a notion they found dangerously wrong. With the church challenged in this way, another council, held at Trent in northern Italy between 1545 and 1563, issued a stout defense of this and the other sacraments. Insisting (incorrectly) that confessing privately to a priest had been the church's practice from the very beginning, the council restated the requirement for annual confession. As the western Christian world divided into self-identified Catholics and Protestants, auricular confession remained a necessary sacrament only for the former group.[10]

This theology and the ritual practices that embodied it came to what Europeans called the New World as Catholics began to settle there. Early Spanish missionaries in the territories that would comprise the west and southwest of the future United States wanted to provide basic religious services to their conquering and colonizing countrymen, who usually had other priorities. But the uncertainties of new settlements, the perpetual shortage of clergy, and the vast distances between communities meant that expectations of habitual religious observance, such as annual confession and communion, were often honored mostly in the breach. Missionaries also hoped to convert Native populations to Catholicism, replacing Indigenous rites, which they considered simple idolatry, with the "true" faith and rituals of Christianity. Mission centers could provide basic religious instruction, supplemented with an introduction to European ritual life. The two efforts were connected: teaching potential converts the Ten Commandments, for instance, included pointing out violations of those divine laws that had to be repented and confessed. Such efforts demanded entirely new ways of thinking from the Indigenous people, and most missionaries were probably less successful than they hoped in replacing one set of beliefs with another. Explaining sins of a sexual nature—practices, including polygamy and homosexuality, that Indigenous people considered merely normal behavior—was particularly problematic. Moreover, the question of language was crucial when it came to instructing converts in how to go to confession. Not all missionaries were good at picking up Native languages, which existed in great variety, and they sometimes had to rely on third parties as translators, a practice that would have been completely out of the question in Europe. French missionaries in Canada faced the same problems, frequently calling on interpreters in confession—sometimes even using women for this purpose, again something otherwise unthinkable. As late as the 1850s, a missionary on the American frontier—in this case, near Green Bay, Wisconsin—was still hearing Indigenous confessions "through the medium of an interpreter."[11]

The English colonies along the Eastern Seaboard, founded in the early seventeenth century, were outposts of empire no less than their Spanish and French counterparts, but they were also deliberate attempts to replicate European society in America. Reproducing what settlers thought of as normal religious life, while always an uncertain enterprise, was a part of this plan. Catholics were distinctly unwelcome in most of these colonies, their religion back home considered essentially treasonous, but Maryland had been founded in the 1630s in part to provide a safe haven in which they could practice their faith. An old English Catholic family, the Calverts, led the effort, and Jesuits accompanied the first migrants. They supported themselves with the proceeds from their extensive farms, the land worked by slaves owned by the priests with little thought that slaveholding was incompatible with Christian fellowship. Some effort was made to convert these slaves to Catholicism, but the energies of the clergy were directed mostly toward their fellow English colonists. As settlements spread around the Chesapeake and up the Potomac River, priests rode ever-widening circuits, seeking out small groups of Catholics as they found them. In some places, there were little chapels that were used whenever a priest came through; in other places, services were conducted in private homes or the open air. Itineracy of this kind was necessary for decades. Into the 1750s, one priest, Joseph Mosley, was still describing this pattern to his sister back home in England. "We have many to attend," he wrote her, "and few to attend them. I often ride about 300 miles a week, and never a week but I ride 150, or 200." At every stop, there was Mass to say and confessions to hear, the locals not having had the chance for either in some time. Friends had advised him to be "more moderate in my labours" and to look after his own health, but the priest's sense of duty drove him on. How could he neglect his responsibilities to his parishioners, scattered as they were, "by staying at home? Must I, when at the Chapel, refuse to hear half that present themselves?"[12]

Mosley's experience was the common one for the handful of priests in English America, and it persisted until the time of the Revolution and even after. When a priest arrived in a stopping place, his first order of business was usually hearing the accumulated confessions. That done, the missionary could say Mass, the faithful could receive communion, and then recently born infants could be baptized and older children given some instruction in the catechism. Often, however, so many came forward to confess that everything else had to wait, and the strict rules that governed church practice in Europe had to be set aside so as to accommodate the crowds. Sunday Mass, for example, was technically supposed to be celebrated no later than noon. One priest in 1785 encountered difficulty in adhering to this canonical standard, going so far as to request permission from Rome to extend the deadline to one o'clock "because at times confessions cannot be heard in less than three hours." Even if he started early in the morning, as he usually did, he could not hear all those who wanted to confess, and he thought it better to delay the Mass "rather than send home" without confession those "who with great difficulty and inconvenience had come twenty or thirty miles." (He waxed even more dramatic, hoping to elicit sympathy and a favorable response to his request: among those coming in from afar were "pregnant women, some of them close to delivery.") This one missionary had sought official approval for bending the rules; presumably, others simply did it on their own without asking.[13]

Because confession was so infrequent for most American Catholics of the time, priests often encountered those who had not mastered the proper form for doing it or who were just out of practice. Most laypeople had probably been instructed to a greater or lesser extent at some point in their lives, but many were often unsure how to go about it, and missionaries had

to devote time to reminding them of the basics. Joseph Greaton, a Jesuit slightly older than Mosley, had a stock sermon
on the subject that he delivered at least half a dozen times at
various stops in Maryland and Pennsylvania between 1723
and 1748. He wanted to instruct his listeners in how to make
a "good" confession, by which he meant something both theological and practical. Humility and sincerity were the proper
dispositions with which to begin; the sinner had to genuinely
acknowledge the wrongs he or she had done and had to signal to the priest acceptance of responsibility for them. Those
who "relate their sins with the same indifferences [*sic*] as if
it were an idle story" were obviously not in the right frame
of mind. But Greaton emphasized more prosaic factors as
well. The confession had to be clear so that the priest knew
exactly what the offense was without cross-examination—he
assured his hearers that priests disliked doing this as much
as laypeople hated being questioned—and it also should be
as brief as possible, "not relating any unnecessary circumstances." Missionaries frequently recommended prayer books
that Catholics could use, both in the specific task of preparing
for confession and for more general devotional purposes as
well. One of these, a *Manual of Catholic Prayers* published in
Philadelphia in 1774, even contained a "Form of Confession"
that a lay reader could use to replicate the experience when a
priest was not in town to preside over the real thing. It lacked
any kind of absolution (which only a priest could impart), but
it led the reader through a series of possible transgressions,
each one preceded by the phrase "I accuse myself of . . ." and
concluding with "I ask God pardon for it."[14] Both by hearing sermons and by their own pious reading, laypeople who
had the opportunity for confession only infrequently might
yet develop good religious habits, and they might be better
prepared when the next opportunity presented itself.

New possibilities for regularizing Catholic religious life emerged after the Revolution with the appointment of John Carroll as the first bishop for the new nation in 1789. Until then, American Catholics had theoretically been under the jurisdiction of a vicar in London, an arrangement that became clearly unacceptable with independence. Carroll's family had been in Maryland almost as long as the Calverts, and he had been educated in English-speaking seminaries in Europe and ordained there before returning home in 1774. He immediately became familiar with the rigors of circuit riding. From a base at his mother's house in Rock Creek, he was always on the go. "I have care of a very large cong[gregatio]n," he told a friend; "have often to ride 25 or 30 miles to the sick; besides which I go once a month between 50 & sixty miles to another congn in Virginia." He was the obvious choice to be appointed bishop, with his diocese centered in Baltimore and encompassing the entire United States, consisting at the time of the original thirteen colonies and the unsettled lands as far west as the Mississippi River. "The prospect before us is immense," he said, and he had little in the way of helpers. "In Maryland there are nineteen priests," he reported to Rome, "in Pennsylvania five," and this reality was even worse than it sounded. Of those available clergy, "two are beyond, and three others are approaching seventy years, and thus they are incapable of sustaining the labor necessary."[15] It would be the work of his lifetime—he died in 1815—to recruit young men for the priesthood, get them ordained abroad, and then returned home for pastoral work. He was also forced to rely on foreign-born priests, not all of them reputable or reliable, who wanted to come to America.

At first, Carroll's appointment as a bishop only added to his own burdens. He himself still traveled widely, but now he had additional duties to perform, including administration of the sacrament of confirmation. This was a ritual for young people (usually about age twelve), literally confirming their membership in the church into which they had been baptized as infants, and it could only be performed by a bishop. At every stop, there were children that age waiting for the ceremony, along with a good many adults who had never had the opportunity for it, and this always required extra time and effort. "The ministry of Confirmation would not be much of itself," he wrote to a friend in England, "if, for want of coadjutors, I were not obliged to bear a great share of the Confessionals [*sic*] wherever I go."[16] Only gradually was he able to promote a larger institutional infrastructure for his church throughout the new nation. Catholic communities gathered in seaboard cities, the members drawn by commercial possibilities, and with time these grew more substantial. Philadelphia had a small church from earlier in the eighteenth century, and New York opened a parish in 1785. Settlers from Maryland and Virginia were also streaming over the mountains into Kentucky (a new state as of 1792), enough of them Catholics so that an area in the central part of the territory earned the nickname of "an American Holy Land." Even in Puritan Boston, once a seat of hostility to "popery," a congregation of about one hundred people was able to buy an abandoned Huguenot church and open a parish in 1788. In addition to his own local responsibilities, Carroll now had general supervisory authority over these churches as well.

Those duties included oversight of all priests serving around the country, and it was necessary for him to step in occasionally to settle disputes. These might range from ethnic tensions within parishes to conflicts between clergy and laity, usually driven by strong personalities on both sides. Complaints about particular priests often came to him for resolution, and some of these involved confession. Priests who were routinely too rigorous with laypeople constituted a new kind of problem.

One who was doing missionary work near Detroit in the 1790s was, like his future colleague in Saint Louis, particularly harsh with penitents on the subject of dancing, but Carroll tried to soften his approach. The bishop acknowledged that restraining supposed sensuality was a worthy social goal, but this had to be handled "with much circumspection," he told the priest in question. "To prohibit dancing entirely would, I fear, be a rash exercise of authority" and as a practical matter would probably "drive some out of the Church." Another priest, this one in Kentucky in 1807, was stern with couples who had married before civil authorities or a Protestant minister, usually because a Catholic ceremony had been unavailable to them. The priest even "forbade married persons to use the conjugal privilege"—a carefully worded euphemism—"which the bishop directed him to cease," Carroll wrote, referring to himself in the third person. The constant demands put on them could also wear on priests, leaving them occasionally short-tempered with laypeople. Another missionary in Kentucky complained of being "everywhere followed and pestered for confession."[17]

Not all was conflict in the growing American church, and many pastors were successful at encouraging their parishioners to a new regularity of religious practice. In New York, a priest named Anthony Kohlmann arrived to take charge of Saint Peter's Church at the corner of Barclay and Church Streets in 1808. Consisting mostly of immigrants to the emerging metropolis, the parish drew a diverse group of worshipers from all over the city: day laborers, artisans (such as butchers and masons), small-time merchants (grocers and clothiers), a handful of professionals (the occasional teacher, doctor, or lawyer), and their families. A succession of priests (two of them named O'Brien) with short tenures had preceded Kohlmann there, but he would stay until 1815, and this gave him the opportunity to establish routines for parish life. He was a good choice for the assignment. Originally from Alsace, he was fluent in French and German as well as English, and this allowed him to speak to the principal ethnic groups represented in the parish; there was also a small Black population. The largest ethnicity was Irish, but enough Francophones had left behind the revolutions in France and Haiti to populate the church, and Germans were pleased with a pastor whose native language was their own. Kohlmann could now address all these parishioners from the pulpit. Getting them into the habit of Mass every Sunday had been his first priority and, at least with those to whom he was preaching, that effort had apparently paid off. Now, he could try to add other markers of Catholicity to their religious habits, and none was more important to him than regular confession. Of all the distinctive practices of their religion, he told his people, this one was "the chief, most essential, and most inviolable."[18]

Manuscripts of some of the sermons that Kohlmann delivered during the first six months of his pastorate survive, and in that period he preached on confession at least three times, once in German. He also conducted a two-week mission for the parish, not very different from the one that Joseph Fichter would observe in New Orleans a century and a half later, and he emphasized the subject in those talks too. Repeatedly, Kohlmann offered practical advice on how parishioners should prepare themselves for the sacrament, often drawing on traditional forms of the "examination of conscience" that believers could use to review their actions, right and wrong. He addressed the problem of those who found themselves falling into the same sins over and over — "habitudinaires," he called them — suggesting ways for them to break these cycles. He reminded his congregation that anything they said to a priest in the confessional remained secret by divine injunction, a foreshadowing of his involvement a few years later in a court case (to which we will return) in which that principle would be tested in law. Above all, it was the salutary nature of confessing that constituted its greatest benefit. Admitting one's offenses, aloud if only in a whisper, was "so humiliating, so repugnant" to human dispositions, he thought, that it had to be of divine origin. Moreover, the fact that no Catholic was exempt from the requirement to confess offered its own reassurance. All believers, no matter how high or low, "the pope as well as the least member of the church, the monarch upon the throne as well as the meanest of his slaves," were required "to submit and bend their necks." There are no records to measure precisely how successful these exhortations were. Kohlmann left no accounting of the number of confessions that he, together with a younger priest who joined him at Saint Peter's, heard regularly. But the message was clear: "We do not well what we do too seldom," he said, summarizing his message during the mission. Thus, the parishioners should "confess and receive [communion] every month at least once," he said flatly. Without those two linked practices, there was "no true Xtianity."[19] Not every parishioner heard this message, as he and priests elsewhere would learn, but a great many of them did.

As the church continued to expand nationwide throughout the first half of the nineteenth century, Catholics were, like those in Kohlmann's parish, increasingly accustomed to exercising their faith. By the time of the Civil War, American Catholics were becoming a churchgoing people in a way that they had previously been unable to, setting patterns that would persist. New dioceses were created one after another as the population grew and spread out around the country, and church leaders worked to provide the institutions of their church to support steadily rising levels of participation. Beginning in 1829, the nation's bishops met periodically to standardize some of these practices. Less concerned with matters of theology (though traditional Catholic doctrines

e endorsed), these gatherings focused more on such mat-
's as the recruitment and training of clergy, the ownership
of church property, and the religious education of the young.
Providing for the uniform administration of the sacraments
in local parishes was also important, and confession was high
on that list of concerns. The centuries-old requirement for
annual confession was restated, but practical matters got the
most attention. The construction of new church buildings
was encouraged, for example, with the injunction that they
should always contain confessional boxes *in loco publico et patenti* — in a public and conspicuous place. Care was to be taken
that confessions, particularly those of women, were heard
regularly in these confessional boxes, providing the requisite
anonymity; exceptions to this rule were allowed only when a
priest was visiting a parishioner's sickbed at home. The age at
which children should go to confession for the first time was
left to the discretion of local pastors. But all parishes were
urged to standardize and announce the times when confessions would be heard — before the first scheduled Mass every
Sunday, for example, and also during the evening on other
days of the week — so that laypeople would have consistent
access to the sacrament. There would be "no lack of penitents," said the published statement of the bishops' meeting
in 1866 confidently, "if only the confessors are there to hear
them."[20] With these and other directives, the groundwork had
been laid for regular confession by American Catholics.

✠

THE BISHOPS HAD BEEN right: by then, there was "no lack
of penitents." As Kohlmann had observed, sooner or later all
types of Catholics found their way to the confessional, and the
broadly democratic nature of the sacrament was everywhere
visible. One priest tallied up a list of some of the penitents he
encountered during an ordinary week: a policeman who had

been away from the confessional for almost ten years but felt
the pull to return; "a well-dressed man having the appearance
of a seaman," about to embark on a voyage; "another man of a
rather low station who had led a sinful and neglectful life" but
who repented himself and then urged others to do the same; a
lady "moving in the gayest and most fashionable circles, and
much addicted to amusements." She had not confessed in several years, the priest noted, but for reasons that he did not
know or at least did not record, she had then formed the habit
of doing so twice a month.[21] By the beginning of the twentieth
century, regular confession had taken hold as a defining characteristic of American Catholic religious life.

In parishes everywhere, the weekly schedule turned on
this reality as much as it did on Sunday Mass. Saturday was
always busiest, with hours set aside both afternoon and evening, a consequence of the link that had been forged between
confession and communion. When priests like Anthony
Kohlmann recommended that the people of his parish form
the routine of doing both every month, he was presenting an
ideal that many parishioners found they could achieve. Most
laypeople were reluctant to take communion on Sunday
unless they had gone to confession on Saturday, and church
life was structured to accommodate this joint demand. The
experience of Father James Walsh, a newly ordained curate
in a working-class parish in the Roxbury neighborhood of
Boston, full of second-generation Irish and Germans, became
standard for Catholic clergy. He did regular Saturday duty
in his confessional box: three to six o'clock in the afternoon;
a short break for supper; back at it between seven thirty and
nine thirty that evening. Like Patrick Healy, he sometimes
noticed changes in the pace: one February Saturday, the
numbers were "solid" between three and five, "straggling"
from five to six, then steady again in the evening. Even far
from the Eastern and Midwestern cities that were centers of

(handwritten margin note: ↳ the effect this has on catholic culture)

the Catholic population, parishioners could count on confession being available to them at stated times. At the Cathedral of the Madeleine in Salt Lake City, just up the street from the Mormon Temple, confessions were heard every Saturday from four to six o'clock in the afternoon and seven thirty to nine in the evening, and the people—there were about 2,500 parishioners—came. In the early 1950s, the two priests of the parish reported that they were hearing about two hundred confessions every week.[22]

But this was only the beginning, as many churches routinely set aside other times for confession, too. A busy parish in Detroit in the 1920s assigned at least one priest to the task on weekday mornings after the six o'clock Mass (which probably lasted only about half an hour) and before the eight o'clock Mass, and a priest was also there every evening for half an hour starting at seven thirty. We do not know how many parishioners availed themselves of these occasions, but this much "supply" clearly indicated a certain level of "demand" and may even have helped create it. Parishes with schools, both elementary and secondary, sometimes designated Friday afternoons as the time for children's confessions, a practice intended to keep them out of the way of adults on Saturday. The priest at one French Canadian church set *pas d'enfants* (no children) as a rule for the Saturdays leading up to Christmas. In 1900, a parish in suburban Boston set a pattern that would persist there for decades. Four priests heard confessions from three thirty to six in the afternoon and again from seven to nine thirty in the evening every Saturday, but the children of the parish were told to confess on Friday afternoon beginning at four o'clock, and they might be shooed away if they came outside that window. Other parishioners were also steered toward one time and not another. "Housekeepers and all others whose duties will allow them to do so," the pastor announced on a Sunday in

June, "should go to confession in the afternoon" on Saturday, "and leave the confessionals free in the evening for working people" who could not get there during the day. In 1920, his successor even saw to it that a priest would be ready to hear confessions on Sunday mornings before the eight thirty Mass. This was "for the convenience especially of the older people of the parish," who would thus not have to come to the church twice on the weekend (for confession on Saturday and again for Mass on Sunday), a particularly welcome benefit in the wintertime.[23]

Regularly scheduled confessions such as these were supplemented when the sacrament was connected to the other devotions that grew in popularity as the century advanced. Few had more impact than the "First Friday" devotions to the Sacred Heart of Jesus. These traced their origin to seventeenth-century France, when Jesus was said to have appeared to a nun, promising special benefits in return for special practices. Believers who went to Mass and communion on the first Friday of nine successive months were given the assurance that they would not die without having the chance to confess and receive communion one final time, thereby guaranteeing the opportunity to unburden themselves of sin just before facing God in judgment. American Catholics embraced this devotion enthusiastically, and local churches were crowded for Mass on the designated Friday mornings. Many parishioners completed the cycle several times during their lives and, if for some reason they happened to skip a month, they simply started over. "I missed communion on Fri.," a young man in Michigan told his family in May 1905, but he was philosophical about it: he "wasn't very far along in the number because I missed in December anyway." In June, he was back at it, and by the next winter he had finished the requisite nine.[24]

Confession was not necessary before a First Friday communion, strictly speaking, but priests consistently recommended

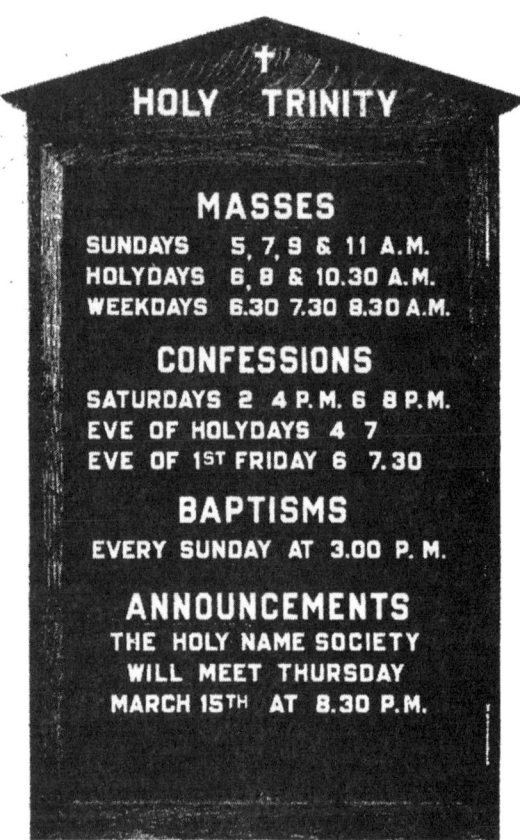

Church sign listing hours for confessions on Saturdays and other days, 1935. Advertisement for the Acme Outdoor Sign Company, *Official Catholic Directory, 1935* (New York: Kenedy Publishing 1935), advertising page 72. Credit: O'Neill Library, Boston College

it in theory and encouraged it in practice. Parish schedules were supplemented in anticipation of an expected surge of confessions on the applicable Thursdays, with more priests assigned to the task on those afternoons and evenings than would otherwise be the case. Sometimes they faced even larger crowds than on a typical Saturday. On one "first Thursday," a priest in Boston counted 147 confessions, while he had heard a mere eighty-seven the Saturday before. Patrick Healy in New York once heard 169 confessions ("a fair number," he thought) on a Thursday afternoon, most of them probably from school children. In the 1950s, Joseph Fichter tabulated about 165 confessions on average during Saturday afternoons at "St. Mary's" in New Orleans, but almost five hundred every first Thursday, again the number swelled by kids from the parish school who were routinely brought to Mass the next day. Only rarely did other devotional exercises get in the way, decreasing rather than increasing the number of those seeking to confess. At Healy's church in New York, one first Thursday in February happened to coincide with the Feast of Saint Blaise, a figure (perhaps legendary) from the ancient church who was thought to protect his devotees from diseases of the throat. American Catholics flocked to church every year on his saint's day for a simple blessing of their throats by a priest, a hopeful spiritual precaution in the dead of winter. Even though the church was crowded all afternoon with parishioners who had come for the blessing, Healy observed, fewer of them than usual stayed for confession as well.[25]

The "Forty Hours" devotion was another extraliturgical practice that priests used to encourage confessions among their parishioners. These services commemorated the exact amount of time (according to Saint Augustine's reckoning) that Jesus had spent in the tomb between Good Friday afternoon and Easter Sunday morning. Once a year, following a schedule that moved the devotion from parish to parish in a given city, Catholics were encouraged to visit their local church for prayer before a consecrated Eucharistic host, displayed on the altar in a piece of church hardware known as a monstrance. Societies of laypeople were enlisted to ensure that at least one parishioner was present in the church for a time of private prayer around the clock during forty consecutive hours. Wives and mothers usually got the morning, school kids the afternoon, men the overnight shift. At the end of the designated period, a public service in the church would conclude the observance, with the monstrance carried in a special procession followed by Mass, during which participants were expected to receive communion. This was understood to imply confession beforehand, and again priests scheduled special hours so that their people could take advantage of the opportunity. Two priests at Sacred Heart parish in Newton Centre, Massachusetts, heard confessions at expanded times (though not around the clock) during one Forty Hours period in 1900, and they also brought in two visiting priests to assist with the crowds. At a nearby church in Boston, a single priest heard almost 375 confessions over two days when the devotion came to his parish.[26]

Most significant of all in increasing the number of confessions was the periodic parish mission, like the one conducted by Anthony Kohlmann when he first went to New York. Small teams of priests, usually members of religious orders rather than the diocesan clergy, traveled the country as a "mission band," stopping at one church after another, for a week or two of intense preaching. Priests of the Redemptorist, Paulist, Passionist, and Jesuit orders specialized in this work, which consisted of a series of services over several days and evenings. Often, one week of the mission was designated for the women of the parish, followed by a second one for the men. In larger parishes, the visitors might stay longer and further differentiate their programs for the married and unmarried men and women, along with distinct after-school sessions for children. Regardless of format or audience, confession was the best way to measure the mission's success, more meaningful than counting the crowds in attendance, which might include the merely curious and the unconvinced. The entire purpose of the effort was to reinvigorate the faith of the already-committed and to call the lapsed back to routine religious practice, and therefore getting parishioners to go to confession was the crucial turning point. This was the climax of the mission, the Catholic equivalent of the "altar call" in Protestant revivals, in which the believer stepped forward to make a new commitment to live a godly life. If mission preachers were doing their jobs effectively, they would spend hours in the confessional—and they usually did.[27]

The numbers could be impressive. The pastor of an isolated parish in Monroe, Louisiana, about one hundred miles east of Shreveport in the northeast corner of the state, reported that he was accustomed to hearing barely a dozen confessions every year at Easter time. When the Redemptorists came through town in 1869, they heard 165 in just ten days; on their return a year later, the number hit 200, an upward trend that continued in subsequent years. Saint Patrick's Church in Seneca Falls, New York, was visited by successive teams of Paulists, and they saw some improvement over time: about thirteen hundred confessions when they first stopped there in 1880, almost nineteen hundred on a return visit a few years later. Over the course of the 1890s, the number of mission confessions at a parish in Manhattan nearly doubled to more than eleven thousand. Other stops by the Paulists produced more stable results: around three thousand every other year at Saint Patrick's in Pittsburgh and numbers holding steady on either side of thirty-five hundred over a ten-year period at Saint Elizabeth's in Chicago.[28]

The priests directing these missions knew that some of their success was attributable to the fact that they were only in any one place for a limited time, and this worked to their advantage. Some parishioners, particularly those who had been away from the sacrament for a long time, preferred to tell their sins to a stranger than to their own pastor, who they feared might recognize their voice or at least guess their identity. "The local clergy offered to help in the confessional," a traveling Paulist reported on one occasion, "but the people would not go to them." Pastors even advertised this in advance of a mission. "Prêtres étrangers" ("unknown priests") would soon be coming to a French Canadian parish in Massachusetts, the pastor announced shortly before Christmas one year, hoping that this would bring out the otherwise reluctant. As often as not, the tactic worked, especially with men. At one stop, a missioner noted, "it actually seemed as if no man making the mission had been to confession within five years, and most of them not for twenty." Two visitors to Saint Brendan's parish in San Francisco thought that they set an all-time record for confessions in a single day; one of them counted 215. "We were both very tired," the other concluded, no doubt with reason. "Such success were it to continue would be fatal to the missionaries," another priest said of a stop in Chicago, suggesting that next time five priests be sent to that parish rather than three so as to distribute the workload. As the numbers rose, so did priestly expectations, which might or might not be realized. The count of confessions at a mission in Omaha one year — more than thirteen hundred — was "not great," a priest said afterward. A Paulist campaign over three weeks at another stop brought in nearly six thousand penitent men, women, and children, but the priests nonetheless left town trying to understand the "reason for the small no. of confessions."[29] American Catholics, priests and laity alike, lived in a mental world in which thirteen hundred confessions were "not great" and six thousand of them was a "small" number.

So much confessing — but what was it that all those parishioners were confessing? Because it was an oral encounter,

leaving no traces once it was over, we cannot recover the substance of any individual confession. Still, we want to know:
What were the two participants saying to each other? What
did parishioners think they needed to confess? How did
priests judge what they heard? For people and for priests,
the whole process turned on the highly articulated Catholic
understanding of sin.

2

Sin

THERE WAS ALWAYS AN answer—a correct answer, a definitive answer, a The Answer. American Catholics reading diocesan newspapers and devotional magazines knew that, if they had a question about their faith or the demands it put on them, there was a way for them to get a clear and straightforward response. Publications of that kind, weeklies and monthlies, proliferated throughout the first half of the twentieth century, circulation numbers attesting to their popularity, and almost every one of them contained a regular feature called something like "The Question Box." Readers who wondered about some aspect of church life, whether the proper way to understand a point of doctrine or what they should and should not be doing, both in church and out, could send in their question and receive an authoritative reply from a priest. He might or might not be identified by name ("Monsignor Conway's Question Box" was syndicated in several newspapers), but the mere fact that he was a priest meant that what he had to say was reliable. There were even monthly magazines for the clergy, trade journals of a kind, offering the same sort of service. A priest, perhaps especially one newly ordained, could inquire about how to address a particular problem in working with the people of his parish. Both kinds of readers, laity and clergy, could be reassured that their doubts would be resolved, their questions answered.[1]

Many of the questions that laypeople posed were about sin. What was a sin, and what was not? If it was a sin, how serious was it? Virtually any edition of one of these columns had at least one question on the subject. Many of the concerns that prompted these inquiries seem trivial today, but the narrowness of their focus is itself a measure of how seriously Catholics took the whole matter, how much they had internalized the teachings of the church—indeed, just by asking, how much they wanted to internalize them. In the summer of 1964, for instance, a person identified only as A. G. (questioners' names were never printed) from New York City wanted to know how sinful it was to blurt out "Damn," and got an answer from *Sign* magazine, a monthly produced for a middle-class audience by the Passionist Fathers. It was a characteristically nuanced reply, beginning with "That depends." If said "to curse anybody or anything holy," the exclamation was quite serious, "the worst possible use of the word." If, as seemed more probable, there had been no intention literally to wish for someone's eternal damnation, it was "a mere safety-valve for pent-up feelings" and "ordinarily not sinful," though its use around children should be avoided. Some questions did not need detailed analysis. In 1943, someone had asked the *Messenger of the Sacred Heart*, published by the Jesuits, what kind of sin was committed by a person who ate meat on Friday, prompting an unambiguous, one-sentence reply: "The deliberate violation of the law of abstinence on Friday is a mortal sin." End of discussion. Questions about dieting (fine if done for reasons of health; mildly sinful if done out of vanity), about women wearing makeup (permissible to "hide a defect" or even "just to look well and 'be in style'"; wrong if done "for the purpose of enticing or encouraging others to sins of impurity"), and almost any other conceivable topic got serious consideration.[2] Moreover, by publishing the questions and the answers, the editors of the periodicals in question thought the moral issues involved were serious enough that a nationwide audience should know the answer—the The Answer.

Beyond such petty concerns, more substantial issues got the same analytical consideration. Immediately after the end of the Second World War, for example, as American racial laws and customs were coming under new challenges, the *Messenger* was asked whether discrimination by "Catholic landlords, restauranteurs, employers, etc." was a sin. To "discriminate unjustly and insultingly" was obviously sinful, the magazine replied, though sadly "the full education of white people, Catholic and non-Catholic, to a correct attitude in this matter is a slow process." The *Messenger* might have noted—but did not—that most Catholic school systems across the South were segregated at the time and that, in racially mixed parishes, Blacks usually sat in the back and received communion only after all the whites had done so. Even more vexing were the questions that were published periodically concerning contraception. "Does the Church permit birth control?" a reader wanted to know in 1943, particularly when a family's meager income could not adequately support another child. The reply was as clear as the one about meat on Friday, restating what was and would remain official Catholic teaching. "Voluntary abstinence from the exercise of marital rights" might be acceptable in such a case, but "contraception, or artificial birth control, is intrinsically evil. . . . No set of circumstances justifies this course of action." In 1964, another question on the subject prompted an addendum from the *Sign* that any priest who heard the confession of someone who practiced the forbidden methods of birth control—and intended to keep doing so—would be forced to withhold absolution. Persisting in the practice was "tantamount to refusing to repent."[3] Contraception would continue to bedevil both priests and people in the confessional, as we shall see.

All these questions and answers reinforced the Catholic conviction that sins could be readily identified and their relative gravity weighed. From their earliest education in the faith, ordinary laypeople were accustomed to thinking in these terms and to using a specialized language for expressing them. They knew how to identify what they had done wrong. They knew how to describe their failings in a few words, and they knew both why these offenses were wrong and why they should ask forgiveness for them. They knew, when necessary, how to draw fine distinctions in complicated circumstances. They knew who to ask if they were unsure. Armed with this certain knowledge, Catholics could approach the confessional with confidence. They were not theologians, but they had learned to apply to themselves the theological ideas that the church presented to them. By virtue of their membership in the church, they accepted its larger understandings of human nature and behavior, and this gave even the least of them a facility in talking about sin. Those understandings shaped the mental universe of American Catholics in profound ways.

✠

THE CHURCH HAD BEEN thinking about sin for a long time, and a finely detailed sense of it was passed from one generation of Catholics to another. Perhaps the most effective instrument for disseminating these concepts in America was the Baltimore Catechism, the standardized tool of religious instruction both in parish schools and in special classes for public school students. Teaching was so dependent on it that these classes, in either context, were known in shorthand simply as "Catechism." The text, first published in 1885 at the

behest of a general meeting of the nation's bishops in Baltimore and revised in a new edition in 1941, remained in wide
use until the 1960s, replacing a variety of volumes that individual prelates had produced over the years for use in their
own dioceses. Employing a format of simple questions and
answers (in all, there were just over four hundred of them),
the Catechism presented the basics of the Catholic faith in
a systematic progression, covering the Ten Commandments,
the Apostles' Creed, and the prayers and sacraments of the
church. It came in three versions, designed respectively for
elementary school children, for students in higher grades,
and for adults. The questions were the same in each one,
the answers growing more complete and sophisticated with
the rising age of the intended user. Pedagogy, especially in the
lower grades, consisted mostly of the teacher assigning a number of questions to be memorized each week and then recited
in class and reproduced on examinations. "Who made us?"
the first question asked; "God made us," was the reply. "Who
is God?" came next; "God is the Supreme Being who made
all things." The answers grew longer, but the cadences of the
responses were ingrained in students from their first exposure to them. Unwittingly, the book even introduced them
to the passive voice. "What is meant by the resurrection of
the body?" question number 78 asked. "By the resurrection
of the body is meant . . ." the answer began. Such a refined
literary style, coming from the mouth of a ten-year-old, was
at once anomalous and unremarkable, and the clarity of the
answer to every question made this volume, as one historian
has said of it, "the central text for workaday Catholics."[4]

   The Baltimore Catechism laid the groundwork for Catholics' understanding of sin, and the story began with Adam and
Eve. Because of their disobedience of God in the Garden of
Eden, all humans after them "share in their sin and punishment." (Only the Virgin Mary had been exempted from this,

the Catechism was quick to point out, alluding to and reinforcing the distinctive Catholic doctrine of her Immaculate
Conception.) Students, particularly the youngest of them,
might think it odd that children should be punished for the
misdeeds of their parents, so a teacher's guide to the Catechism suggested that they be given examples from situations
they might experience or at least imagine in their own lives:
a father who drank away an inheritance, perhaps, punishing
his children by leaving them destitute. The effect of Adam
and Eve's action was permanent and all-encompassing, the
text went on; it "darkened our understanding, weakened our
will, and left us a strong inclination to evil." All this was identified as original sin—original "because it comes down to us
from our first parents," defining the human condition irre-
versibly: "we are brought into the world with its guilt on our
souls." Even after baptism, which, as another lesson pointed
out, cleansed this sin, "the corruption of our nature and other
punishments remain."[5]

The matter did not end there: "there is another kind of sin
which we commit ourselves, called actual sin." The categories presented by the Catechism now became increasingly
complex, and they began to hit home in individual lives. To
begin with, there were two general kinds of actual sins: those
of omission (skipping Mass on Sunday, the teacher's manual
offered by way of example) and those of commission (stealing). The latter kind might seem more apparent and easily
recognized, but both were serious: "it is not enough to simply
do no harm, we must also do some good." More important
was the distinction between actual sins identified as mortal
and those that were venial. A mortal sin was one "which kills
the soul," like a fatal wound to the body. It was "a grievous
offense against the law of God; . . . it deprives us of spiritual life . . . and brings everlasting death and damnation on
the soul." At death, an unforgiven mortal sin sent a person

directly to hell. Built on many earlier sources, the Christian understanding of hell as a place of eternal torment for those who separated themselves from God was as old as the faith itself, part of what one scholar has called the "geography of the other world." A venial sin, by contrast, was "a slight offense against the law of God in matters of less importance" and, unforgiven at death, it sent the sinner only to the temporary punishment of purgatory prior to admittance to heaven. Even so, its effects could not be minimized: "it wounds the soul, it weakens it just as slight wounds weaken the body." Moreover, it prompted a "lessening of the love of God in our heart," leaving us "less worthy of His help." Worse yet, a venial sin was often the first step on a downward slope to something more troubling, representing "a weakening of the power to resist mortal sin."[6]

These basic definitions were clear, but they led to new questions. Since it was obviously important to know, how was a Catholic to determine which sins were mortal and which were venial? The catechism provided a framework for analysis. For an offense to rise to the level of a mortal sin, three conditions had to be met. First, the action in question had to be a serious one, and the instructor was encouraged to pause here to be sure that students understood the word "grievous." Suppose you stole your mother's cheap decorative pin, the teacher's guide suggested; that would clearly be wrong, but since the stolen item had cost almost nothing, the sin would be merely venial. But suppose you stole a diamond pin; given its value, that "would surely be 'grievous,'" and the offense would be a mortal sin. A second condition, "sufficient reflection," demanded even more careful scrutiny and another pause to explain what the phrase meant: "you must know what you are doing at the time you do it." Teachers might at this point recur to the case of the pin. If, at the time of the theft, the perpetrator thought it was only made of glass, the sin would be venial. But if subsequently "you found out that what you had stolen was a valuable diamond," the lesser offense would assume a different character, and the sin would, in retrospect, have been mortal. Finally, a mortal sin required "full consent of the will." This was perhaps an even more difficult idea to get across, particularly for the very young, and the teacher's guide was forced to explain what it was with an example of what it was not: shooting an arrow at a target, for example, and accidentally killing someone instead. That death was unintended and thus had been done without full consent of the will, whereas deliberately aiming at the victim rather than the target elevated the seriousness of the offense.[7]

This method of explanation and instruction promoted a way of thinking that was deliberately evocative of legal reasoning. Though not a perfect comparison, the distinction between mortal and venial sins was readily likened to that between felonies and misdemeanors. When laypeople applied these distinctions, they were encouraged to imagine what they were doing in confession as a kind of courtroom drama. "In what sentiments should we place ourselves" when approaching the confessional, a precursor volume to the Baltimore Catechism had asked, and the answer was clear: "In the sentiments of a criminal" facing justice. Father Joseph Greaton had made the same point a century and a half earlier. In his often-repeated sermon on confession he had noted the salutary effects of the "confusion fear & shame" experienced by "a criminal convicted of heanous [sic] crimes" when facing his judge: "with the same sentiments ought a penitent to appear at the . . . tribunal of confession." The analogy long preceded both Greaton and the Catechism, and it would last well after them. Confession was "a judicial process," a pamphleteer was still writing in the 1950s, with the priest as judge, "impersonal and neutral," and the penitent in multiple roles as "accuser, prosecutor, [and] witness" in his own trial.[8]

In this courtroom as in secular ones, the motives and intentions of the perpetrator could dictate exactly what the charges
were. "A. G." had probably felt a little guilty about having
said "damn," but the reasons behind the outburst made all the
difference. Purposely cursing someone was a serious business, fulfilling the three mortal requirements; merely letting
off steam was something less—and maybe no crime at all,
though still behavior best avoided. The nature of the offense
was determined by the circumstances: A. G.'s answer from
the magazine had, after all, begun with "That depends." Everything depended. It was necessary but not sufficient to know
that stealing, for instance, was wrong, but was it petty theft or
grand larceny, a worthless pin or a diamond? Those accused
had to reconstruct and to acknowledge their own train of
thought in the commission of the crime. Thoughts, as well as
words and deeds, mattered. Had sinners reflected on what
they were doing beforehand and, even knowing that it was
wrong, had they gone ahead anyway? This sounded very
much like "malice aforethought" in a trial, crucial for deciding
what was murder and what was only manslaughter. The instruction of the Catechism gave Catholics the analytical scaffold-
ing for assessing their behavior.

Just as important, it gave them a glossary of terms that
they could adopt in describing and confronting moral problems. It was a vocabulary both highly elaborated and mar-
velously precise, one whose contents, strange at first, became
habitual through use. "Venial," "grievous," "sufficient reflection," "full consent of the will"—these were not phrases that
came up in everyday usage, but such language grew to be
common among Catholics. It was most fruitfully employed by
adults and applied to adult circumstances, useful in drawing
important distinctions. How serious a sin was racial discrimination or use of the proscribed methods of birth control? To
find out, sinners would have to examine their intentions in

such matters, and even in dieting or wearing makeup, to get at the true nature of their sinful acts. There was a way for motives to be parsed and analyzed, with clear moral conclusions the result. And while it was one thing to ask adults to become familiar with such concepts, the Catechism and the memorization at the heart of its use in instruction asked even grade school children to learn this language, to think in these terms. In fact, the church assumed that children *could* think this way, and the repetition of the classroom was devoted to training them how to do so. Children were routinely advised, in the words of another instructional manual (directed in particular at elementary school students) that "it is well to begin your Confession with the most serious sin," advice which accepted as given that they would be able to rank their offenses in order of seriousness.[9] Such habits, instilled early, persisted as the child grew up, and a framework for knowing right from wrong had been established and embedded. Even "workaday Catholics" had the mental tools for sophisticated moral thinking.

✠

LAYPEOPLE BECAME FAMILIAR WITH these tools in part because their priests had themselves been trained extensively in how to use them and in how to convey that skill to their parishioners. The nature of moral problems and the means of addressing them had been at the heart of clerical education for decades. From the time of John Carroll, bishops had worked to establish their own seminaries on American shores, cultivating a native-born clergy so as not to have to rely on foreign imports (who varied widely in quality) or to incur the expense of sending American boys abroad for their priestly preparation. At first, these seminaries were ad hoc affairs, a bishop often taking prospective candidates for the priesthood into his own rectory for spiritual reading and direction. With time, more formal educational institutions were established, and the same council of bishops that had authorized preparation of the Baltimore Catechism urged both their continued growth and the steady expansion and upgrading of their curricula. By the beginning of the twentieth century, a six-year program of post-secondary study had become the standard, with preliminary coursework in philosophy followed by immersion in theology. Practical subjects that would be needed by a priest in a parish—Latin above all, since that language was used in all the services of the church—also got attention. By the 1950s, there were more than forty such seminaries scattered around the United States for the education of the diocesan clergy. Religious orders, such as the Jesuits and Paulists, also maintained seminaries of their own, and some places even had "minor seminaries," high schools designed to channel boys toward the priesthood from their earliest adolescence.[10]

In the seminary curriculum, only the study of Catholic dogma got as much time and attention as the classes in moral theology: an average of five instructional hours each week for the former, according to one national survey, four hours a week for the latter, both of them through all six years of study. Since so much of a working priest's life would be spent in the confessional, helping his parishioners confront their sins, it was crucial that he be fully grounded in the church's understanding of such work; practically speaking, moral theology was simply more useful than anything else. (The study of Scripture, by contrast, got only three hours of class time.) As early as 1813, Carroll, desperate as always for personnel, had expressed his preference that candidates for the priesthood be ordained as quickly as possible, even "tho they may not have studied all the Treatises of Divinity, provided they know the obvious and general principles of moral Theology." The "doubts and difficulties" that ordinary parishioners were likely to bring to their confessors, a later seminary rector said, were "almost all of a practical kind. Their doctrinal misconceptions are usually of little account compared with a mistaken apprehension of their duties." While still a student, a future priest thus had to be readied to meet those human problems and to remind Catholics of their duties. The teaching of moral theology was based on the use of standard manuals, similar to those that had long been employed in Europe. Most influential of these in the twentieth century was the *Summa Theologiae Moralis* (a "summa" was a comprehensive treatment of a subject) by Jerome Noldin, an Austrian Jesuit who taught the subject at his order's seminary at Innsbruck for decades. First published in 1902, its twelve hundred pages over three volumes gave exhaustive coverage to the sacraments of the church, particularly confession, and to the Ten Commandments, with special attention to the sixth, the prohibition against adultery according to the Catholic numbering of the Decalogue. Also in wide use was the one-volume *Moral Theology* by Heribert Jone, a German Franciscan, first published in 1929, followed immediately by a French edition and then in 1945, happily for American seminarians, an English translation. At a mere six hundred pages, it was not as encyclopedic as Noldin, though it was, said a reviewer of the English version, "a ready and handy reference book . . . for quick and accurate" consultation.[11]

Seminarians probably spent as much time with these volumes as with any other books on their course syllabi, and Noldin represented a particular challenge since that work was available only in Latin. One seminarian in Boston in the 1950s did what others elsewhere may also have done: he had the third volume, which covered the sacraments, disbound and then rebound with a blank sheet between each printed page, on which he could write his own notes, in English, based on his teacher's explanations in class. Section 280 of the text, for example, dealt with *Peccatis Dubiis* ("Doubtful Sins")—what to do when someone in the confessional was unsure whether a sin was mortal or venial, or, indeed, whether it was a sin at all. The professor obviously reviewed the three requirements for a mortal sin, presenting some examples, and the student abstracted practical advice from the discussion. As to the necessary grievous nature of the offense, the seminarian wrote, if it was a "common person" who was unsure, it was best to be strict, erring on the side of having him or her consider it mortal and confess it as such. "If the person is well instructed, do not make them confess it." It was the same with the requirement for full consent. "If it is person of tender conscience who ordinarily does not sin in this [whatever it might be], give him benefit of doubt. If person has very lax conscience, make him confess it," probably in the hope of instilling a little more earnest attention next time. Other issues, large and small, got the same detailed scrutiny. Noldin section 265, for example, discussed the requirement for annual confession by all Catholics. "What does annual mean?" the seminarian wrote, probably repeating the rhetorical question of his teacher. "Church has never decided this." Some authorities said "Jan. 1–Dec. 31. . . . Others say Easter time to Easter time." The consensus "nowadays" seemed to favor the Easter calculation, but there was "no automatic penalty attached" to those who were keeping track in another way.[12] How closely the student followed any of this advice once he was out of school and in a parish assignment is impossible to know. One suspects that the easygoing Father Dominic, whom Joseph Fichter met in New Orleans, was less inclined to an exacting enforcement of these standards, perhaps especially with "common" people. But he, like the seminarian in Boston, had nevertheless been instructed in how to convey to his parishioners the church's approach to sins and how to confess them.

This careful analysis of the details of particular cases brought to America another longstanding church tradition: the practice

of casuistry. Thomas Aquinas and other theologians since the
Middle Ages had fashioned systems for exploring the nuances
of sin and for assessing the degree of guilt incurred by sinners.
Specific circumstances affected the level of an offense, either
enhancing or diminishing it, and by the seventeenth century
there was a growing body of what lawyers would have recognized as a kind of "case law." Past examples and decisions
could be applied anew when facing problems that were similar but just different enough to require scrutiny. Too rigid
or mechanical an approach verged on petty logic-chopping,
however, and denunciations of that way of proceeding gave
the word "casuistry" (derived from the Latin *casus*, for "event"
or simply "case") an enduringly negative connotation. At its
best, however, this was a serious moral and ethical system
that did not rely solely on broadly stated ideals—"do good
and avoid evil"—but rather provided practical advice on how
individuals should behave in real-life situations. "Students
of Moral Theology," said one authority, "get a better grasp
of the universal laws of their science when these are applied
to particular instances." Such analysis would help a priest in
"the acquisition of that habit of mind which will enable him in
forming the consciences" of the people entrusted to his care.[13]
    A number of texts were available to seminary professors
and students to help in developing these habits of mind, both
in themselves and by extension in their parishioners. *The
Casuist: A Collection of Cases in Moral and Pastoral Theology* first
appeared in five volumes between 1906 and 1917, and these
were quickly revised and reissued in 1924 to take account
of a revision of the universal canon law of the church a few
years before. The cases had originally appeared in the pages
of the *Homiletic Monthly*, a magazine for priests that contained
advice on pastoral issues, together with sample sermons that
could be delivered by those who lacked the time or inclination
to write their own. In 1920, the journal would be renamed

the *Homiletic and Pastoral Review*, and its regular question box took up the work of guiding priests through the dissection of cases. Many of those published in the original volumes had to do with various points of church law, particularly the rules governing marriage: what kind of special permissions were needed for Catholics to marry non-Catholics, for example, and how far should priests go in discouraging such unions? But questions about sins and how to handle them in the confessional were also persistent. A number of these concerned the restitution of ill-gotten property as a condition of forgiveness: bank and insurance fraud; a buyer who paid an unaware seller less than an item's true value; pilfering goods from a store; even a street-car passenger who managed to elude paying his fare. The cases could, in some instances, seem fanciful and even wildly improbable. In one particularly convoluted example, an old woman left the confessional box before the priest had granted her absolution and was replaced there by a young man, who had yet to say a word as the priest began to recite the forgiving formula over him. Which of the two had actually been forgiven? (The woman.) Still, amid all the detail, the compilers of *The Casuist* hoped to fully prepare readers, both the seminarian and later "the priest whose duty brings him into intimate relations with souls, either as confessor, or adviser, or friend."[14]

A contemporary reader of these intricate, sometimes outlandish, cases can perhaps understand why casuistry as a method got a bad reputation. But it allowed for flexibility when circumstances warranted it, and priests in the United States leaned decidedly toward flexible interpretation. In this, they were strongly influenced by the approach to sin and forgiveness of Alphonsus Liguori, an eighteenth-century priest and bishop from Naples. His noted devotion to the poor made him an especially sympathetic listener when hearing confessions, and he articulated a moral theology that tried to strike a balance between uncompromising rigor at one extreme and lax permissiveness at the other. Priests in the confessional, he thought, should not be looking for reasons to deny forgiveness and absolution. Catholics certainly had a duty to know God's law and to follow it, but if they conscientiously believed that something was not sinful—or that it was merely venial rather than mortal—and acted accordingly, they should not be held to the strict letter of the law. The manual that he compiled prompted many later imitators, and the religious order he founded, the Redemptorists, embodied this style in their work, particularly in parish missions, at first in Italy and then in America after their arrival in 1832. American theologians generally adopted this attitude, and references to him were common in *The Casuist*, the *Homiletic and Pastoral Review*, and other sources. In one case, he was even advanced as an authority in concluding that what had seemed like an act of perjury in court, which would of course be grievously sinful, was in fact "a permissible act of self-defense." A few sterner priests considered Liguori, as one had said, "too sweet," but the majority followed his lead in helping their parishioners come to terms with their sins.[15]

✠

ALL THESE CLASSIFICATIONS OF sin, their dimensions and boundaries on display in a seemingly never-ending string of cases, were the basis for the church's teaching on the subject. But they remained general and theoretical. How could lay Catholics place their individual acts of wrong-doing—specific thoughts, words, deeds—within these larger frameworks, both in preparation for confession and in the confessional box itself? Here again, the church provided ways of structuring the thought process. The so-called Deadly or Capital Sins had long been one way of compiling a list of possibilities. From ancient times, theologians had attempted to identify certain attitudes or traits that together encompassed the full range of bad behavior. Lists varied, but eventually agreement settled on seven: pride, envy, anger, sloth, avarice, gluttony, and lust. They were confirmed in the cultural imagination through tradition and literature. Chaucer's Parson delivered a sermon on them to his fellow pilgrims in the *Canterbury Tales*, and Dante applied them as labels for the successive levels of purgatory in the *Divine Comedy*. By the twentieth century, a few attempts had been made to translate these for a modern American audience. An instructional pamphlet, *These Are Our Seven Deadly Enemies*, published in 1952 by the Knights of Columbus, the largest national organization for laymen, tried to explain each one to its members, though it lumped lust and gluttony together as essentially the same ravenous urge, merely directed at different objects. Pride, "an exaggerated love of self," was the worst, "prompting a man to make a god of himself." Avarice (the pamphlet used the more common word greed) was the inordinate desire not just for money, but also for "knowledge and dominion over others," and it "raises havoc in homes, shops, and businesses." Envy, "sorrow at another's good fortune," was "as common as grass"; anger "makes of man the most irrational and the most predatory of all animals"; sloth was "a lack of interest in the things of God."[16]

Despite this attempt to update the traditional ideas, the Deadly Sins never achieved a prominent place in American Catholic thinking. The Baltimore Catechism did not mention them at all, and it seems unlikely that they came up very often in sermons, except perhaps indirectly. Their appearance in devotional and other publications was, if not entirely unknown, rare; no one asked a question box for fine distinctions among different kinds of sloth or pride. A Catholic reference encyclopedia from the 1910s had quoted a theological authority describing them as the "chief sources" that led to "the commission of many sins," distinguishing them from the kinds of specific behavior that ordinary parishioners were familiar with.[17] They were morally unhealthy, to be sure, but they seemed more like general dispositions, underlying causes ("sources") of sin, rather than specific offenses in particular circumstances that could be pinpointed, described, and confessed. How did knowing what anger was, generally speaking, help one decide whether saying "damn" was right or wrong? Better to focus more narrowly on individual thoughts and actions and to judge them according to clearer standards. For this, Catholic catechisms and preaching had to look elsewhere.

The biblical Ten Commandments were the logical place to start. While agreeing on their substance, Catholics and Protestants numbered the commandments differently. Catholics collapsed the prohibition against "graven images" into the first one, which required worship of the one true God, while Protestants listed images separately as number two on the list. This would have left Catholics with only nine so, in order to get to the normal count of ten, they then split the "covets" at the end — of neighbor's wife and of neighbor's goods — into two separate items, while Protestants listed these together. Some Jews and others also used different numbering schemas. The Commandments were succinct and firmly fixed in Western culture, and their implications for behavior were easily comprehended, starting with the requirement for the worship of God alone. Accepting their duty to affirm God's sovereignty, Catholics could know when and how they may have transgressed, perhaps by asking themselves a series of direct questions. "Have I willfully doubted things revealed by God?" a guide to confession suggested as one possibility in 1941. "Have I refused to be resigned to God's holy Will?" — or even, "Have I consulted the Ouija-board or fortune tellers?" Those who answered yes to any of these questions (or to several others besides) had challenged the supremacy of

God and therefore sinned against the first commandment. In the same way, the injunction to honor father and mother prompted a reader a decade later to ask the *Messenger of the Sacred Heart* whether disobeying one's parents was not just a sin, but a mortal sin. Usually, this was a venial sin, the magazine replied with its usual precision, but if a parent's instructions concerned "a serious matter in which they have a right to command you," the offense would be mortal. If, instead, the parental orders were illegitimate on their face—a directive, the *Messenger* suggested, "to give up all thought of a vocation to the priesthood or the Religious life," for instance—then disobedience became a positive duty.[18]

Some commandments and the sins of violating them got more attention than others, and none were more fraught than those relating to sexuality. To this end, Catholic writers and preachers frequently linked numbers six (adultery) and nine (coveting a neighbor's wife). The plain meaning of the words in the former, "Thou shalt not commit adultery," was only the starting point. That was obviously sinful, one priest explained to an adult audience in 1952, because it was "a selfish seeking of pleasure, without reference to the natural purpose of the union of man and woman, and without assuming the corresponding obligations, which is the very purpose of marriage." Moreover, with this commandment, "every deliberate thought, word, deed is mortally sinful"; there was simply "no such thing as a deliberate venial sin" against the sixth commandment. The implications went well beyond the narrow case of illicit affairs between consenting adults; rather, it was a more inclusive virtue, chastity, that was really at stake. Defending chastity was the ultimate goal: "to be pure and modest in our outward behavior," as the Baltimore Catechism put it. The words of the ninth commandment enlarged and reinforced this concern. Coveting alone, even when it resulted in no action, was also sinful. It was not just "outward behavior" that Catholics had to monitor and control; they were also "commanded to be pure in thought and in desire," the Catechism said.[19] More clearly than with some of the other commandments, the connection of these two opened up the range of possibilities for transgressing the divine law. Sin might come not just from what someone did or said, but also from what he or she thought.

This interpretation gave to these two commandments a wide purchase, prompting another cleric to itemize a fuller list of sinful possibilities when it came to sex. A priest in the confessional, he said, had to know what "kind of sin (self-abuse, immodest embracing, fornication, adultery, and so on)" a parishioner was talking about before he could begin to address it with the offender. With adolescents and young adults, the dangers were heightened, and a Jesuit speaking to a college group in 1963 graphically itemized a number of situations that threatened "the chastity of their precious God-given bodies": "the 'theater balconies,' the 'drive-ins,' the 'parked cars,' the college week-ends, the beach parties." Such temptations were particularly worrisome in the case of women. Questions about female dress and deportment were not infrequent whenever the general subject of chastity came up, not only because improper behaviors were sinful in themselves but also because they might prompt impure desires (that is, coveting) in someone else. There were other issues too. Women smoking and drinking might not be sinful, a popular writer allowed in 1956, "as long as they are temperate"—though, he added, "I know very few girls who are able to smoke neatly and comfortably"—and it was probably best if "sun dresses and shorts" were worn only in private, not in public and certainly not in church.[20] The line between formal moral judgments and a generalized, vaguely Victorian sense of propriety could be porous, but the connection between the sinful actions of one person and the sinful thoughts they evoked in another had been established.

Concern for the potential perils of parked cars and back rows at the movies was heightened by yet another category of behavior that the church identified as morally problematic: not sin itself, but occasions of sin. These were like a leaky pipe that caused the plaster in a house to fall, the teacher's guide to the Baltimore Catechism suggested as an illustration; the pipe demanded attention before the plaster. "Stop the leak, take away the occasion, and then you will not fall into sin," it said, adding a realistic "at least not so frequently." Catholics had a responsibility not to commit specific transgressions, but they also had an affirmative duty to avoid any situations, even those that seemed innocent, that might lead them into sin. True to form, the church offered a detailed typology for recognizing these dangerous occasions, which might be of several overlapping varieties. First, they might be either proximate or remote. The former were "those persons, objects, actions which, for an individual, constitute a strong temptation to sin," the *Messenger of the Sacred Heart* explained in 1962, any circumstance in which it was more likely than not that someone would give in to temptation. These were probably different for everyone—what, a Catholic should ask, were the particularly dangerous occasions of sin for *me*?—and thus they demanded that the sinner be constantly on watch for them. Some were only too obvious. Men on the line in a factory, one turn-of-the-century pastoral theology textbook had suggested, who "relish immodest talk and carry on conversations on nasty subjects," were plainly sinning themselves, but to the extent that they might induce an otherwise decent coworker to join in, they constituted for him an occasion of sin. "It is a grave sin to expose one's self [*sic*]" to a proximate occasion, another authority said in the 1960s. Other occasions were remote, carrying only "a slight or improbable danger" and usually easy to avoid: walking past the neighborhood bookie joint on the way to the grocery store and being tempted inside to bet one's wages recklessly, for instance. Exertion of even a little bit of willpower by taking another route, one priest thought, could help sidestep that trap.[21]

But occasions of sin could be more dangerous than this, as a second set of distinctions made clear: those that were necessary and those that were unnecessary. A necessary occasion was one a person "cannot avoid even though he puts forth a reasonable effort to do so," whereas an unnecessary occasion was "one to which a person freely exposes himself." An adolescent who "would like to conquer a habit of impurity," for instance, a pamphlet writer said in 1962, obviously talking about masturbation, but who kept buying "cheap and suggestive magazines" was exposing himself unnecessarily to an occasion of sin, thereby doubling his culpability. Not avoiding this occasion demonstrated that there was apparently "no true sorrow," and it would be difficult for a priest in confession to impart forgiveness. The factory worker surrounded by crude colleagues was in a tougher spot. The textbook writer suggested that he ask the boss for a transfer, but if he could not get one, he was forced to endure this occasion, and he would have to try all the harder not to fall. Other necessary occasions were much more serious: a husband or wife who found their spouse "trying to persuade them to sins of contraception," or a doctor "expected by hospital or civil authorities to perform an immoral operation, such as abortion or sterilization."[22] In cases of this kind, Catholics might not be able to remove themselves from the occasion of sin, and heightened vigilance was essential.

Such considerations had helped bring the larger question of contraception to the fore by the middle decades of the twentieth century. Most Protestant churches had changed their views on the moral standing of married couples who limited or spaced their children, but the Catholic church held to its traditional teaching that any such practice was grievously wrong. A papal encyclical in 1930 had stated the matter in language that was convoluted but nonetheless clear. Since "the conjugal act is destined primarily by nature for the begetting of children," the pope said, "those who in exercising it deliberately frustrate its natural power and purpose sin against nature and commit a deed which is shameful and intrinsically vicious; . . . those who indulge in such are branded with the guilt of a grave sin." Sexual activity ("the conjugal act") was legitimate only if it was at least open to the possibility that a child might be the result. Any form of "birth prevention is wrong," said a priest from Wisconsin who was chaplain to a laywomen's group, "for the same reason that a lie is wrong; because it uses a faculty"—he could not actually bring himself to say "sex"—"and defeats the purpose of that faculty," just as a lie abused the faculty of speech. As the *Messenger of the Sacred Heart* had said in answer to an inquiry, "No set of circumstances justifies this course of action."[23]

Some Catholic couples might think they had valid reasons for using "artificial" methods of birth control, but priests were uniformly certain that they were misguided or simply incorrect in such thinking. "It is better for the layman not to attempt to judge the right to limit offspring," one Dominican wrote confidently, "he should have recourse to someone trained to make judgments in moral matters." Monsignor J. D. Conway, who was the head of the marriage court overseeing annulments for the diocese of Davenport, Iowa, and whose question box appeared in many diocesan newspapers, was even more pointed. In 1955, a woman told him that she had been reading various publications that favored contraception, thinking that she should honestly try to "see both sides" of the issue. "Your zeal for honesty is misleading you," Conway told her, pulling priestly rank. "If you were a moral theologian," such wide reading might be harmless, since she would then be able pick out the errors. "But in your case, your fervent desire for seeing both sides of the question convinces me that you are gullible enough to simply devour those errors." Two years later, a seminary professor in Boston stated the matter coolly in print. "Even when an excusing cause is present, often it will be more advisable and more praiseworthy for a couple to continue to build a family, placing their trust in Divine Providence." In class, this same professor had made clear that the confessional was the place where the church's firm position had to be enforced. Any priest, the professor's student recorded in his notes from the discussion, who "tells [a] penitent that contraception is not sinful for him, priest is guilty."[24] Such institutional certainty aside, the question of contraception in the confessional would persist, even as lay Catholics grew increasingly unpersuaded by the church's arguments, particularly after approval of the birth control pill for sale in the United States in 1960.

Equally firm was the church's long-standing position on abortion, based on the apparently unambiguous prohibition of murder in the Ten Commandments. Jone's *Moral Theology* had settled the matter succinctly: "The *direct killing* of the foetus [*sic*] is murder and therefore always gravely sinful" — so sinful, in fact, that abortion was a "reserved sin." Only a bishop (or a priest acting with a bishop's specific permission) could absolve it. Still, the case analysis of the theology manuals had to be applied here as with other issues. To restore her own health, for example, a gravely ill mother could take medicine which caused an abortion even though that was not her purpose, "presupposing that there is no other remedy for the illness and the restoration to health does not result from the abortion but from the medication." Here as always, the intentions of the participants mattered to a determining degree, but the prohibition against abortion was as absolute as anything could be. Attitudes of American Catholics about abortion were beginning to change throughout the period before the legalization of the procedure nationwide in the *Roe v. Wade* decision of the Supreme Court in 1973. In the meanwhile, the fixity of the church's position seems to have precluded laypeople asking about it from the usual authorities: why ask if you already know the answer? The subject virtually never came up in the question box columns of Catholic periodicals. One writer addressed a general question to *Sign* magazine about the conditions under which a priest might withhold forgiveness in the confessional, and it was the magazine that offered abortion as an example, even though "H. C." had not specifically asked about it. Again, clarity was the hallmark: "in every case of abortion," the sin was mortal and "excommunication is incurred" automatically.[25]

The rest of the Ten Commandments covered territory of possible sins that was less contested than these sexual issues but still serious. The injunction to keep the Sabbath holy, for example, prompted near-Talmudic concerns about what activities were and were not permitted on Sundays. The catechism here introduced the idea of "servile" work, defined as "labor that is more of the body than of the mind." Such work was forbidden, but what constituted servile work? Was it right or wrong for a housewife to sew on Sunday, someone wanted to know. Wrong, the *Messenger of the Sacred Heart* answered in 1946, "unless the need is immediate and pressing," though permitted in the case of "artistic work, such as embroidery." Paying the rent was not sinful. Washing the family car, however, was indeed servile work, and in fact it might be two sins at once. It clearly violated the command to rest on the Sabbath, but it was also the sin of giving scandal to others if it was done "in full view of the neighbors." Some authorities tried to draw finer distinctions yet, attempting to specify how

much time could be spent at a servile task. Three hours probably crossed the line between venial and mortal sin, more
than one priestly authority said, though two and a half hours
was sufficient "in the case of very laborious work." Genteel
notions of the proper way to spend Sundays in America were
not very far beneath the surface of all this and, as with other
sins that laypeople worried about, the insignificance of the
concern seems apparent today.[26] But it is a testament to the
hold that these ideas had on the minds of American Catholics
throughout the first half of the twentieth century that such
questions troubled them in the first place.

✠

NO LESS IMPORTANT THAN the Ten Commandments in prescribing good and proscribing bad behaviors were what the
Catechism called the Six Precepts of the Church. As with so
much else, these had a history of development, taking explicit
form in the aftermath of the Reformation. They provided
readily apparent badges of denominational identity, specifying things that Catholics did which Protestants did not do.
The church's emphasis on the importance of obeying them
thus acted as a powerful tool in resisting Catholic "leakage"
to other faiths in the pluralistic United States, a problem bishops and priests worried about perhaps more than they needed
to. Laypeople found it easy to ingrain most of them in regular
family habits. The precepts were presented succinctly, beginning with the requirement that all Catholics attend Mass on
Sundays and on the church's special "holy days of obligation"
(that is, the obligation to go to Mass), of which there were
six scattered throughout the year. Second came obedience
to the laws of fasting (only one large meal allowed, with no
snacking between meals) and abstinence (no meat) on certain
days. The latter applied most obviously to every Friday, but
there might be other occasions during the year, such as Lent,

when both practices were required on other days as well. The next two rules covered the necessity for confession and for communion, respectively, at least once a year, followed by the responsibility "to contribute to the support of the Church." Last on the list was simply stated but it involved a good deal of detail: the obligation to observe the church's laws regarding marriage. This covered such questions as the impossibility of divorce, but it was most immediately intended to apply to cases of "mixed marriages"—Catholics marrying non-Catholics—which the church did not explicitly forbid, though it did try to discourage them as much as possible.[27]

Because these precepts involved direct personal actions, it was easy for almost all Catholics to know when they were obeying them and when not. Sunday Mass attendance, for example, became ingrained, though some effort had been needed to instill this habit early on as the church's infrastructure began to spread. At the turn of the century, a priest sent to open a new church in the rural town of Yale in Michigan's "Thumb" had had to work at convincing his parishioners on this score. "For one hundred successive Sundays," Father Patrick Cullinane recalled in later life, most likely exaggerating for effect, he reminded them from the pulpit of their weekly obligation. It was hard for him not to get discouraged about spotty attendance until someone finally confessed to missing Mass on a Sunday. "I said to myself—Thank God," he concluded, "not indeed because the person had failed in his duty," but because the man had at last recognized his lapse as a sin that had to be repented and confessed. In ensuing decades, weekly Mass attendance by American Catholics rose steadily. Precise statistics are hard to come by, but all observers agreed that until the 1960s rates of practice were well above 50 percent. Attendance on holy days (such as Ascension Thursday in the spring, commemorating Jesus's return to heaven, and the Feast of All Saints on November 1) was also high: most parishes had almost as many scheduled masses on those days, which were otherwise normal work days, as on Sundays. But the desire of some Catholics to be exacting in following the rules could always prompt new questions. If, as the guide to the Baltimore Catechism had urged teachers to tell their pupils, "we should keep the holy-days of obligation as we should keep the Sunday," questions about servile work on those days might arise, a nice conjunction of a biblical commandment and a church precept. As late as 1962, one troubled Catholic had many uncertainties on this score: Could one go shopping on holy days, even for groceries? Should Catholic barbers and shopkeepers close for the day, as they did on Sunday? By then, the *Messenger of the Sacred Heart* was becoming less exacting. Going shopping for anything other than absolute necessities might not be formally sinful, but neither was it "in keeping with the spirit of a holy day." As for the barbers, "it would be a good thing" if they took the day off as a kind of public witness to their faith, though the magazine refrained from condemning them if they did not.[28]

Whether from God himself in the commandments of Sinai or from the authoritative requirements of the church, the standards for discerning sinful behavior had many sources, and Catholics could use them to identify sins beyond those that existed in theoretical cases. More to the point, they could recognize as blameworthy or blameless things they themselves had done and not done. They had a larger framework in which to place and to understand human behavior—*their* behavior. That framework was complicated and expansive, filled with categories and distinctions: original and actual sins; mortal and venial sins; sins of omission and sins of commission; grievous matter, sufficient reflection, and full consent; proximate and remote occasions of sin; necessary and unnecessary occasions. Detailed though it was, this method of mental analysis was, the church believed, capable of being mastered by ordinary parishioners and even by children. The church had given Catholics the tools, the words, to judge the moral and ethical dimensions of their lives, to know right and wrong. When they did the right thing, they could be confident that they had done so. When they did the wrong thing, they could be equally confident in recognizing it as wrong, and they could take the necessary steps to regret, to repent, and to do better in the future.

Sin was everywhere—or, better, it *might be* anywhere. Even the most mundane actions of everyday life were freighted with moral significance, a significance that was a truly serious business. The big sins were obvious: murder, adultery, theft, and so on. But there was a potentially unlimited number of smaller sins, still sinful even if of lesser gravity, and possibly more sinful than they at first appeared. Perhaps dozens of times a day, perfectly ordinary believers, "workaday Catholics," had the chance to sever their connection to God, sometimes minimally, sometimes completely. What they did, what they said, what they thought, what they did not do—it all mattered to a profound degree. In the worst of cases, their ultimate fate hung in the balance. Every single day, they had the ability to send themselves to hell for all eternity. That consequence would be terrifying indeed without the remedy that confession offered.

3

Confessing

IN THE 1880s, $3,000 was a lot of money, several times greater than the total annual wages of an ordinary immigrant in Boston. For more than a decade, some of those immigrants had been lucky enough to find steady work, which paid them about a dollar a day, by helping to build a massive new cathedral, replacing a smaller, decaying structure that had been in use since the beginning of the century. This new Cathedral of the Holy Cross was of impressive proportions. Occupying an entire city block, it was by far the largest church building in New England—one of the largest buildings, period—and, in a nod toward interurban competition, it was even bigger than Saint Patrick's Cathedral in New York, itself just recently finished. It could hold up to two thousand people when fully packed, and the taller of its two front towers, at three hundred feet, dominated the city's skyline. Acknowledging the closer-to-home competition with the local Yankee Protestant establishment, a priest there liked to point out that this tower was fully eighty feet taller than another local landmark, the Bunker Hill Monument, which commemorated an early battle of the American Revolution. The building was, the priest said, "grand enough to meet our wants and to satisfy our aspirations."[1]

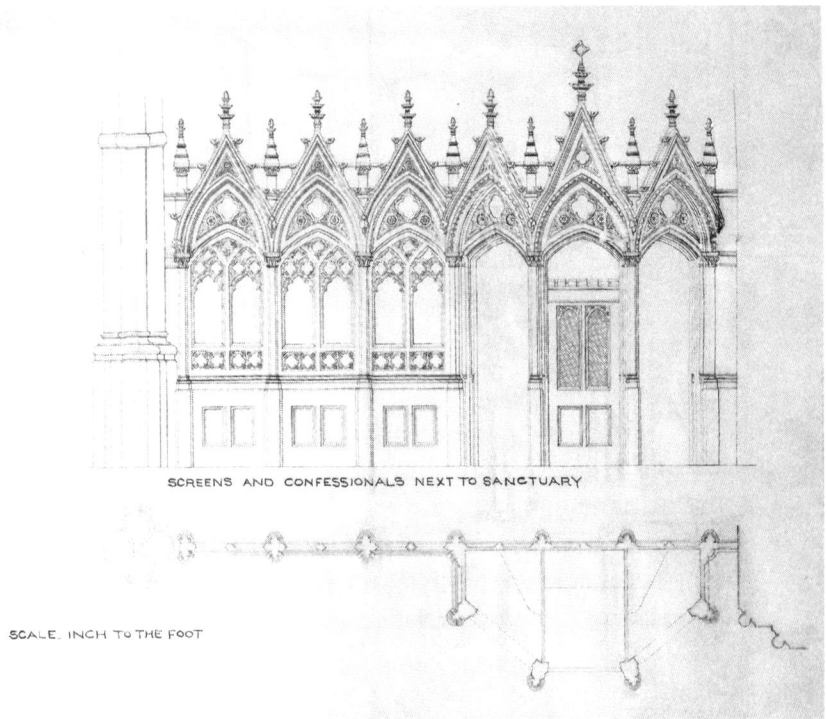

SCREENS AND CONFESSIONALS NEXT TO SANCTUARY

SCALE. INCH TO THE FOOT

Architectural drawing, Cathedral of the Holy Cross, Boston, 1880s, showing plans for confessionals (at right); below, a view of the confessionals as seen from above.
Credit: Archives, Archdiocese of Boston

But a cathedral is more than just a big building that makes a big statement about big aspirations. It is also a parish church like any other, serving the Catholics of its surrounding neighborhood, and so Holy Cross needed everything that any church had to have: altar, pews, choir loft, organ, and all the rest. It also needed confessional boxes, where parishioners could go, as they so regularly did, to confess their sins and to receive God's pardon. A builder and furniture maker from the nearby industrial city of Lowell named John Welch won the contract to erect four confessionals inside the new cathedral for the total price of $3,000. Each one, standing against a side wall, would be built of "the very best black walnut lumber and my best Calumet finish," Welch said, and it would have three compartments. In the middle was a small doored space, roughly three feet square, with a seat, just big enough for a priest to sit in. On either side was a similarly sized enclosure, to be covered by a curtain, where a parishioner could enter, kneel down, and talk in a low voice to the priest through a screen or grille. Each of those small openings was covered by a sliding wood door, at about the sitting priest's ear level, and he could close off one side for privacy while listening to the penitent on the other. By alternating from side to side, he could keep the line waiting outside moving.[2]

Not every Catholic church in America was as grand as Holy Cross in Boston, and not every confessional box was as expensive to make as these had been. A few years before, in a small church in the town of Columbia in Lancaster County, Pennsylvania, a carpenter had built one for just over twenty dollars.[3] But no matter the cost of their construction, confessionals of the same basic design became the site for the usual practice of this sacrament. Parishioners came to know these darkened, anonymous spaces as they went about the business of confessing.

✠

PRIESTS HAD ALWAYS URGED their parishioners to approach the confessional soberly and with earnest intent. When Father Joseph Greaton, the missionary in early Maryland, warned his people in the 1740s against treating their confession "as if it were an idle story," he hoped to prompt them to careful reflection and sincere sorrow, and he was striking a theme that later generations of priests would repeat over and over. "It is a serious business," one Jesuit told a class of college students

in the 1940s, one to which they should "give the same attention you would to a serious business affair." He even suggested that they imagine themselves "making out your income
tax." In that case, they would have to tell the truth even when
it was to their disadvantage, though they should also consider
any factors that counted in their favor. "You want to remember all your exemptions," he noted. "Remember all the money
you gave to charity." At the same time, they should not err
in the opposite direction, inflating the number of their sins
just to cover anything they may have left out: "it's wrong to
give too high a number too," he said. Confession demanded
a full and honest moral accounting, and it needed to be done
"seriously and carefully."[4] When American Catholics went to
confession, they tried to act on their priests' instructions.

Catholic theology described the sacrament as having three
successive stages: contrition, confession, and satisfaction. The
first of these had many subordinate steps, but it was both
the most important and, in many ways, the most difficult to
accomplish since it took place entirely inside the heads of
ordinary believers. The real work of confession began with
them. Penitents' task was to take the church's detailed understanding of sin and, after prayerful consideration, apply it to
themselves, to their own lives and actions, and in particular
to what they had done since the last time they had been to
confession. This process was called the examination of conscience, and they were expected to conduct it before they
ever entered the confessional box or spoke to the confessor.
Originally a monastic practice, the examination could be
done by laypeople too. A great many guides were available,
in pamphlet form and otherwise, to help them in this, and
most of these agreed that reviewing the Ten Commandments
and the Six Precepts of the Church was, as one textbook said
in the 1920s, "perhaps the easiest method." Even the youngest or least sophisticated Catholic had a general sense of what

those standards were, of what they required and what they forbade.[5]

In conducting this scrutiny of themselves, penitents were told to strive for completeness. "Hasty preparation" undercut the value of the entire exercise, one priest wrote, producing only "thoughtless acknowledgment" of one's faults and leaving open the possibility that some wrongdoing would be overlooked. As a guard against this, most of the texts guiding lay people through the process offered detailed lists of questions that they could ask themselves. The second commandment, for instance, prohibited taking the Lord's name in vain. The *Saint Joseph's Missal*, a popular devotional volume that contained translated texts of the Mass (still entirely in Latin) together with other prayers, accepted this general injunction on its face. "Have I taken God's name in vain?" was the logical place to begin. Then, it raised several more specific possibilities, such as "have I made false, unlawful or unnecessary oaths?" The fifth commandment, proscribing murder, got more expansive treatment, identifying some possible precursors to an act of killing that might, in effect, constitute its functional equivalent. "Have I been angry? Have I been violent toward another, or caused violence without just cause? Have I been jealous of others?" Even "have I been guilty of drinking to excess" came under this rubric. As always, the dangerous territory of the sixth commandment demanded attention: "Have I deliberately taken pleasure in impure thoughts? . . . Have I gone to places of amusement that I knew would lead me into sin? Have I kept away from other occasions of sin?" If completeness was the goal, this kind of detailed cross-examination of oneself was obviously useful, though by the middle of the twentieth century, some Catholics were beginning to see its limitations. A priest of the early 1960s worried that a quick run-through of basic moral requirements threatened to become "a matter of picking out a few sins from this entire

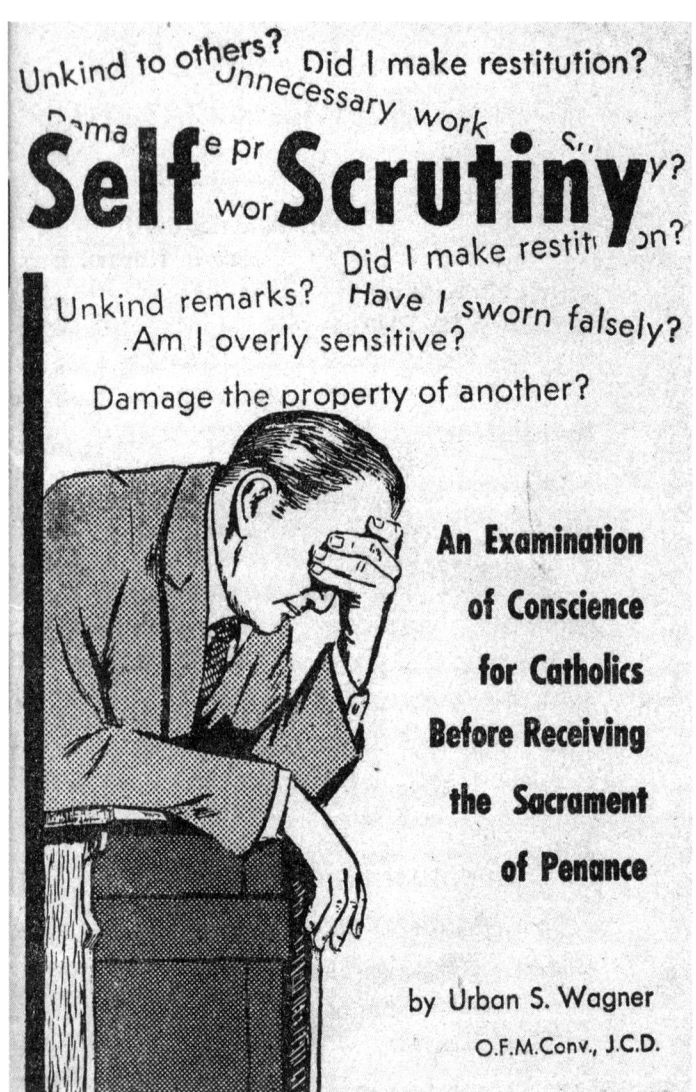

A guide to the examination of conscience, 1960.
Urban Wagner, *Self-Scrutiny: An Examination of Conscience for Catholics Before Receiving the Sacrament of Penance* (Chaska MN: Conventual Franciscan Fathers, 1960).
Credit: Burns Library, Boston College

catalogue," and was thus not a thoughtful enough reflection on one's own behavior. A laywoman agreed, saying that "the standard list of sins" did not, in her experience, "yield much" of value. But the enumerations of sins persisted. "We can make a good examination of conscience," the Baltimore Catechism told generations of Catholic schoolchildren, "by calling to mind the commandments of God and of the Church, and by asking ourselves how we may have sinned with regard to them."[6]

Theoretically, such a detailed approach could go on indefinitely, but actual practice enforced common limits. To begin with, as the *Messenger of the Sacred Heart* said in response to a questioner in 1947, "a good Catholic who goes to Confession regularly does not have to make this entire review in every examination of conscience," though it was profitable to attempt a more comprehensive effort periodically. The magazine agreed with many writers in thinking that fifteen minutes was about the optimal outer boundary; a few years later, *Sign* magazine thought that regular penitents might need only five minutes. Either way, since there was usually a wait, most people would normally have sufficient time between their arrival at church and their entry into the box. Even so, the "examen" (the Latin was often used as a shorthand) consisted not merely of assembling a random assortment of sins—mentally, of course; no one should be urged to write them down, except perhaps "very dull children"—but also of classifying them according to what were called "number" and "kind." The question of number was simple: how many times had one missed Mass on Sunday or eaten meat on Friday? In more serious matters, how many times had one stolen something, or coveted someone, or taken delight in an impure thought? The penitent had the duty to try to remember specific instances, to note the tally, and to be precise. "If person *knows* he has committed a sin 5 times," wrote the seminarian in Boston who was noting his teacher's comments in his copy of Noldin, "and says to priest *about* 5 times," that was itself sinful. "About" was an acceptable measure only when the penitent was genuinely unsure, and a "person who can't remember must come as closely as possible." There might even be a responsibility to amend the record in a future confession if one or more episodes of sin had been initially missed but remembered later.[7]

Consideration of "kind" demanded more care, since it asked penitents to differentiate between their mortal and their venial sins, as defined by the church. Priests and popular devotional writers were only too willing to help penitents decide which was which. Strictly speaking, only mortal sins had to be confessed and forgiven, but parishioners were always urged to confess their venial sins as well, particularly since the line between the two might be a thin one. Classifications and distinctions multiplied. As we have seen, a child's disobedience of a parent was normally venial, though in serious matters it might be mortal. In the same way, lying was usually a venial sin, though if it "violates other virtues, like justice or religion, it can easily be a mortal sin." In some cases, of course, there was no doubt. Those who insisted that there was "no such thing as a deliberate venial sin" when it came to chastity allowed for no ambiguity. Printers' gimmicks could reinforce this way of specifying the level of gravity of any offense. One pamphlet from 1960, written by a Franciscan, put all the mortal sins in capital letters, thereby ensuring that they would stand out on the page: "Have I SWORN FALSELY? . . . Did I deliberately DENY A TRUTH REVEALED BY GOD OR TAUGHT BY THE CHURCH?" A Jesuit publication from the 1920s had been even more creative with its typography. Mortal sins were in capital letters, venial sins were in lowercase italics, and venial sins that might under certain circumstances become mortal were in boldface: "Did I MISS MASS ON SUNDAYS . . . THROUGH MY OWN FAULT? Did

Fourth Commandment

Did I *disobey my parents?*
Did I *disobey my teachers?*
Did I *make fun of old people?*
Was I *mean towards my parents?*
Was I *mean towards my teachers?*

Fifth Commandment

Was I *angry? Stubborn?*
Was I *unkind or mean to others?*
Did I look down on others? (Pride)
Did I **wish evil** to others?
Did I **hate** others?
Did I **try to "get even" with others?**
(Revenge.)
Did I *fight or quarrel?*
Did I *make others fight?*
Did I **lead others to sin by my bad
example?**

— 4 —

Sixth and Ninth Commandments

DID I WILLINGLY TAKE
PLEASURE IN USING IM-
PURE WORDS?

DID I WILLINGLY TELL IM-
PURE STORIES AND TAKE
PLEASURE IN THEM?

DID I LIKE TO LISTEN TO IM-
PURE TALK?

DID I TAKE PLEASURE IN
SINGING IMPURE SONGS?

DID I WANT IMPURE
THOUGHTS, AND DID I
TAKE PLEASURE IN THEM?

DID I TEACH OTHERS TO
COMMIT IMPURE SINS?

DID I TAKE PLEASURE IN
TOUCHING MYSELF OR
OTHERS IN AN IMPURE
MANNER, OR LET OTHERS
DO SO TO ME?

— 5 —

An examination of conscience depicting the different levels of sins with
different typefaces, 1927.
A. J. Wilwerding, *Examination of Conscience for Boys and Girls* (St. Louis:
Queen's Work, 1927).
Credit: Burns Library, Boston College

I *misbehave in church?* Did I **come late to Mass through my
own fault?**"[8]

How often or how closely any individual penitent relied
on one of these precisely crafted and imaginatively designed
guides is impossible to know. Some people may have thumbed
through them while doing their examen or consulted them
occasionally. Most parishioners probably did not, and we
should therefore resist the temptation to over-read these texts.
Still, this approach to the process helped to frame Catholic
thinking on the subject. The very profusion of publications

testifies to at least the perception of the need and the demand for them, and priests always felt a responsibility to stress the importance of careful self-surveillance, however it was accomplished. "Inculcate need of examination of conscience," one professor in 1964 told a classroom of seminarians preparing for the priesthood, "in pulpit, in catechism classes, on visitations" to parishioners' homes. "Show them how to do it, following the commandments of God and of the Church as adapted to their own lives."[9] Preaching, particularly that which was conducted during parish missions, reinforced the idea that Catholics had to assess their behavior according to the standards the church had articulated for them. The distinction between mortal and venial sin was not an abstract point of theology, of concern only to the clergy. Rather, it was objective and knowable; laypeople could grasp it and then apply it specifically to their own lives and actions.

So much attention to the kinds and levels of sin produced, perhaps inevitably, a steady inflationary pressure that constantly expanded the list of mortal sins. If lying could "easily" be something more than venial, the risk of grievous offense was ever present. Apparently, it was easy to commit a mortal sin, a conclusion that underlined, even if only implicitly, priestly calls for frequent confession. "How often has the fell shadow of mortal sin been on my soul!" one preacher urged his parishioners to ask themselves. "Had death suddenly snapped asunder the thin thread of life, I would be tortured forever in that pool of fire prepared for the devil and his wicked angels." (His listeners probably did not know that he was borrowing, without attribution, the image from the eighteenth-century Puritan divine, Jonathan Edwards.) The amount of time spent at servile work on Sunday, for instance, ratcheted up the seriousness of the crime, possibly without one even knowing it: in such a case, it was the clock that turned venial sin into mortal sin. Reading the whole of a book that was on the Index of Forbidden Books (a catalog of writings condemned by Rome for their presumed heretical or immoral content) was clearly a mortal sin, but reading just a part of it that constituted "a serious danger to one's faith or morals" was probably mortal too, according to the *Messenger of the Sacred Heart*. "Complete" drunkenness (as opposed to mild intoxication) was a mortal sin, added the *Sign*. Even writers who sought to take a more positive approach to the examination of conscience found that graver sins outnumbered lesser faults. Donald Miller, a popular writer and Redemptorist priest committed to the more lenient Liguorian tradition, urged what he thought was a better general method. Monthly penitents, he suggested, might try to focus first on a different virtue each month—faith in January, love of neighbor in May, humility in December—and only then to identify how they had sinned against those noble traits. When he outlined some of the common transgressions associated with each one, however, he found more mortal than venial sins. His was, he thought, "a fairly complete list," and for the year he identified 220 possible mortal sins, but only 147 venial. In July, there were twenty-eight mortal sins that went against justice, including paying inadequate wages and failing to make restitution, with just twelve venial sins, including cheating at cards.[10] Sophisticated theologians might object, but ordinary parishioners had grounds for thinking that most of the sins they were likely to commit could well be mortal. Better, perhaps, to assume that than not; all the more reason to come to confession often.

However thorough or hasty, however guided by the clergy or self-directed, however thoughtful or habitual, the examination of conscience was only the first step. Once it had been completed, penitents moved on to the core of contrition itself: feeling sorry for what they had done. This, too, was not to be approached, as Greaton might have put it, idly. "We do not merely grieve for our sins in words," said one instructional manual, originally published in Britain but widely available in the United States, "but also detest them in our heart, . . . and sincerely wish we had not committed them." Moreover, it was important to be sorry for the right reason, and in guiding penitents toward that ideal the church spelled out two different kinds of contrition: perfect and imperfect. (Since the Middle Ages, the latter had also sometimes been called "attrition.") Perfect contrition was achieved when penitents were sorry for what they had done simply because sin offended God, who deserved better from his creatures. Imperfect contrition resulted from the fear of punishment, however just it was, or from inadequate motivation. "Let us consider how terrible are the pains of hell or of purgatory, which we have deserved; how beautiful heaven, which we have lost," the British catechism went on. In the confessional, such fears were sufficient as an expression of sorrow in order for the sacrament to have its effect, but it was always better for penitents to strive for perfect contrition, which was by its nature "supernatural." Priests often thought that, with a little effort, they could convert the one into the other. A priest in Washington, DC, in the first decade of the twentieth century described for some colleagues how he had the children in his parish school, particularly the girls, write a short note to their fathers every month, urging them to go to confession. He was hoping that Daddy would be embarrassed if he failed to respond to an entreaty from such a source. (As a practical matter, the priest suggested that the exercise could be done as part of a penmanship lesson.) Reluctant fathers' motives for going to confession in this instance might not have been the right ones, but once on the spot the pastor believed that, through words of encouragement, he could "make their sorrow supernatural," thus perfecting otherwise imperfect contrition.[11]

As usual, there was often a gap between official theology and popular understanding, and the fear of dire eternal consequences always had its uses, especially when dealing with children. The Baltimore Catechism itemized the reasons why they should feel contrition for a sin, particularly if it was mortal: "because it is the greatest of all evils, gravely offends God, keeps us out of heaven, and condemns us forever to hell." Offense to God was sandwiched in the middle; the prospect of hell was the clinching argument. Another guidebook, this one "especially adapted to the age and circumstances of the average boy or girl," also seemed to promote imperfect rather than perfect contrition. "One mortal sin is enough to keep my soul from Heaven; one mortal sin is enough to send my soul to Hell," it said. Fear of punishment was exactly the inverse of what theologians described as the right approach to contrition, but it may also have been the more potent one in implanting the idea of contrition in young minds in a way that would endure. Later on, adults could be given more nuanced explanations. "Motives founded on fear" never disappeared entirely when it came to contrition, wrote Bernard Häring, a German theologian who exerted a strong influence in American seminary education in the 1950s and 1960s. "Rather they are purified, invigorated, and elevated to the dignity and value of the sorrow whose motive is love."[12]

Whether with adults or with children, there was an obvious way to test the sincerity of a penitent's contrition, and this was called the purpose of amendment. Getting sinners to the point of regretting that they had ever committed their sins in the first place, as the British catechism had put it, was complemented by asking them to resist those same sins in the future. "It is not enough," Häring offered as an example for his students, "for an adulterer to resolve never to commit the sin of adultery again, if he is not prepared to banish the evil desire for his accomplice in sin from his mind and

heart." John B. Sheerin, an American Paulist priest, made
the same point for a more popular audience. "A man who
does not really intend to amend his life had better not go to
Confession at all," he wrote in 1951. "He is only wasting his
own time, wasting the priest's time, and in addition committing a sacrilege by hypocritically feigning a sorrow he doesn't
feel." It was easy enough to say that one was sorry, but the
words were empty if new sinful inclinations were not resisted.
Unfortunately for good intentions, reality usually intervened,
and most penitents recognized that they were committing
and confessing the same sins over and over. Priests knew it
too. This problem was often called "recidivism," a term that
reinforced the judicial metaphors surrounding confession.
"When there is no improvement from Confession to Confession," the *Messenger of the Sacred Heart* had told an inquirer in
1936, "there is reason to suspect a lack of true sorrow for our
sins and of determination to amend." In practice, however,
most priests applied a loose construction to the whole idea,
even while adding (as they often did) the reinforcing adjective "firm" to the purpose of amendment. As long as one was
"making a serious effort and taking due precautions to avoid
sins," Sheerin concluded, that was probably good enough.
No penitent could "promise that he will not sin again for he
cannot control the future." Forming a "resolve to cooperate
with God's grace" as best one could, perhaps especially by
avoiding familiar occasions of sin, was sufficient to fulfill the
requirements.[13]

When penitents reached this point, they had completed the
first of the three stages that made up the sacrament of confession. Done correctly, it had been a detailed and frank inner
conversation. They had called back to their memory specific
things they had done or said or thought in everyday life, and
they were able to recognize those which failed to meet the
moral standards that the church—and they themselves—had

[margin note, handwritten:] the strange state of mind this creates

set. They had not simply identified general categories of wrongful behavior. Rather, they had recognized particular instances, they had counted up the number of times they had done each one, and they had acknowledged that some were more serious than others. They had achieved an appropriate level of sorrow for their behavior and expressed their desire—their hope, perhaps—not to fall into the same failings again. Now they were ready to enter the box and to proceed with their actual confession.

✠

ALMOST ALL CONFESSIONAL BOXES in America had the same basic tripartite design, though minor variations were not unknown, depending on the size and layout of any given church. Sometimes, they stood out from the inner walls; elsewhere, given the architectural plan for a church's interior, they might actually be built into the wall. However arranged, these private spaces, set apart exclusively for this purpose, had long been familiar to American Catholics. Bishops checked regularly with local pastors to make sure the mandate that all churches contain them was being implemented. In Detroit, for example, every pastor had to file an annual report with his archbishop's office, providing summary data, both statistical (number of baptisms and weddings, enrollment in the school if there was one) and financial (regular and special collections, any debts or mortgages on the property). "Are there Confessionals *in loco publico et patenti in ecclesia*?" the reporting form asked in the 1880s, quoting the official rule. The answer always had to be yes, apart from unusual circumstances, which would have to be explained: a church that was still under construction, perhaps. In later years, the questionnaire requested more detail: How many confessionals were there in each church, it was asking by the 1940s, and were they "conspicuous? Are they provided with gratings and sliding doors? Is there a crucifix or devout image in the penitent's side of the confessional?"[14] Local priests needed little encouragement to meet the expectations of their diocesan superiors, since they knew that they and their people would be spending many hours in these boxes.

While a few other lights in the church might be illuminated, the procedure of confession itself was conducted in the dark. There were no lights in the compartments that parishioners used and no adornment other than the "crucifix or devout image" that was expected in Detroit and common almost everywhere. Penitents might look at it as they entered and left, and this helped set the right spiritual mood for what they were doing. Once inside, there was a place for them to kneel (the normal posture) and perhaps a little shelf on which they could rest their folded hands as they confessed. By the early years of the twentieth century, these compartments were often equipped with an electrical switch that turned on a light outside over the entryway, signaling that the space was occupied. The priest's section of the box usually had a light, which he could switch on to read if times were slow. Though it seems implausible given the number of confessions he heard every week, Father Patrick Healy in New York said that, on at least one occasion, he was able to complete the daily reading from his breviary (required of all priests) while waiting for penitents to come. Most of the time, however, confessors had little opportunity for that, and the light remained off. This helped preserve the anonymity of the process, ensuring that the faces of those confessing could not be observed through the grille, even in reflection. Priests were also trained to avert their eyes or to stare straight ahead to foreclose any possibility of recognition. Efforts were usually made in construction to muffle the sound inside the box, though in any case both confessor and penitent spoke as softly as possible to reduce the chances of anyone else overhearing their interaction. Some churches also roped off the immediately adjacent pews during regular confession hours, keeping other parishioners at a safe enough distance to preserve privacy.[15]

Whatever the particular design of the space they encountered, laypeople were taught the standard formula for confessing early and then followed it throughout their lives. There might be minor variations in wording (depending on distinct ethnic traditions, perhaps), but the essence was always the same. "When the priest opens the little slide," instructed an elementary school textbook from 1936, written by a sister of the Cenacle order, "make the sign of the cross, and then ask the priest to bless you, saying: 'Bless me Father, for I have sinned.'" Next, they should say how long it had been since the last time they had been to confession. "After that, tell all of your sins, and always tell how many times you have committed each sin." Once this list, the product of the examination of conscience, had been presented, the priest might or might not ask a question or two for clarification. If he did, "be sure to answer the questions clearly and truthfully." Next, he could offer some heartening words before assigning a penance, usually in the form of a certain number of prayers to be said by the penitent afterwards. The ritual then moved to its conclusion. While the penitent recited the short prayer known as the Act of Contrition, beginning with the words "O my God, I am heartily sorry for having offended Thee," the priest quietly pronounced the prayer of absolution in Latin, making the sign of the cross in the direction of the person on the other side of the screen as he did so. The priest then closed the "little slide" between them, opened the one on the other side, and the penitent left the box, quickly replaced by someone else.[16]

None of this took very long. The renowned moral theologian John C. Ford, SJ, told a class of seminarians that, under normal circumstances, they would be able to listen to a penitent, form the necessary judgments about the completeness

and sincerity of the confession, "say a few words of advice
or encouragement or consolation, [and] give absolution—
all in the space of a minute and a half." He was not far off.
Father James Walsh, the newly ordained curate in Boston's
Roxbury district at the turn of the century, once counted 125
confessions (including "many men," he noted in his diary)
in four and three-quarter hours. On average, he was speaking with a new penitent every two minutes and fifteen seconds. A month later, he heard the confessions of 105 children
from his parish school in four and a half hours; a new child
was entering his confessional about every two minutes and
thirty seconds. Patrick Healy sometimes averaged less than
two minutes per penitent: three and a quarter hours one day,
102 confessions, one minute and fifty seconds each. From his
scholarly perch in New Orleans, Joseph Fichter concluded
that, depending on how many priests were available and how
many of their neighbors were also waiting, parishioners in
"St. Mary's" spent about fifteen minutes from the time they
entered the church for confession until the time they left it to
return home, their sacramental work done. In 1950, a magazine for the diocesan clergy worried about "how it looks"
when confessors turned over penitents too quickly, thereby
undercutting the seriousness of confession. Priestly "speedkings," it said, should not pride themselves on their pace; they
might think they were being efficient, but it was nonetheless
unseemly.[17] Even so, many parishioners, like the man who
told Fichter approvingly that one priest in his parish "didn't
take all day," appreciated the speed. Like an uneventful trip
to the dentist, it was all over quickly.

Certain factors might slow the pace down, and none were
dreaded more by penitents than those occasions when the
priest had to ask some direct questions. If the penitent,
prompted by even the anonymous embarrassment of it all,
had not made clear exactly what sins had been committed,

the confessor's duty was to find out in order to make a proper assessment. Was the sin mortal or venial? As long as he was unsure, he could not absolve the sinner's guilt or assign the appropriate penalty. Lack of clarity might accompany any sin, but to no one's surprise it was most common when the transgressions went against chastity. The penitent did not, said one moral theologian, have to "give a detailed description of his thoughts and acts; such details are entirely unbecoming in the confessional." But priests did have to seek out at least some additional information when it was necessary. The "priest needs to know," John Ford told a group of all-male seniors enrolled in his class on the sacraments at Boston College in 1948, and then he spelled out some of the details that had to be clear: "married or single, thoughts or deeds, alone or with others, same sex or opposite sex, other person married or single, complete act or incomplete act"—further clarifying this last item on his list by adding a blunt "(i.e., orgasm)." If, for example, a young man said "I was guilty of impure touching with my girl friend, 3 times," that was enough. "Further details <u>unnecessary</u>," Ford stressed, underlining the final word in his lecture notes. But if a married adult man was having a long-term affair with his secretary and said only "I was guilty of impurity with a girl," that was insufficient; a fuller picture of the circumstances had to be elicited through questions. By laying down the law in such explicit detail, Ford was probably hoping that his students would internalize the lesson in advance and thus spare future confessors from having to press them, a hope that may or may not have been realized. When he was speaking to seminarians, however, he was more equivocal, perhaps acknowledging how awkward an interrogation might get. "If in doubt as to the prudence of a question," he told these Jesuits on their way to ordination, "don't ask it." Better, he thought, that "afterwards, when you have the time, try to figure out if and how you could have gotten more information with a prudent question."[18]

Laypeople did not always think so but, as Ford's modest backtracking indicates, priests disliked questioning too. "As a rule," an early textbook in pastoral theology told young priests, "you should always let the penitent speak first and not interrupt him." Any questions could follow if needed, "but do it in a kind and discreet way." The experienced clergy concurred with this general approach, though it was implemented unevenly. Father Urban in New Orleans seems to have been routinely more gruff than his curate, Father Dominic. The Jesuit Gerald Kelly, a theologian of equal stature with Ford who taught at his order's seminary in Kansas and published widely for both clerical and lay audiences, produced an influential manual in 1951 entitled *The Good Confessor*. He included a long list of "prudent don'ts" for priests, and the first of these was "Don't ask unnecessary questions." Close behind it was "Don't overemphasize sex," the area in which circumlocutions from penitents were most frequent. Not only were such questions embarrassing for all concerned, he knew, but they might open the door to something worse, suggesting behaviors and sins that the penitent had not previously known about or thought of doing. "Do not teach evil," still another teacher warned his seminarians, "it is often better to be silent on this matter." Priests faced a tricky balancing act, weighing the need for questions when required against the countervailing need to avoid prurience. The student in Boston taking notes from his teacher summarized the conclusion of the class about the right approach. "I want penitent to return to confession," he wrote, "hence I must not make confession odious by asking too many questions which are not absolutely necessary."[19]

While extended interrogation about details was discouraged, priests were consistently urged to give each penitent

a few words of what Ford had called "advice or encouragement or consolation." Other than being punctual in keeping a parish's posted hours for confession, a 1962 guide for
newly ordained priests said, the most important quality for
a good confessor was "giving every penitent some words of
advice." For children, this might be as simple as telling them
to try harder to obey their parents; for adults, it might be a
more pointed pep talk about avoiding the occasions of common sins. Whatever it was, "a brief reminder, encouraging
thoughts or words of correction are welcomed by the penitent," the guidebook said—adding, realistically, "provided
he is not kept in the box too long." More ambitious priests
could try to go further. In the 1940s, *The Priest*, a monthly
journal of practical pastoral advice for the diocesan clergy,
sought to provide more substantial comments for use in the
confessional. It began a regular feature called "Fervorinos for
Confession." The unusual word was a term of art for priests,
denoting quick, punchy stories that made a religious point or
stoked the spiritual fires. The confessional seemed the right
place to insert these brief exhortations, and the magazine
suggested several in each issue. Most had little to do with
confession, however, focusing instead on the story from the
gospel that would be read at Mass the following Sunday or
on an upcoming feast day. (They thus had the added benefit
of helping the priest organize his own thoughts for his sermon that day if he had not already done so.) However good
the idea may have been as an attempt to prevent confessions
from becoming "merely mechanical," the magazine quickly
abandoned the feature, recognizing its impracticality. If a
confessor gave a short mini-sermon to each penitent, everyone in line would certainly have been "kept too long," and
attendance may have suffered as a result.[20]

Long or short as any particular confession was, both confessor and penitent believed that they were doing something

real. The words they used encapsulated the church's understandings of what was happening. The penitent's Act of Contrition expressed not only regret at having done wrong, but it also signaled acceptance of the proper basis for that regret. After the opening formula, it continued: "And I detest all my sins, because of Thy just punishments, but most of all because they offend Thee, my God, who art all-good and deserving of all my love." Fear of punishment was not absent, but "most of all" it was the offense given to the Almighty that was the legitimate motive for the sorrow. This was a sign of perfect, rather than imperfect, contrition. The prayer went on: "I firmly resolve, with the help of Thy grace, to sin no more and to avoid the near occasions of sin." Here was the purpose of amendment, intended genuinely enough at the time but achievable only with God's help. The priest's words in Latin—which the penitent probably could not distinguish, though they had to be audible at least to the priest himself—likewise expressed the theology of what he was doing on his side of the grille. There were several possible formulas that a priest could use, but the key phrase in all of them was *Ego te absolvo* (I absolve you), described by one textbook as "the essential minimum." A longer form, not always used because of the pressure of time, made it clear that this forgiveness actually came from God. "May our Lord Jesus Christ absolve you," the prayer began, "and by His power I absolve you, . . . so far as my power allows and your needs require." Lest anyone be confused, the Catholic understanding was that it was through divine authority, not that of the priest himself, that sins were forgiven. Jesus had given his first disciples the power to forgive sins or not (often called the "power of the keys"), and the priest was now exercising it centuries later by delegation and "so far as my power allows."[21] These deeper theological understandings of the sacrament were embedded in a simple and straightforward practice, accomplished in two minutes.

✠

BUT THE RITUAL WAS not over quite yet. Penitents still had
to complete the third and final stage of the sacrament, known
as satisfaction, by performing the penance the confessor had
just assigned them. "God in His mercy forgives the guilt of
the sin," the *Messenger of the Sacred Heart* explained to a reader,
"but in His justice He must demand that satisfaction be made."
Several metaphors were commonly applied to the penance as
a way of expressing the church's beliefs about its nature and
purpose. It was first of all a punishment, pure and simple—in
effect, the time sinners had to do for their crime. The penitent
had to undertake "something contrary to his own ease and
pleasure to compensate for satisfying his own ease and pleasure" in violating God's laws. The language of trials, of felonies and misdemeanors, so often applied to confession, was
used unapologetically when it came to this, the sentencing
phase of the proceedings. If penitents were hoping for parole
or commutation, they were mistaken. "Will a judge permit
the criminal at the bar to dictate the verdict of the jury?" one
priest asked rhetorically in 1938. Just so, the criminal in confession had to accept "exactly what God has decreed" through
the priest, and failure to do so displayed an arrogance that
"invites only additional punishment, and a severer sentence."
Penance was also a repayment of the debt that the sinner had
incurred by sinning, a debt that had to be cleared "either in
this life or in Purgatory." Or perhaps in both. While the penance was understood to exact spiritual punishment for sin,
there was still a "temporal" punishment (the precise nature
and duration of which were left undefined) that the sinner
would have to experience, whether through sufferings in this
world or after death. More positively, penance might also be
seen as a "cure for [the] infirmity" that had caused the sins
in the first place, "a remedy adapted to a new life," another

priest called it. If the cure took, the sinner would avoid sinning in the future.[22]

There were no hard and fast rules for determining which
penances should be meted out for which sins. In medieval
times, priests had relied on "penitentials," detailed catalogs of
sins with precise sentences (often called "tariffs") applied to
each one, but the practice in modern America was less exact.
A general sense of proportionality was thought to apply: the
punishment should fit the crime—"neither too great nor too
light," according to an advice manual for priests from 1940.
Mortal sins were more serious than others, and so the penances imposed for them had to be serious as well. Gerald
Kelly articulated a principle for priests to follow in such cases.
An appropriately "grave penance" for a mortal sin was one
that involved "the equivalent of something that the Church is
accustomed to impose under pain of mortal sin." The obligation to abstain from meat on Friday, for example, was such a
requirement, and so telling a sinner not to eat meat on an
additional day of the week would be a proper penance for any
confessed mortal sin. Requiring someone to attend Mass on a
second day besides Sunday was in the same category. It was
not necessary, another theologian added, to increase the number of these penances to match the number of mortal sins
committed—no strict one-for-one equivalence was needed—
though "a confessor should not allow penitents to think lightly
of mortal sin by imposing light penances for it." Moreover,
except in the most unusual of cases, Kelly said, anything resem-
bling a penance that had to be performed in public should be
avoided. Asking a penitent to pray the Stations of the Cross
adorning the church's walls, for instance, a devotion that
might take fifteen to twenty minutes, should be avoided. That
would probably be embarrassing to the penitent, not least by
prompting those who saw someone doing it after leaving the
confessional to speculate about what sins had merited such a

punishment. Nor should a confessor require as a penance that a parishioner apologize personally to someone who might have been offended by word or deed.[23]

Despite the often stern official language, most penances were not harsh. "Today, prayers are given most of the time," the seminarian in Boston wrote in the pages of his textbook. "It is custom nowadays to impose prayers as penance," he added, "because prayer is a good medicine for any moral evil." Requiring a penitent to recite some of the more common Catholic prayers a few times was usually sufficient. "The most practical penance is the Rosary, the Lord's Prayer, the Hail Mary, etc.," said the adviser to priests new to the confessional box. It was especially useful to do this with children. Their sins were less likely to require serious punishment, and a penance of having them say their prayers after confession gave them some practice with the words. The priest could also be reasonably "sure that they say it, and not forget it." Children might also be directed to remember an exemplary saint while they performed their penance: for boys, Saint Stanislaus Kostka, a sixteenth-century adolescent who wanted to become a priest (against his parents' wishes) but died before he got the chance; for girls, Saint Agnes, a third-century virgin and martyr. With adults, an even more targeted approach might be attempted, with the form of the penance geared to the particular sins in question: "for sins of the flesh, some mortification; for stinginess, alms according to means; for pride, prayer; for those ignorant of doctrine, the hearing of sermons or reading of spiritual books." Another adviser to the newly ordained suggested penances that were more blunt still: for sins of impurity, he suggested requiring "frequent thoughts of death." Whatever the theoretical benefits of creative sentencing, the constant pressure of numbers from those awaiting confession on any given day usually inclined priests to keep things simple by assigning a number of prayers, which the

penitent could recite immediately on leaving the box. Technically, it was not required that the penance be said before leaving the church for home, though most parishioners usually
did. In theory, the penance could be performed within any
reasonable time, but it was always a good idea to do so right
away, against the possibility that the penitent, whether child
or adult, would neglect to do it at all.[24]

Sometimes, however, more complicated penances were necessary, most obviously when the sin involved stealing. Then,
penitents had to make restitution of their ill-gotten goods as a
condition of being forgiven. It was a matter of simple justice.
They could not hold on to what they had stolen simply by
saying they were sorry; they had to give it back. The amount
of attention accorded this subject in *The Casuist* and other
moral theology textbooks suggests that restitution cases arose
frequently, or at least that confessors had to be prepared to
encounter them. Priests often had to serve as intermediar-
ies. In 1800s New York, Anthony Kohlmann had mandated
the return of stolen property, having learned of the crime in
confession; when the police asked him about it, the resulting legal case helped establish the privacy of the sacrament
in American civil law, as we shall see. Traveling priests who
conducted parish missions, perhaps precisely because they
were otherwise unknown in the local community, also seem
to have encountered many penitents who had to be told to
return what was not theirs. "Among the restitutions," wrote a
Redemptorist preaching at a parish in Cleveland in 1853—his
opening words suggest that cases requiring restitution were
common—was a bag of children's shoes that had been stolen from a foundering steamer on Lake Erie. Two years later,
colleagues visiting Rutland, Vermont, oversaw the return to
their rightful owner of $40 in cash and several promissory
notes worth even more, missing for over two years. If a restitution was done privately by the penitent alone, priests could

not be sure that, once told to do so, the sinner would in fact fulfill the demand. But they could delay granting absolution (or grant it only conditionally) until the penitent came back on another occasion with assurances of having done the right thing. Someone who promised to return illicit property and then did not do so sinned twice: once for the original theft and again for failing to perform the required penance.[25]

That a priest might withhold absolution and not assign a penance was always a possibility. Jesus's words from the gospel about "retaining" as well as forgiving sins, the text that was understood as the very foundation of the sacrament, gave the priest the authority to decide in each individual case. If he determined that the penitent did not deserve forgiveness— insufficient contrition, perhaps, or absence of an intent to avoid occasions of sin in the future—the confessor was not bound to impart it; in fact, he had an affirmative duty to refuse it. Confession was not like the Automat, John Sheerin said, alluding to the popular New York City self-service restaurant, where "you put your coin into the slot and out comes the cup of coffee." Making an honest effort to be better (even with the knowledge that the sinner might not succeed) was essential: "no amendment, no pardon." *Sign* magazine made the same point to a reader. "A refusal or a postponement" of penance and absolution "might be a confessor's obligatory exercise of the retaining power," it said. Handing out penances "too quickly, too mechanically," rushing people in and out of the box, John Ford told a class of seminarians, risked dereliction of duty. In any given circumstance, it might seem callous for a confessor to turn a penitent away unforgiven, but it might also be necessary.[26]

Nowhere was this more likely than when a penitent confessed to the sin of practicing contraception. As Protestants and others moved decisively away from the position that any overt effort to avoid pregnancy was always wrong, Catholics held firm. The pope's encyclical of 1930 had warned priests in the confessional "not to allow the faithful entrusted to them to err" on this subject. Diocesan priests had long been reluctant to discuss the topic at all, seldom speaking about it publicly in sermons or privately in premarital counseling. They showed no inclination to inquire about contraception in confession if the matter did not otherwise come up. Mission preachers, by contrast, were less hesitant, and the parish clergy seem to have been willing to cede the problem to them. Missioners did not have to worry about building and maintaining ongoing pastoral relationships with the people in local churches. Their success depended largely on the fact that they were outsiders ("prêtres étrangers," as the Franco-American pastor had put it), in any one place for only a week or two, and they could therefore be both more direct and more demanding. "I know many of you are guilty of this crime," an uncharacteristically harsh Redemptorist said in his stock sermon for the married women sessions of his mission. He told them to think about their practice seriously and "talk it over with your husband. . . . Then come to confession, acknowledge your terrible sins and be ready to promise God to give them up forever." If they were not ready to make that promise—and to make good on it—"then don't come to confession at all."[27]

Whether with parish or missionary priests, the difficulty here was not merely the sinful contraceptive practices themselves, but also the equally problematic matter of "recidivism." Priests thought they could be reasonably certain that anyone who confessed to violating the church's teaching on birth control had been doing so over an extended period and would probably continue. That seemed prima facie evidence of a lack of the necessary purpose of amendment. "If a person were of a mind to continue the practice of birth control," *Sign* insisted in 1964, "his confession would be futile and his attempt to obtain absolution would be sacrilegious. For this

reason, once the confessor is aware of the penitent's insincer-
ity, he has no other choice than to refuse absolution." Ford,
who would play a key role in reaffirming the church position
only a few years later, made the same point even more forcefully to a seminary class. "Nowadays good faith on contraception is very rare," he told those who would soon enough be
hearing confessions. "Do not absolve a penitent who refuses
to submit to the teaching of the church after it is explained.
Even if they are in 'good faith,' the common good requires
that you refuse them absolution." Many Catholic laypeople
were by then making their own decisions on the controverted
question but, in the minds of Ford and others in authority,
this meant that the clergy had to be all the more vigilant.
"The vice of contraception is now so widespread," he said
on another occasion, "that confessors have a more pressing
obligation to warn their penitents of its dangers, to speak out
against it, and to make sure of the firm purpose of amendment
in those who confess it." Priests who, perhaps in an effort to
be understanding, allowed a person "to confess this sin time
and time again, without ever checking them up to make sure
that they have a sincere purpose to give up the practice, are
gravely negligent in their office." The entire authority of the
church, on this and on other matters as well, would be seriously undermined if priests looked the other way. "Word gets
around," Ford warned.[28]

Such apparently firm strictures aside, many among the
diocesan clergy were uncomfortable with having to enforce
these rules. They had been told that they needed to be vigilant, but they still often found it hard to do. Immediately
after the papal encyclical, Chicago's Cardinal George Mundelein (perhaps alone among the American hierarchy) had
ordered priests there always to ask adult penitents—at first
only women, but later, men too—whether they were violating
the church's teaching, even if they themselves never brought

it up. The extent to which his clergy followed the cardinal's orders is unknowable; some surely did, others probably not. The steady pressure of the long lines of parishioners awaiting their turn in the confessional certainly served as a disincentive for extended cross examination of every individual, and in any event many priests were more inclined toward Gerald Kelly's view of what made for a "good confessor." He recommended questioning only when the confessor had a reasonable suspicion that the penitent was guilty, but that was difficult to know with birth control if the penitent had said nothing. Could guilt be inferred from the amount of time since the last confession, on the theory that those practicing contraception were staying away so as not to have to address the issue? Maybe, but there were other reasons for long absences too. Did a nervous demeanor signify that the penitent had something to hide? Again, there might be many causes of nerves. Enthusiastic younger priests, just out of the seminary classroom, may have been disposed to press the matter, but as they gained more practice they often eased off. "As we became more experienced in the pastoral field," a priest ordained in 1950 told an interviewer, "we questioned less and less." Another agreed with that approach. "The very fact that the person's coming into confession shows a good disposition; . . . what more can you ask?"[29]

For the normal run of sins, priests assigned a simple penance that was easy for most parishioners to accomplish. In a matter of a few minutes, they could say the required prayers either at the church's altar rail or in any unoccupied pew, and then they would be ready to leave for home or the day's other occupations. They were expected to perform only the penance that the confessor had given them. The pious and spiritually ambitious should not try to add anything to it on their own, perhaps hoping to build up a kind of extra credit. One reader of the *Sign* in 1958 wanted to know where to buy "penitential instruments, such as a hair shirt, chains, and the like," but the magazine firmly discouraged that. Dismissing such things as "gadgets," it said that "extraordinary penances, self-imposed," were conducive only to "spiritual pride" and therefore a form of "sin by excess."[30] The sentence that the priest had handed down as the condition of absolution was enough and, once they had completed it, penitents could be certain that God had indeed forgiven them.

The encounter in the confessional box was normally a brief one, but penitent and priest both had a meaningful experience. Routine might blunt its emotional impact on any given occasion, but even familiarity did not diminish its power. The very fact that many parishioners returned to repeat the experience — some in a week or two, others over a longer interval — testified to the hold that the practice had on them.

4

Experience

FOR SOME PEOPLE, CONFESSION was meaningful and consol-
ing. One woman remembered the time when she told a priest
she didn't want to delay him because of all the people waiting
behind her. "At this precise moment," she gratefully recalled
him saying in reply, "you are the only person in this church
who matters." Another woman found the sacrament "quite
moving, earth-shattering when you really understand what
is going on." Though her verbal exchange was with a priest
on the other side of the grille, she told an interviewer, "you
are talking to God Himself, and being forgiven! The more
seriously you take it, the more joyous the experience." A man
agreed. "Confession conveyed a sense of love," he said, "it
meant I'm worth something"—worth enough to be personally
pardoned by God and set on a new path. Still another woman,
who said that she usually went to confession a couple of times
a month, experienced "a deep reminder of the Lord's loving
acceptance of me." Priests, for all their long hours in the box,
often felt much the same way. An older cleric in Minnesota
had been hearing confessions for nearly fifty years and, he
said, "sometimes I'm amazed at all the wonderful things that
have happened in the confessional. People have come in dis-
turbed, distraught, at odds with God, and through the grace
of the sacrament, they've found peace with themselves and

anecdotes like this add a lot to the book (with drawback of anonymity)

God."[1] For Catholics like these, confession fulfilled the purposes, both spiritual and emotional, that the church intended for it.

Other people had not had such positive experiences. For some, confessing was merely a rote fulfillment of the conditions of church membership. "You want to be a practicing Catholic," a woman said matter-of-factly, "you gotta go to Confession. Certain things go with the territory." A man, however, objected to what he took to be a similar offhand attitude from a priest. Once, after wrestling with his conscience about an unspecified personal matter and "gearing up emotionally," he sensed indifference in the confessor, who seemed not to be paying attention. "It had taken so much out of me to confess," he said, but "it was like I hadn't spoken." Another woman had been scolded during one confession for saying that she had committed a sin "several" times; the priest insisted, as he had been taught in the seminary, that a specific number was required. When she went again a few weeks later, she made an effort to be more precise, but nerves caused her voice to quaver, prompting an eruption from the other side of the screen. "All right now, come clean!" she quoted the priest as exclaiming. "You wouldn't be this nervous if you weren't concealing something. Cut the lying and tell the truth!" She left the box filled not with consolation, but with "pure unadulterated anger and indignation" at the way she had been treated.[2]

Personal accounts such as all of these, called to mind by individuals after the fact and then recounted to interviewers, can be both true and not true—real enough, but in memory often exaggerated in one direction or the other. Most American Catholics had a confession story of some kind, a story they repeated to themselves and on occasion to others, a story prone to getting better or worse every time. Because the sacrament depended on particular persons and circumstances, any confession was equally open to the possibility that the experience would be positive or that it would be negative. It had been a private conversation between the confessor and "the only person in this church who matters." Penitents had had to admit, aloud if quietly, to not having lived up to standards of behavior they endorsed in theory, and that was hard. The anonymity of it all surely helped, limiting the chances that a priest would be able to associate specific offenses with specific parishioners. "I feel shy and uncomfortable discussing my faults face to face with a fellow human being," a woman from Maine said in the 1970s, and the darkened confessional removed that obstacle. Priests felt the same way. "It is much easier to avoid embarrassment in dealing with people outside of confession," Gerald Kelly noted, "when we have no confessional knowledge of them." The constant stream of penitents was also a benefit. "You don't have much capacity for remembering the sins of any individual," another priest said. "All the stories blur together," and all the separate voices become "like one great voice of humanity."[3] The experience of confession was always one-on-one, singular as to time and place, but patterns among various kinds of penitents nonetheless emerged from its sustained practice by American Catholics.

✠

AMONG ADULTS, THE DIFFERENCES between the confessions of men and those of women seemed obvious. "All you need to do for a woman is to put her on the train to Heaven and she'll stay aboard; but you have to watch out for the men at all the way stations," one Jesuit in the 1890s said more than once when describing his approach in the confessional, according to his obituary. Priests consistently worried that men came to the sacrament less regularly than women, and their concerns had some foundation. Patrick Healy had (unfortunately for us) not separated his weekly "score" into

distinct tallies for men and women, but evidence on the subject is available elsewhere, in part from the detailed records
kept by traveling missionary priests. Since parish missions
usually included separate sessions for men and women, it was
easy to count the confessions these prompted from each sex,
and the results were usually clear and stark. A Paulist mission
at Saint Joseph's Cathedral in Dubuque, Iowa, in 1901, for
instance, brought 1,385 women but only 725 men to the confessionals. A few years later at a little church in McKeesport,
Pennsylvania, the total numbers were smaller, but the gap
between the groups was bigger: 875 women, 150 men. At a
parish in Worcester, Massachusetts, "a state of affairs that
rarely happens" attracted attention when it did happen: more
men (just over 1,300) than women (about 1,200). Much more
typical was the experience of the Paulists who went to New
Brunswick, New Jersey. "Women's mission good," one of
them reported afterwards. "Men 'horse of another color,' . . .
almost rivalled Baltimore," an unspecified earlier stop on the
mission tour where things had apparently been just as bad.
A mission was, of course, an unusual occasion by definition,
and we should therefore be careful in generalizing from these
necessarily fragmentary data; they say nothing about regular week-to-week practice in ordinary parishes once the missioners had moved on to another town. But the experience
of the settled parish clergy was mostly the same as that of
their traveling confreres. That James Walsh in Boston made
special mention of the "many men" who came to his box one
Saturday confirms that this was indeed enough of a departure
from the usual to be worth noting.[4]

Well into the twentieth century, American Catholic priests,
like the clergymen of other denominations, usually presumed that women were the more "naturally" religious seg-
ment of the population. Stereotypes about women retained
their cultural power for a long time and, given that Catholic

priests were celibate and had limited contact with women, such attitudes may have been all the more tenacious in them. Like the Jesuit who fancied himself a train conductor, most priests thought women needed little encouragement to form regular sacramental habits, though at least one writer also warned that "women often pretend to be pious and virtuous whilst in reality they are not." However that might be, men remained horses of another color. The pastor who enlisted his schoolkids to embarrass their fathers into confession may have been more creative in his methods than most, but priests knew that this was an area in which special effort was needed. "It is all-important that the men of your congregation frequently come to confession," said Father (later Bishop) William Stang, the author of an early textbook on pastoral practice. "The grace of God cannot be where confession is regarded as the special duty of the devout sex" only. He made several suggestions for increasing male participation, some of them hard to implement. "Have one side of the confessional exclusively for men," for example, and always hear them first, allowing them to jump to the head of the line on any given day. (He was sure that "women have more patience . . . mothers and daughters are willing to wait.") More generally, if a priest showed "that you are really pleased when men are at your confessional" and that "you consider it a privilege and pleasure to hear" them—he did not say exactly how priests would convey this—he thought the numbers would increase over time. And when it came to assigning penances, he recommended that confessors keep their expectations for men low. They should not lay down any exacting "rules of piety and perfection for the ordinary class of men, but be satisfied if they shun mortal sin and keep the commandments." If none of that worked, the writers of *The Casuist* added, a simple appeal to male vanity was not out of place. Pointing out "that God has shown special predilection for men, confiding to them the most important positions in the family, State, and Church" might be the way to bring them in; after all, "the priesthood is only accessible to men."[5]

Whether in the confessional itself or in sermons, priests might also try to cast regular confession in the context of generalized notions of manliness, hoping that men could be induced to become "sober, honest, industrious, and practical members of the Church," Stang said. "Of course to confess one's sins is unpleasant," a priest from New York admitted flatly; all the more reason that "one should do the manly thing, bend his pride, humble himself, be a man, face and toe the red line of Christian duty, [and] make his confession." A Catholic who did "the manly thing" was doubly commendable, a contrast to those who followed the "soft and namby-pamby" approach to life promoted in the self-help "peace of mind" books of the 1940s and 1950s, John Sheerin said scornfully. (He did not name any names, but he was probably thinking of Norman Vincent Peale's *Power of Positive Thinking*.) A devotional guide book for members of the Knights of Columbus made the same point. "Confession of one's guilt to God's representative is seldom easy," it said, "not a pleasing prospect." But that was exactly its highest recommendation and value. "The Sacraments are not devices for making us pleasing to ourselves. They make us pleasing to God." More than one layman absorbed this outlook. A thirty-year veteran of the Air Force echoed the parishioner who had told Joseph Fichter that it was sometimes useful to get "bawled out" for his sins. "There's something to be said about discipline in this life," the former officer said, "something to be said for an injection of fear." He was not endorsing terror for its own sake, but there was value to "staying enough on the edge to keep you moving. Confession gives you that little rush, that bit of fear that keeps you on your toes." Catholic teaching had long endorsed the idea of "heroic virtue," embodying worthy traits to the highest degree possible, regardless of personal cost. Such intensity was one of the requirements for the canonization of saints, but ordinary believers might strive for it too. "Get the habit of doing hard things because they are hard," an examen from 1949 said.[6]

Demonstrations of manliness had particular appeal with adolescent boys, some writers thought, promoting ideals to which they were being encouraged to aspire. If that approach did not work, there might be other ways of connecting with youthful male interests. Confession was like a tune-up for your car, a teacher at an all-boys Catholic high school in Cincinnati thought in 1967. "Just as an owner of an automobile needs to have his car checked over periodically," he said, so his students needed the sacrament "to keep yourself going in the traffic temptations bring on." Similarly, the problem of recidivism was akin to trying to correct a golf swing, and it might not work the first time: "You intend never to slice again, but force of habit may lead you to." The purpose of amendment was like studying the Xs and Os on the blackboard in the locker room. "No football coach waits until a big game has begun to plan his strategy. . . . You must plan your strategy in advance so you are not surprised by a temptation." The principal temptation he had in mind, the teacher was frank to tell his students, was masturbation. But, he added, like a good baseball coach who helped get a player out of a batting slump, "God is a good manager, is patient, and will wait it out."[7] Such analogies may have drawn a smirk from the students in class, but they were part of a larger effort to accustom men of all ages to think that confession was not something to be left to the "devout sex."

Organizations of laymen helped make the same point, and they were often conducted in such a way as to encourage regular confession. The most popular of these, with nearly two thousand local branches across the country by the 1920s and

more thereafter, was the Holy Name Society. It promoted
devotion to the name of Jesus through a pledge to keep the
second commandment, which forbade taking the Lord's name
in vain. On the most basic level, this meant giving up "blas-
phemy, profanity, and obscene speech," but it was broadened
into larger campaigns against indecency in books and movies.
The society had a slogan — "Every man a Holy Name man" —
and that ideal was nearly achieved in churches everywhere.
"The American parish," its handbook proclaimed, "needs
spirituality, especially of that masculine type which the Society has been promoting." Manly piety and respectable male
behavior reinforced one another: a man could still be a man,
even if he did not curse, tell dirty jokes, or read questionable
literature. Parish societies met quarterly or monthly, attending Sunday Mass and receiving communion in a body, often
followed by a simple breakfast in the church hall. To prepare
for those occasions, members were encouraged to go to confession the day before, and most of them did. "128 Conf[es-
sions]," Father Walsh in Boston noted one Saturday at the
turn of the century, "H.N.S. turned out well — heard many
more men than women to-night." A colleague in a nearby
suburb made plans for a similar surge in his parish. "On next
Sunday the members of the Holy Name Soc'y will make their
quarterly communion at the 8.30 mass," the pastor of Sacred
Heart parish in Newton announced one week. As a result, "on
next Saturday afternoon + evening we shall hear confessions
of *men only*. There will be three priests hearing confessions to
afford *all* the men of the parish an opportunity."[8]

Not everyone responded to these urgings, of course, and
so priests were always grateful when they encountered a penitent who had not been to confession in a long time. In the
spring of 1929, for instance, a Jesuit described the people
he and other priests of his order were able to attract as they
fanned out to missions in the parishes around Los Angeles.

"All the missionaries were consoled and encouraged by the number of negligent Catholics brought back to their duties after periods of five, ten, twenty and more years." The parish clergy experienced this too, and the common metaphor applied to someone who returned to confession after years of neglect was "big fish." On a January weekday in 1899, for example, Patrick Healy had sat in his confessional in Manhattan until 10:30 at night, during which time, he later told his diary, he encountered a "big fish of many years." In a similar case a few weeks before, he had expressed his satisfaction in French: "Quelques gros poissons!" In Boston once, James Walsh "landed a 17 y[ea]r fish" and then "landed" another one the very next day.[9] The allusion was to the passage in the gospels in which Jesus referred to his disciples, former fishermen, as "fishers of men." In the modern confessional, such fish could in theory be of either sex, but the term was most often applied to men. Walsh identified (not by name, of course) both of his catches as male: one of them, he concluded from the man's account, was a sailor just returned from a long time away from home. It was occasions such as these, perhaps, that provided the opportunity Father Stang had hoped for when priests could show how pleased they were with the confessions of men.

Though women were more regular in coming to the sacrament, female penitents could potentially raise problems of their own. Priestly condescension toward women colored these encounters, with some authorities believing that confessors had to be especially watchful when dealing with the "devout sex." Women might appear to be genuinely sorry for their sins, but "be not deceived by tears," Stang cautioned, "they may be sincere, but women's tears are always cheap and handy." Any semblance of "familiarity" was to be carefully avoided, and the slightest indication that a woman was becoming close to a particular confessor (or wanted to) had to be met with a swift rebuff. A cool, detached distance — "in-difference," Stang called it — was always the proper stance. Women were sometimes "carried away by their feelings of admiration" for certain priests, another textbook advised, and the clergy, especially those new to their duties, had to "be on the lookout" for that possibility. "If a female penitent should, directly or indirectly, show that she is attached to her confessor, she must be told, rudely and abruptly, never to come near him again, but to seek another." Maintaining the authoritative male persona, even if done "rudely," was essential. "Do not address the penitent in words that are too sweet and too soft," admonished one writer, reinforcing this rule with an aphorism in Latin: "*Patres summus non matres*" — we are fathers, not mothers. "Whatever you say should be short, grave, and to the point. Long conversations, extensive discussions even of spiritual subjects, both inside and outside the confessional, are wrong." In part, these concerns were fueled by the desire to head off any suggestion that supposedly celibate priests were taking advantage of women. But they were also grounded in a fear that women could sometimes be the sexual aggressors, using their "cheap and handy" tears to seduce a priest and to undermine his authority. In a case involving women's confessions, *The Casuist* had warned against women of "malicious intention, either of confusing young and inexperienced confessors, or even to lead them into temptation."[10] Whether or not this ever happened, it was better for all priests to be wary.

In posing questions to female penitents, confessors (who were, of course, all male) had to be very careful indeed. "Guard your tongue," Stang said bluntly, and "put the fewest possible questions." That was always good advice, but it was especially so in the case of women. In particular, an adviser to new priests said in 1940, "questions concerning sins of impurity" should be avoided to the extent possible. The concern here was that questions could "excite curiosity" about previously unknown activities or teach women about "depravities they need not know." But by then such seemingly ironclad rules were beginning to work at cross purposes with the church's concerns about contraception. How could that especially troublesome sin be identified and rooted out if penitents, male and female, were not routinely asked about it, as the cardinal in Chicago had instructed his clergy to do? At first, many priests assumed that the wife was the one who introduced the practice of birth control into a marriage. "The modern up-to-date girl or woman pride themselves," a Passionist missionary said in a grammatically challenged sermon, "on knowing the different tricks and expedients whereby they may escape the results of conjugal intercourse and shirk the burden of child bearing." Another priest thought that, faced with such a woman, sometimes "a man allows himself to violate the commandments of God," and that was obviously wrong. Instead, this cleric insisted, the husband "ought to offend his wife rather than sin against God." With time, however, preachers seemed more inclined to think that the contraceptive initiative came from men and that, as another Passionist said, women "are frequently influenced, even perhaps forced, by thoughtless and selfish husbands."[11] The potential for awkward encounters in the confessional that resulted from detailed questioning on the subject only increased the reluctance of some priests to broach it if penitents did not. Still, priests had been given—and had accepted—the responsibility to be enforcers of church teaching in the confessional. One wonders if the sins that prompted the angry outburst of "cut the lying and tell the truth" had concerned birth control.

While the confessions of women presented many potential pitfalls, women were more likely than men to make what were called devotional confessions. Since the Middle Ages, the church's rules had been simple: confession was a requirement only once a year during the Easter season. Apart from that, it was also mandated for anyone conscious of having committed a mortal sin. If a penitent had only venial sins to account for, confession was not absolutely necessary, though it was a good thing to do. Lesser sins could be forgiven in other, informal ways too, through such things as sincere private prayer, voluntary self-denial, or almsgiving. Notwithstanding the constant expansion of the number of mortal sins in published examinations of conscience, most priests recognized that serious mortal sinning was actually rare among their parishioners. If those parishioners adhered only to the strict once-a-year standard, the number of confessions every week would be small. But the clergy regularly promoted the idea of more frequent confession (inspired by "devotion or piety," one writer said) of venial sins. Penitents might indeed have only venial sins to confess, but they should go to confession anyway. "Should persons conscious of no mortal sin stay away from confession so as 'to save the priest's time'?" someone asked the *Messenger of the Sacred Heart* in 1940. No, the magazine answered forcefully. Removing the penalties for mortal sin was "only one of the effects of the Sacrament." Confession also "imparts graces to strengthen the soul to resist temptation, to advance in virtue, and to acquire greater merit before God." Just by going, the penitent received "an increase of sanctifying grace," another writer said, and what penitent would not want that? Confessing frequently was thus "highly recommended."[12]

With no mortal sins to be forgiven, penitents engaging in devotional confession could focus on their venial sins. If for some reason (rare, perhaps, but nevertheless possible), they had no venial sins either, they were told to mention some sins already forgiven in a previous confession—no more than four or five, one authority suggested—just so they would have something to say. This did not mean that the earlier confession had been invalid or that the sins were being forgiven a second time; rather, it merely enabled the penitent, as the *Messenger* said on another occasion, "to obtain the special graces of the Sacrament." There was no uniform standard for determining the proper frequency of devotional confessions, with anything from monthly to weekly the most common recommendations — recommendations that remained remarkably consistent over time. A catechism from the 1840s had restated the earlier position of Anthony Kohlmann that once a month was the bare minimum for "a Christian who is careful of his salvation," while a Jesuit in the early 1960s was still maintaining that "once a week is not too often." The long lines in churches everywhere were visible evidence that laypeople were hearing this message and forming their confessional habits accordingly.[13]

The promotion and the practice of devotional confessions were also linked to increasing frequency in reception of the Eucharist. For centuries, receiving communion at Mass by Catholics had been rare, even by those who attended regularly. Motivated by a deep and lasting sense of their unworthiness, most Catholic laypeople, though faithfully in their pews on Sundays, did not come forward for this purpose. One prayer guide had expressed the common attitude. When the priest began to distribute communion, parishioners could remain in their seats and say a silent prayer, addressed to God, which opened with the words "Conscious of my infirmities and sins, I dare not now receive Thee sacramentally." One mid-century Jesuit remembered the practice of his grandfather, a retired blacksmith in the early twentieth century, who hobbled through arthritis to Mass in his local church every single day of the year and yet took communion only on Christmas and Easter. A priest in Boston at about the same time counted roughly seven hundred people at his 7:45 Mass one spring Sunday morning, and he noted that exactly forty of them received the Eucharist, a number he actually found hearteningly high. Beginning in 1905, however, prompted by papal encouragement, priests began to urge more frequent communion by their parishioners. One of the underlying motives for such parish groups as the Holy Name Society, together with the comparable sodalities for women, had been to instill the practice of monthly communion. No matter how conscious of their sins and infirmities individuals might be, the pressure of group participation helped overcome hesitation, allowing them to "dare" approaching the sacrament. And usually, Sunday communion had been preceded by Friday or Saturday confession. As Joseph Fichter noted of parishioners in New Orleans in the 1950s, "frequent communicants are also frequent confessants, because they realize that both sacraments bring special graces to the soul."[14]

A separate confession was not actually required before every single reception of communion, but the two remained intertwined in the lay imagination into the 1960s. Still, some parishioners wondered whether the rules were really as rigorous as they seemed. How long after any given confession could one continue to go communion at Mass without having to confess again, a woman wanted to know, and the *Messenger of the Sacred Heart* had to admit that there was "no strict obligation" to confess every single time. "For greater purity of soul and better preparation to receive our Lord," however, once a week was best and once every two weeks was acceptable. Similarly, another parishioner wondered whether someone pursuing the nine First Friday devotions always had to confess on the Thursday before; what if they had confessed the previous Saturday for a Sunday communion? Was a five-day gap too long? Again, the *Messenger* allowed for some leeway, and even tried to shift the focus from one sacrament to the other. "The mere fact that one has not been to Confession should not cause one to lose an opportunity of receiving Holy Communion." Most Catholics, however, male

and female alike, apparently continued to think that communion without confession was spiritually risky. The especially
devout might attempt it, but more ordinary parishioners
did not think of themselves as such. At the Jesuits' massive
Church of the Gesu in downtown Philadelphia in the 1910s
and 1920s, Mass attendance and communion were so impressive as to require a marshalling of priestly forces in advance.
"The confessionals were crowded on Thursday, Friday, and
Saturday of each week," one of them wrote in the eulogy of
a former pastor; "ten confessors on those days and fourteen
confessors on each Saturday, on the eves of holydays [*sic*]
and the eves of First Fridays."[15] Even allowing for exaggera-
tion when extoling the accomplishments of a previous parish
leader, this account underlines how confession and communion had become two halves of the same whole for laypeople.
Those halves might indeed be decoupled, but it was best not
to "dare" pushing that practice too far.

Those given to frequent confession often got into whichever
line was shortest, but some tried to find one particular confessor to hear them every time, and this was easy to do. Not
only did parish priests normally occupy the same confessional
from week to week, but in most places their names were also
posted on the door of the box, so parishioners could know
which member of the parish staff was inside. Penitents who
found a priest especially understanding—like Father Paul in
New Orleans—could make a point of seeking him out again.
But there were less worthy motivations too, and priests were
quick to denounce what they perceived as confessor "shopping," with parishioners deliberately choosing one priest who
might go easier on them than another. Selection gave laypeople, who otherwise exercised limited control over the experience of confession, some degree of power in determining
its successful (from their perspective) outcome. The parishioners who took advantage of the visits of traveling mission

preachers to unburden themselves, rather than confessing to their own local clergy, were doing this, as were those who went to so-called service churches, located in a number of cities around the country. In New York, for instance, Franciscan priests staffed "the church of 1,000 confessions a day" on West Thirty-First Street. At least one priest, and sometimes as many as five or six, were available for confessions every day from just before seven in the morning until nine o'clock that night. Shoppers and workers from nearby offices could stop in at any time, and others made special trips from all over the tri-state area. The church even installed automatic counters in the kneelers of the confessional boxes to keep track, and these recorded more than 275,000 in one year (1970) alone. The Franciscans, an account of the church said, were "aware that the anonymity of confessing to a friar in Manhattan plays a part in attracting penitents."[16]

Shopping for a confessor, whether because he was sympathetic or because the penitent would be a complete stranger to him, was also common enough in normal circumstances to call forth periodic warnings from the clergy. "Good Catholics," one priest said, "will not talk about what was said in confession, nor will they discuss whether the confessor was severe or lenient." Informal networks among parishioners existed anyway, and every priest probably earned a reputation of one kind or another for how he treated those with whom he talked. "Good" penitents, however, should not try to take advantage of the system. A student at Georgetown University in the 1870s received a long and difficult penance from one confessor and then immediately went to another and confessed all over again, hoping for a lighter sentence. The second confessor discovered the scheme somehow, and insisted that the original penance be completed. Others might try to be even more crafty. One parishioner asked an authority whether it was sinful to go to a particular confessor because

he was hard of hearing and thus might not understand enough
of what was said to be severe or to pose too many questions.
The answer was "definitely," though slightly deaf priests were
probably popular whenever they could be identified as such.
Still, "a person who started shopping around for a confessor,"
another priest said, "would certainly be putting himself in a
false position as a Catholic."[17]

✠

JUST AS THE CONFESSIONS of adults, whether male or female,
had dynamics of their own, so too did the confessions of children. With the exception of converts to the church, most
Catholics learned how to go to confession when they were
young. The age at which they should begin doing so, usually
called the "age of reason," had been left loosely defined in the
nineteenth century, though Father Stang urged that priests
"not wait" too long before introducing the children of a parish to the practice. Since they were expected to comprehend
and then apply to themselves the church's understandings of
sin and forgiveness, children had to know the basic difference between right and wrong, and local pastors interpreted
this differently. In some places, confessions might begin at
around age ten, in others as late as twelve or thirteen. But at
the beginning of the new century, the same pope who promoted frequent communion also lowered the age for a child's
first reception of the Eucharist to seven. Given the close connection between the two sacraments, that now dictated the
age for a child's first confession as well.[18]

The more detailed examinations of conscience available for
adults were modified for a younger audience. One priest in
the 1930s suggested a list of age-appropriate questions: "Did
I talk back to my father, my mother, my teacher, older people?" "Did I copy in school?" "Did I tell lies, or say wrong
things about anybody?" "Did I think, say, or do anything to

be ashamed of? alone or with others?" "Did I stay away from Mass on a Sunday or a holy day?" Another priest added such possibilities as "Have I been ashamed of my religion before Protestant boys and girls?" and, probably thinking of slightly older children, "Did I smoke and thereby endanger my health?" (This last was interpreted as an infringement of the fifth commandment's injunction against killing.) Other questions, aimed particularly at adolescents, covered missing "the principal parts of the Mass" and missing all of the Mass after communion—in other words, no coming late or sneaking out early. All such questions, like their adult counterparts, were designed to accustom children to thinking about themselves as personally responsible for their behavior and as capable of recognizing that their smallest daily actions had serious moral implications. We should not presume that children used these examens any more consistently than their parents used theirs, but the texts nonetheless acculturated children to the church's ways of expressing these ideas. Familiarizing kids with the process of confession itself was also useful at an early age. "In preparing the children for the first Confession," said a religious educator at Catholic University in Washington in the 1920s, "it is well to take them to the confessional. Show them the place to kneel; show them the slide; show them how to turn their face when talking so that the priest can hear them."[19]

For better or worse, the habits instilled in children in this way often stayed with them for years. "I truly believe," a laywoman said, that "your initial instruction in the Sacrament of Penance has a big influence on your attitude toward Confession. It's so important that you get good instruction initially, training that doesn't frighten you and make you fearful of God." She wanted young people to develop a healthy attitude toward the sacrament, one that was capable of maturing over time, but things did not always work out that way. A priest

Two children going to confession, 1920s.
Credit: Burns Library, Boston College

might be too abrupt or too severe, and an adviser to new priests
insisted that any correction of children in confession, whether
of substance or simply of form, must be done "without signs
of displeasure." Even so, the templates established by childhood confessions were not always what the church wanted.
For one thing, they may have helped children acquire skills in
euphemism at an early age, finding ways to phrase their sins
so as not to attract too much notice, and priests knew that
this was happening. "Must we forever go on confessing the

way we did as grade-school kids?" one asked in exaspera-
tion in 1966, citing an example (perhaps drawn from his own
experience) of a man who confessed to having "disobeyed"
his wife. The "adult patterns expected of us in dealings with
people in business and social contacts," this priest went on,
should be applied in confession as well, though many laypeople found that hard to do. Only some—like one man who said
confidently, "we can make moral decisions"—could make the
transition. Promoting a more "advanced spiritual life" was
always difficult, another priest acknowledged, and for many
Catholics the habits of childhood were impossible to break.[20]
Dissatisfaction with those patterns would eventually contribute to the widespread turn away from the sacrament, a story
for later.

✠

No LESS SIGNIFICANT THAN gender and age in shaping the
experience of American Catholics when they went to confession was their ethnicity. All nationalities were to a large extent
reenacting traditional practices in their new surroundings,
and ethnic groups adopted the habit of frequent confession
unevenly. Some of them came from cultures in which confession only once a year had been an acceptable norm, while others were used to the greater frequency that priests in America
routinely advised. Irish immigrants were probably the most
regular. Their church back home had gone through what historians have called a "devotional revolution," in which the
previously negligent Irish became the fervent churchgoers
of their later reputation. Many German immigrants had fled
Bismarck's Kulturkampf, an aggressive government policy of
severe restrictions on the church, and they may thus have been
all the more resolved to practice their faith. Hispanic immigrants in the Southwest often came from rural settings, where
access to clergy for Mass and confession had been spotty and

other popular devotions had more cultural resonance; regular confessing was therefore less engrained among them. As the small number of African American Catholics—a "minority within a minority"—moved from the rural South to the urban North throughout the first half of the twentieth century, they hoped to be able to fulfill the requirements of church membership, including regular confession, though they sometimes encountered hostility in white parishes. One pastor in Detroit refused absolution to a Black penitent, telling him that he should confess in his own parish down the street, designated exclusively for African Americans. Of course, people of all ethnicities had to concentrate on the immediate problems of finding work and adequate housing, and so religious impulses were always acted upon within constrained limits.[21]

For many first-generation immigrants, language proved an enduring obstacle to overcome in confession. Most of those who came from Ireland were English-speakers, though this had not always been the case. Missioners to Irish workers in the navy yard at Portsmouth, Virginia, in the 1850s—"the most thoroughly ignorant [Catholics] we have ever met with," one priest said—made little headway until they were able to find a nearby priest, himself an immigrant, who could speak Irish and thus hear confessions in that tongue. (Even then, he reported "the same abject ignorance.") For other groups, the ability of confessors and penitents to understand one another could be problematic to a greater or lesser degree. By the beginning of the twentieth century, while there were variations from place to place, the American priesthood was overwhelmingly Irish by background, dominated by the sons of second- and third-generation families, and English was their only language. They had been force-fed enough Latin to be able to perform their basic sacramental functions, and a few had even been exposed to some Greek and Hebrew. But the study of modern languages was largely absent from seminary curricula, leaving priests unprepared to work successfully with non-English speaking parishioners. Bishops tried mightily to recruit priests who were native speakers of the other languages represented in their dioceses, and these could be assigned to ethnic or "national" parishes, but in many places there were never enough to meet the demand. Moreover, for a long time a seemingly obvious solution to the problem — taking a seminarian of whatever ethnicity and training him in Italian or Polish or some other language, just as Anglophone priests today learn Spanish — was seldom attempted. The cultural gaps between groups, most clearly expressed in language but also something more than that, were presumed to be simply too wide to cross. An Irish American priest who knew German, it was thought, would never be completely successful in a German parish.[22]

Where there were sufficient numbers of parishioners so that distinct ethnic parishes could be formed and staffed by priests who spoke the appropriate language, the problem was lessened: Portuguese speakers could confess to Portuguese speakers in Portuguese parishes. For the most part, parishioners stayed within the confines of their own ethnic league. Most of Milwaukee's Polish parishes, for instance, reported in the 1940s that fewer than 5 percent of their confessions were in languages other than Polish. These might come from the younger parishioners, or they may have been neighboring non-Poles who simply found a particular church a shorter walk from home or work. Elsewhere in the city, the crossover rates were sometimes higher. The pastor of Saint Wenceslaus, a tiny Bohemian church at the corner of West Scott and South Fourteenth Streets, reported that about 80 percent of the confessions he heard were in English, and some Irish pastors also said that they encountered "many Germans" who knew enough English to get by. As one generation succeeded another, English-speaking children and grandchildren grad-

ually replaced the original immigrants, and language presented fewer difficulties. Until that happened, priests and
people who were most comfortable in different languages
struggled to achieve something less than the ideal. The Paulist priests who visited "a rather mixed" church in New Jersey in 1894 had to enlist "the help of a German, a Polish
Bohemian, an Italian, and a Greek priest to get through the
confessions."[23]

The theological understanding of the sacrament was that
a confessor had to grasp enough of what a penitent was saying in order to impart absolution. In particular, he had to be
able to determine whether the sins in question were mortal
or venial before he could assign a suitable penance. Absent
clarity, his first response should be to send the penitent to
another priest who was able to understand, but that might
be neither possible nor desirable. If penitents were sent off
to another priest somewhere else, would they actually go?
Wouldn't it be better, now that they were already in the box,
to try to make the best of it? In such circumstances, the priest
was left largely to rely on his own judgment. If "the penitent acknowledges his sins at least by means of some general
signs" (unspecified), an adviser to inexperienced priests said,
that was probably sufficient, though the confessor should also
encourage the penitent to find a priest more fluent in his own
tongue the next time.[24]

A few priests tried, with good intentions but probably limited success, to compile multilingual manuals that could be
put to use in the confessional. Around the time of the First
World War, one Paulist with the indisputably Irish name
of McSorley published *Italian Confessions: How to Hear Them*,
suggesting methods that confessors could try out when
encountering an Italian-speaking penitent. In a series of
short chapters, he presented model sentences in English and
Italian, the latter also spelled out phonetically. "Ditemi vostri

peccati," the priest might say when the penitent entered the box. "Dee-tay-mee vaw-stri pec-cah-ti. Tell me your sins." Then came similar guidance through the possible sins against the Ten Commandments—including, at the sixth, the always relevant "solo o con altre persone" (alone or with others)—and then the penance: "Ditte sette Pater Noster. Dee-tay settay pah-ter naw-stayr. Say seven Our Fathers." In the 1940s, John Sheerin, another Paulist, published a similar volume for confessions in Spanish, perhaps a recognition of the increasing presence of Hispanic Catholics in some previously all-white parishes. A Dutch priest prepared a little handbook, subsequently distributed in the United States, which gave the prayers, formulas, and prompting questions for confession in eleven languages: English, French, German, Dutch, Italian, Spanish, Danish, Polish, Bohemian, Slavic, and (leaving nothing to chance) Esperanto.[25] Presumably, a priest could turn to whichever section he needed when occasion arose, though it is difficult to imagine such guides being very helpful. Like tourist phrase books, they were a better idea in theory than in practice.

Apart from language, distinctive ethnic customs also affected the experience of confession. One of the most troublesome was the use of what were variously called "confession cards" or "Easter tickets." Precursors of this system had a long history, going back to the Reformation, and although they had died out in most places in western Europe, they managed to survive and come to America with immigrants from Poland and Lithuania. It was a simple enough procedure. After each penitent confessed, the priest passed a small card or certificate through the grille attesting to the fact; sometimes, parishioners brought blank forms with them, which the priest could sign and then return. No penitents' names were written on these small pieces of paper, thereby safeguarding the secrecy of the confessional. Rather, their

1944

FIRST PRINTING JANUARY 5,000
SECOND PRINTING MARCH 10,000

•

Imprimi Potest:

JAMES P. SWEENEY, S.J.
Provincial New York Province.

•

Nihil Obstat:

ARTHUR J. SCANLAN, S.T.D.
Censor Librorum.

•

Imprimatur:

† FRANCIS J. SPELLMAN, D.D.
Archbishop of New York.

Feast of the Immaculate Conception

•

Copyright 1944 by
REV. ANTHONY RUSSO-ALESI, S.J.
Nativity Church, 44–2nd Ave., N. Y. C.
United States and Canada
Printed in U. S. A.

ANGLICE — ENGLISH

Do You Wish to Go to Confession?

1. How long is it since your last good confession? How many weeks? How many months, years?
2. Have you cursed? Have you read bad books?
3. Did you miss mass? How many times?
4. Do you belong to any society condemned by the Church? Willing to give it up?
5. Did you sin seriously against your parents?
6. Did you quarrel? Injured anyone unjustly?
7. Did you consent to bad thoughts?
8. Did you do bad actions alone? How many times? With a man or woman?
9. Are you married? In the Catholic Church or by a protestant minister or by a judge?
10. In your marriage relations have you prevented children? Have you caused abortion?
11. Did you steal? Much? Willing to restore it?
12. Did you lie? Injured anybody's good name?
13. Have you gotten drunk? How many times?
14. Did you eat meat on forbidden days?
15. Have you other sins to confess?
16. **Are you sorry for all your sins?**

Penance: Hail Mary. How many times?

Contrition: My God, I am sorry for having offended Thee; give me grace never to sin again.

ITALICE — ITALIANO

Vi Volete Confessare?

1. Da quanto tempo vi siete bene confessato(a)? Quante settimane? Quanti mesi? Quanti anni?
2. Avete bestemmiato? Letto libri cattivi?
3. Avete perduta la Messa? Quante volte?
4. Appartenete a qualche società proibita dalla Chiesa? Volete voi abbandonarla?
5. Avete offeso gravemente i vostri genitori?
6. Avete litigato? Ingiustamente ferito alcuno?
7. Avete consentito a pensieri cattivi?
8. Avete fatto cose oscene da solo(a)? Quante volte? Con altri? Uomo o donna?
9. Siete sposato(a)? Nella Chiesa Cattolica, o dal ministro protestante o dal giudice civile?
10. Nell'uso del matrimonio avete fatto cose per non avere figli? Avete procurato aborto?
11. Avete rubato? Molto? Volete voi restituirlo?
12. Avete mentito? Avete parlato male del prossimo?
13. Vi siete ubbriacato(a)? Quante volte?
14. Mangiaste carne nei giorni proibiti?
15. Avete altri peccati da confessare?
16. **Chiedete perdono dei vostri peccati?**

Penitenza: Ave Maria. Quante volte?

Contrizione: Mio Dio, mi pento d'avervi offeso; datemi la grazia di non peccare mai più.

HISPANICE — ESPANOL

Quiere Confesarse?

1. ¿Cuándo se confesó Ud. bien la última vez? ¿Cuantas semanas? ¿Cuantos meses? ¿Años?
2. ¿Ha blasphemado? ¿Ha leido malos libros?
3. ¿Ha faltado a misa? ¿Cuantas veces?
4. ¿Es Ud. miembro de sociedad prohibida por la Iglesia? ¿Esta Ud. resuelto a abandonarla?
5. ¿Ha ofendido a sus padres gravemente?
6. ¿Ha reñido? ¿Ha herido injustamente a alguno?
7. ¿Ha retenido pensamientos malos?
8. ¿Ha hecho acciones malas solo(a)? ¿Cuantas veces? ¿Con hombre? ¿Con mujer?
9. ¿Es Ud. casado(a)? ¿Por la Iglesia Católica, ó por un ministro protestante ó por lo civil?
10. ¿En sus derechos matrimoniales ha Ud. hecho cosas para no tener hijos? ¿Ha procurado aborto?
11. ¿Ha robado? ¿Mucho? ¿Desea restituirlo?
12. ¿Ha mentido? ¿Le ha quitado la fama a alguno?
13. ¿Se ha emborrachado(a)? ¿Cuantas veces?
14. ¿Ha comido carne los dias prohibidos?
15. ¿Tiene Ud. otros pecados que confesar?
16. **¿Se arrepiente de sus pecados?**

Penitencia: Ave Maria. ¿Cuantas veces?

Contricion: Dios mio, me arrepiento de haberte ofendido, ayudame para no más pecar.

Multilingual guide with common questions for priests to ask in confession, 1944.
Joseph L. Healy, *Polyglot Questionnaire for Hearing Confessions in an Emergency.*
Credit: Burns Library, Boston College

"Easter ticket," proving that a parishioner had fulfilled the requirement
for annual confession.
Credit: Author's collection

mere possession was proof that the person had complied with
the requirement for annual confession. Where the tradition
was practiced, the card might have to be produced at some
later date to establish good standing in the church, to join
a parish society, or to enroll children in the parish school.
Some Catholic schools used this system themselves as a way
of reminding students of their obligation and ensuring that
they met it. The possibilities for abuse were obvious, nota-
bly when a pastor insisted on using the custom as a form of
fundraising. At one parish in Rochester, New York, around
1910, fifty cents (later increased to a dollar) was the expected
"donation" for an Easter ticket after confessing, though that
seems to have been demanded from men only.[26]

Bishops strongly disapproved of this, seeing it as a modern
form of the ancient crime of simony, charging parishioners for
religious services to which they had an inherent right. Church
officials did what they could to stamp out the practice, but in
many places it died hard. At Saint Casimir's, a Lithuanian
parish in Nashua, New Hampshire, as late as the 1930s, the

pastor was still insisting on rigorous enforcement, and when
he learned that some members of his flock were going to confession in other churches to avoid paying, he denounced them,
threatening to "expel" evaders from the parish. But there were
places where the people themselves demanded that the custom be maintained. Another Lithuanian cleric, this one newly
appointed to a parish in Baltimore, reported that "I wanted
to abolish them," but the people insisted that the cards be
continued as they were "an ingrained tradition." Seminarians
were told to be on watch for the practice when they got to
their first parish assignments, and to eliminate it where they
found it. "Confession cards," wrote the Boston seminarian in
his class notes, "Don't use such things." Another authority
agreed: "The practice of giving certificates, if it still exists,
should be abolished." It took the acculturation of immigrant
parishioners to common American practices to end the tickets and other ethnic variants in confession, and this was the
work of generations for most groups. "Many of our penitents
were young men + women of German parentage," wrote an
English-speaking Paulist in Evansville, Indiana, noting the
shift in the parish from one language to another and away
from ethnically distinctive customs.[27]

✠

THE PRIEST WHO DESCRIBED the words of his penitents as
blurring together into "one great voice of humanity" had a
point, but certain populations of parishioners stood out as
requiring special attention. Most obvious were those who
were deaf or hard of hearing. Confession was by design an
oral process, relying on speaking and hearing, but accommodations were necessary when that was difficult or impossible.
The likelihood that a deaf penitent would be able to find a
priest fluent in sign language was even more remote than that
of a non-English speaker looking for one who understood a

foreign tongue. Confession in writing might then be the only alternative, though since that would create a record of sins, there was no obligation on the part of a penitent to agree to it; general signs of sorrow, such as striking the breast, might have to suffice. If writing was employed, precautions had to be taken to ensure the confidentiality of the exchange. In such cases, *Sign* magazine suggested that the sinner write out the itemization of sins, hand the list to the confessor, who would read and then return it to the penitent so that it could be destroyed afterward. *The Priest* thought it was better if the confessor kept the paper, tore it into little pieces, and later burned it to ensure its destruction. As an alternative, an interpreter might be used if available, but no penitent could be forced to accept the participation of a third-party intermediary.[28]

A better solution was to hear the confessions of those who were not completely deaf someplace other than in the confessional box—the rectory parlor, for example—so that the two could speak loudly enough to hear each other without being overheard by anyone else. Technology might also offer assistance. By the 1950s, several commercial enterprises were producing various forms of hearing aids that could be installed in the church's boxes. The Audio Equipment Company of Elmhurst, New York, promoted its compact "Confessionaire," which could be mounted on the wall between the confessor and the penitent. Priests could listen to the whispered words of their deaf parishioners as usual, while penitents could place a small receiver to their ear so as to hear the priest's amplified questions and the penance. Another outfit sold a "Hear-All," which took the form of a small closed-circuit telephone on both sides of the divide in the box.[29] Not every priest or parish might require such devices, but their availability indicates a desire not to overlook the pastoral needs of any parishioner.

A BLESSING TO THE AFFLICTED...AN AID TO THE CONFESSOR

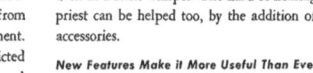

﴾CONFESSIONAIRE﴿

THE CONFESSIONAL HEARING AID SOLVES AN OLD PROBLEM

THANKS to CONFESSIONAIRE, the hard-of-hearing no longer need be kept from the Confessional by fear of embarrassment. No longer is it necessary that these afflicted parishioners, during a crowded Confessional hour, impede the work of the confessor.

CONFESSIONAIRE is simple, compact and easy to use. The afflicted parishioner merely places the convenient receiver to his ear, and can hear the priest's voice clearly—

Take advantage of our two weeks trial offer. Test it, try it. Send for this comforting device today!

even in a faint whisper. The hard-of-hearing priest can be helped too, by the addition of accessories.

New Features Make it More Useful Than Ever
- Illuminated instruction sign • Unbreakable receiver
- Mountable in many ways • Illuminated receiver and hook
- Squeal control circuit
- Metal case — fireproof
- Simple installation
- 3-year guarantee

PRICE $74.00
(Plus small shipping charge)

Send for CONFESSION-AIRE now! No obligation. Use it two weeks.

Use CONFESSIONAIRE for this trial period; then, if you are not satisfied, return it at our expense.

AUDIO EQUIPMENT COMPANY
805 MIDDLE NECK ROAD • GREAT NECK, N. Y.

Help for the hard of hearing in confession, 1955. Advertisement for the Audio Equipment Company, showing its product, the "Confessionaire." *Official Catholic Directory, 1955* (New York: Kenedy Publishing, 1955), advertising page 67f.

Credit: O'Neill Library, Boston College

Growing awareness of the special needs of the intellectually disabled throughout the twentieth century led to an attempt to articulate norms for hearing their confessions. It was an open question as to whether or how well those with disabilities could understand the church's elaborate categories of sin, particularly the distinction between mortal and venial sins. Some priests tried to apply them anyway, unwilling to make too many exceptions to the general rules. In the 1960s, a Redemptorist proposed classifying special penitents according to IQ level—how a confessor would know in any individual case he left unstated—applying such later objectionable terms as custodial, trainable, and educable. Those in the first category, he thought, "cannot commit any kind of personal sin" and simply had no need for confession at all. Those in the last group could be presumed capable of mortal sin, but confessors should not press the matter too closely; any such penitent should be given "the benefit of the doubt and judged as guilty of venial rather than mortal sin." Efforts to render confession less threatening should also be attempted, including hearing penitents in the rectory office rather than the box and prompting a stripped-down examination of conscience that emphasized such behavioral issues as anger and stubbornness. A simple act of contrition—"Jesus, I am sorry; I don't want to hurt You again"—was usually sufficient. Priests had to cooperate with the caretakers of the disabled, and the advice of an otherwise stern seminary professor seemed best in such cases: "Be doubly kind."[30]

Extraordinary circumstances might require similar adjustments with other special populations, including those who were confined in institutions. The Paulists conducted "a memorable mission" at Sing Sing Prison in New York in the 1880s, two weeks of effort that produced nearly six hundred confessions. Some prisoners wrote out private lists of their sins so as to be sure to remember them all, the mission's chronicler noted, and a young man was so moved during Mass one day that he abruptly left his seat and, visible to everyone present, knelt at a priest's feet to confess. Some Protestant prisoners asked for confession, too, "saying they knew they would be better men" for it. The confessions of hospital patients were likewise unusual, requiring particular attention to privacy, which might or might not be available on the wards. Even if it was, too strict an enforcement of the normal rules of confession should not be attempted, regardless of the patient's degree of illness. "Just ask that the sick person be sorry for sins," an adviser to the newly ordained said in 1962; "give a penance which can be said in a moment, . . . and then give absolution." Confessions heard when a priest visited a dying parishioner at home for a final anointing ought to be similarly brief. Such "sick calls" demanded a great deal of the local clergy's time—at one church in the Bronx, New York, in the 1950s, priests logged about a thousand of these every year, probably a typical number at the time for an urban parish—and, in addition to the rite of anointing itself, the occasion offered the opportunity for one final confession. Family members should be told to leave the room at that point, priests were instructed.[31]

Of all the special cases of hearing confessions, none were more dramatic than those of soldiers in wartime. Chaplains regularly accompanied troops into battle, where constantly changing conditions meant that confessions were often heard in ad hoc circumstances. During the Civil War, a French Jesuit was attached to a New York infantry regiment of "Irish Rifles" as they campaigned in Virginia. "Heard confessions in one of the tents, sitting upon a knapsack," he recorded in his diary one day when the unit was camped near Alexandria, and those accommodations later came to seem sumptuous. On another occasion, he listened to penitents in a "ditch" (probably meaning a military trench), and on yet another he "heard confessions the whole afternoon and late at night, until 12.30, in a small tent, without fire and on the wet ground." Given their situation, soldiers on the battlefield usually needed little encouragement to confess. The prospect of death was ever present, and the opportunity to purge themselves of guilt before possibly meeting their end was all the incentive they needed. Catholic chaplains in later wars had the same experiences. On the eve of an impending encounter with the enemy during World War II, one priest heard many confessions before the "big business tomorrow" and then, "as usual," he wrote letters to their parents back home "informing them of the fact of Confession." He was confident that, if the news turned out to be bad, families would be comforted that their sons had had this last chance to clear their moral slate. Another priest attending an army field hospital after the Battle of the Bulge came across a German prisoner, "filled with machine gun bullets." The chaplain listened to the man's confession—it is unclear how much of it he actually understood—and pronounced the absolution. "Gott ist gut," said the man, who happily seems to have survived.[32]

Wartime conditions meant that priests sometimes had to adjust the usual expectations governing confession, and they were willing to do so. A navy chaplain temporarily ashore on Guadalcanal in 1943 found himself, like his earlier confrere, in a strange setting. "To hear confessions I sit on a stone to the right of the Chapel, which is only a canvas of a couple of Army tents stretched from coconut trunks. . . . The men have to speak up to be heard, for all the time the planes are taking off just 200 yards away." This priest also regularly overlooked aspects of the sacrament that would have been rigorously enforced in calmer times and places. On several occasions, when surprised by Japanese air attacks, he imparted a hasty "general absolution" to all on board his aircraft carrier without hearing the confession of any individual. Once, he even

Army chaplain hearing confessions in the Philippines, 1945.
Note portable confessional screen.
U.S. Army Signal Corps, Photographs of Military Activity During
World War II and the Korean Conflict, https://catalog.archives.gov/id
/80682862?objectPage=107.
Credit: National Archives and Records Administration

imparted absolution from afar, having witnessed one of the
ship's own pilots miss his landing and crash into the sea. "No
sign of plane or pilot. Smoke billows up from the deep; gas
tank evidently broken feeding the fire on the surface like a
lamp. I give the dying or dead boy absolution." Yet another
time, he "was just about to raise my hand in absolution at a
distance" when a struggling plane pulled up, came around,
and landed safely. On the other side of the world, a chaplain stationed with the troops preparing for the Normandy

landing heard as many confessions as he could on the night before D-Day, and then he simply imparted a general absolution to the rest.[33] Both priests and penitents knew that these were loose constructions of the church's rules, acceptable only because of the abnormal situation. Even so, they underlined the fundamental belief in the efficacy of confession and absolution. When they returned to civilian life, these Catholic soldiers would not have expected such concessions and would have returned to their peacetime confessional habits.

✠

THE EXPERIENCE OF LAYPEOPLE in confession accounts for only half of the sacramental exchange. On the other side of the screen or grille in every confessional was a priest, and the personal experiences of the clergy encompassed the same range, from positive to negative, as that of their parishioners. The long-serving pastor in Minnesota was not alone in reflecting with satisfaction on "all the wonderful things" he had witnessed in the box and, indeed, had helped enable there. But others occasionally gave in to common enough human complaints. Even Gerald Kelly, the ardent promoter of "good" confessions, conceded that the process could be "monotonous, even distasteful" for a priest to sit through. "The time for hearing confessions comes round with a boring regularity" every week; the "long lines of penitents sap one's energies." A "stuffy box in a stuffy church," another priest wrote, often made for an unpleasant few hours, and the "sometimes unavoidable necessity of getting through as quickly as possible" because of the crowds only made matters worse. The church custodian might have forgotten to sweep out the box or otherwise keep it clean, still another priest said, and in winter "the germ-laden coughs of thoughtless penitents" threatened the transmission of colds, particularly "if the screen is not of a protective type." Moreover, when

Kelly was being completely honest, he had to admit that less than noble thoughts could also affect the attitude of the confessor. "It is not easy to go to the confessional when one's favorite team is advancing toward a thrilling championship" on a Saturday afternoon or evening, he acknowledged, itself a candid confession.[34]

Beyond what might seem like the drudgery of it all, virtually every confessor compiled his own informal list of complaints about penitents over the course of his priestly career. "There are penitents who would try the patience of an archangel," one said. "There are those who will do anything except speak up. Others are so reticent and incomplete in their answers that numerous questions are necessary. . . . Others will insist on going into long details about venial sins, and glide over matter far more serious." The confessions of young children and of adolescents could be particularly trying. Grade school kids might fool around in church beforehand; they might forget the usual formula or even some of their prayers; they might leave the box too soon, before the penance had been assigned and absolution granted. Teenagers could be even worse. Too often, they gave only perfunctory attention to the examination of conscience, "jabber[ing] off a lineup of meaningless generalizations that do not come within a mile of a truly good confession." Those generalizations were most commonly employed when the subject was sex, many priests thought—not without reason—and close questioning might thus be needed to drag the truth out of them. A supposed expert on hearing the confessions of adolescents elaborated a long list of sins in this area, and they were not merely specific infractions against the sixth commandment, encompassing instead all sorts of bad behavior. "If a mother commands her daughter to stay away from certain companions for grave reasons, or to be home at a certain hour of the night," and the daughter disobeyed, that was a mortal sin against the divine injunction to honor one's parents.[35] Patience was a noble ideal that priests should strive for, but it was sometimes hard to come by.

Even so, all seminarians knew that, in becoming priests, confession would be an essential part of their lives and ministries. But how they actually learned to do it, how to conduct themselves in the sacrament, and how to guide their parishioners through it were all more complicated, since this was not a rite they could practice with real penitents beforehand. They were permitted to conduct certain other rituals of the church—baptisms, for instance—while they were advancing through the so-called minor orders (such as deacon) that constituted steps toward the priesthood. But a confession could be heard only by a priest, and that left them out until they had officially crossed the ordination threshold. They spent a great deal of time in their preparatory studies on the coursework in moral theology, as we have seen, but that equipped them with knowledge that was largely theoretical. "My mind is filled with technical knowledge," said one writer, assuming the persona of a newly ordained priest. "I can rattle off the impediments to marriage, correct the scrupulous penitent, [and] spot the recidivist." When abstract cases of the classroom were "translated . . . into real flesh and blood" on the other side of the confessional grille, it was not so easy to know what to do.[36]

Over time, seminaries developed coursework and other ways of introducing their students to the realities of pastoral practice. By the beginning of the twentieth century, it had become evident that seminarians needed not only the intense study of the ins and outs of moral theology as defined by such comprehensive manuals as Noldin and Jone; they also needed to give explicit consideration to effective ways of conveying and applying those principles to ordinary parishioners. William Stang's pioneering textbook on pastoral theology from

1897, together with the volume produced two years later by
Frederic Schulze, a priest-professor from Wisconsin, essentially defined the field which, Schulze noted happily, was "at
last" receiving the attention it deserved in priestly preparation. Their works covered the entire range of activities in
local churches, and when it came to confession they provided
a way of bridging the gap between theory and practice. Seminarians "study about the sacraments," wrote a later priest
who was a product of this kind of training, "the Ten Commandments, the six precepts of the Church, and just about all
the known ways of breaking them." After that, clerical students were prompted to consider "questions on typical confession problems and try to come up with the proper advice."
As a climax to their studies, an oral examination was admin-
istered by a board of three or four professors "designed to test
the knowledge, wisdom, and prudence of the young priests-
to-be." This could be daunting: the "examiners can dream up
rare cases to puzzle and test the would-be priests."[37]

For years, John Ford, SJ, taught these courses for Jesuit
seminarians at the Weston School of Theology in Massachusetts, and his surviving class notes provide a window into the
process. Ford had joined the Jesuits after graduating from
high school (a common age at the time) and quickly emerged
as an intellectual star within the order. After earning graduate
degrees in Rome, he returned to America and became perhaps the leading Catholic moral theologian of his generation,
with a teaching career that lasted from the 1930s to the 1960s.
Together with Gerald Kelly, he edited the regular "Notes on
Moral Theology" in *Theological Studies*, the leading journal in
the field. Whereas the equally formidable Kelly was inclined
to speak and write for popular audiences as well, Ford was
the recognized academic expert on morality and ethics, and
he published widely on topics ranging from alcoholism to
sexuality. At the height of World War II, he even produced

a controversial essay defending the right of Catholic pilots to refuse orders to participate in the obliteration bombing of civilian targets. Throughout his career, his reputation was such that he regularly received letters from priests around the country, soliciting his advice on thorny problems they had encountered among their parishioners.[38]

In addition to his usual classes, Ford also presided over the oral exams for more than one generation of Jesuits, and his method was characteristic of that used in seminaries everywhere in the country. At the end of two years of coursework in moral theology, students faced the exam *Ad Audiendas Confessiones*—toward the hearing of confessions—known in shorthand as "Ad Auds." This, he told his students, was not just one more academic exercise, "testing the abstract knowledge of the student in the realm of moral principles and canon law." Rather, its goal was to gauge a student's "ability to apply correctly and prudently to concrete human situations the law and the moral principles." The words he underlined in his notes were the crucial ones. Coming up with the correct answer about right and wrong in any particular circumstance was obviously crucial, but that answer had to be applied in the confessional, where prudence was no less essential. The strict letter of the law might point to one outcome, but a looser interpretation could well be called for. This was probably clearest when it came to asking questions, and it was all-important to know when to stop questioning: usually, a confessor could get to the requisite knowledge of the exact nature of a sin without hearing all the details. "Don't ever ask questions while doubting whether they are prudent or necessary," he warned. Sometimes, it was better to be satisfied with too little information than to press for too much: "don't torture them with all the distinctions you learned in class." If those heading to their first parish assignment were going to be able "to hear confessions fruitfully," they had to demonstrate that they had reached the appropriate levels of both "knowledge and prudence." To find out, Ford and the other priests who joined him as "Ad Auds" examiners presented each student with a number of situations, similar to those they had already encountered in *The Casuist* and elsewhere. Over the course of his teaching career, he amassed several hundred such cases for use in exams.[39]

Each began by identifying the "state in life" of the penitent and then proceeded to the specific problem broached in confession. A boy had quit school at sixteen, for example, and gone to work. But somehow he was able to get away with paying only the student fare on the streetcar—Ford was unsure whether that was five or ten cents—thereby saving himself about seventy-five cents a week. If he brought this up in confession, was he bound to make restitution to the trolley company as a condition of forgiveness? Was the seemingly innocuous sin transformed into "serious guilt by accumulation?" Ford himself believed that there was a right answer, but he was interested first in listening to how the examinee addressed the problem. What was at stake here was more a matter of deception than of justice, and the proper response was to call that to the boy's attention. Then, having learned that the case was really about lying, he could be told "to give what he saved to charity" as a part of his penance. If the seminarian being examined was able to get to that endpoint of analysis, the test had been successful. In another instance, an eight-year-old child ("not very bright") confessed to all sorts of things, including "I was fresh with the kids; I hit the little ones and sassed the big ones." The first duty here was to "find out if [the] child knows what a sin is." Then, "teach child essentials and either absolve or give blessing." In every case, the seminarian was not required to defend his reasoning in detail, though the examiners might ask for "a brief indication of why the case was solved as it was." Moreover, these exams were public and could be attended by other seminarians; in fact, others were encouraged to attend, thereby learning from their classmates' mistakes and successes. This no doubt added to the pressure on the candidate, but it also helped prepare his friends for when they had to go through the same exercise.[40]

For all the effort that went into their instruction in advance, priests mostly learned how to hear confessions just by doing it. To that end, virtually every authority recommended that they throw themselves into the work from the very beginning. "Any opportunity for gaining experience in sacerdotal duties during the first days should be taken," the author of an advice manual to the newly ordained wrote in 1962. That included volunteering for funeral masses and sick calls, but it was all the more important to "start the hearing of confessions immediately." New priests might be a little uncertain at first, perhaps especially on the matter of assigning penances. What were the usual expectations on this score in any particular parish? But in that as in other matters, another priest wrote, they could be guided by the pastor and older priests in the rectory. In some instances, the *Messenger of the Sacred Heart* had explained to its lay readers, a priest who encountered "a case which he hesitates to decide" on his own could consult with "another more learned or experienced," with the understanding of course that the anonymity of the penitent be preserved.[41] Pastors could help this process along by letting the younger priests of the parish hear most of the weekly confessions, as Father Urban had done in New Orleans. Soon enough, priests developed their own confessional styles. Hundreds of confessions every week provided all the practice they needed.

With priests as with their parishioners, the experience of confession was personal. No matter how many times they did it, each occasion was particular to them, and the privacy of it was central to keeping it personal. That privacy also provoked curiosity in others, whether Catholics or not.

5

Secrecy

"THIS CASE," SAID ONE of the lawyers afterwards, "like many others of importance, had its origin in a trivial occasion." Late in the winter of 1813 in New York City, Charles Bradley and Benjamin Brinkerhoff—"both coloured men," the lawyer noted, though that seemed to have little bearing on the matter—had stolen some goods from a merchant named Keating. The loot (the exact nature of which was unclear from the trial record; perhaps jewelry) had wound up in the hands of Daniel Phillips and his wife, Mary. The police investigated, and all four culprits were quickly identified and charged: Bradley and Brinkerhoff for the theft itself, Mr. and Mrs. Phillips for receiving stolen property. Before long, however, Keating reported that the missing items had been returned to him. Asked how he had recovered his property, Keating was at first reluctant to say, but when pressed he answered that the restitution had been arranged by Father Anthony Kohlmann, the pastor of Saint Peter's Church, of which Keating and the Phillipses were members. So the investigators went to the priest, who surprised them by refusing to say how he had learned of the crime, how he had taken possession of the purloined articles, and how he had effected their return to the rightful owner. Even though his refusal was made "in a very becoming manner," it exposed him to the scrutiny, and possibly the sanction, of the courts. It was a well-established principle that "the law is entitled to every man's evidence," and a witness could not simply say "no, thanks" when summoned to testify. Father Kohlmann was now subject to a charge of contempt.[1]

The reason he gave for his silence was an unusual one, never before asserted in an American court. Had he learned of the crime "as a private individual," Kohlmann said, he would be willing, indeed eager, to cooperate, but that was not the case here. Rather, he had gained what knowledge he had "in quality of a minister of a sacrament, in which my God himself has enjoined on me a perpetual and inviolable secrecy." He meant no disrespect to the police or to the courts, but he insisted that he could not say a single word about the matter because he had learned what he knew of it in confession. The "seal" of the confessional was absolute, he explained, covering "all and every part and circumstance of what is communicated." Were he to break that seal, he would be "a traitor to my church, to my sacred ministry, and to my God. In fine, I should render myself guilty of eternal damnation." At first, the prosecutor was inclined simply to let the matter drop; he had no interest in prosecuting the priest. Relations among religious denominations had turned in a decidedly amicable direction in the aftermath of the American Revolution. Earlier tensions between Protestants and Catholics were being set aside in the interests of community harmony and fellow citizenship. A draft article in the New York state constitution had been proposed by John Jay, denying Catholics the right to vote and even the right to own property because of their alleged political loyalty to the pope, but it had been soundly rejected. And in any event the present business had ended well: Keating got his property back. Then came another surprise: a petition to the court from several laymen, the leaders of Saint Peter's parish, specifically asking that the prosecution of their pastor go forward, "to the end that a judicial determination may be had" regarding Kohlmann's silence. They were hoping for a precedent that would clearly establish the seal of confession in American law.[2]

They got their wish. Over several days in early June, a trial was held in a court presided over by DeWitt Clinton, then the mayor of New York and a future governor who, among other accomplishments, would oversee construction of the Erie Canal. Neither the judge nor the jurors nor the contending attorneys were themselves Catholics. Appearing for the defense were Richard Riker, a former congressman politically aligned with Clinton, and William Sampson, a Protestant from Ireland who had been expelled from his homeland for nationalist political agitation. After joining with the prosecution in reviewing several cases from British law, none of which offered any clear guidance, Sampson and Riker focused their argument on a section of the New York constitution guaranteeing to all citizens "the free exercise and enjoyment of their religious profession and worship." Since confession was an essential part of the Catholic religion, they insisted, forcing Kohlmann to testify would compel him to violate the rules of his church, thereby limiting his exercise of faith. It was tantamount to saying that, while of course he had the right to practice his religion, he just might have to go to jail when he did. The court agreed in rejecting any such logic. Protestants had only two sacraments (baptism and Eucharist), Clinton pointed out in his ruling; did anyone doubt that legally restricting the practice of one of those would be an infringement of fundamental rights? The same applied to Catholicism's seven sacraments, including confession. True, the New York constitution did bar religious practices that encouraged "licentiousness" or were "inconsistent with the peace or safety of the state," but that was hardly the case here. In fact, the restitution that had been required for forgiveness in confession had had exactly the opposite effect, restoring stolen property and thereby, in a larger sense, restoring justice. Moreover, Kohlmann's sincerity was beyond doubt. "Although we differ from the witness and his brethren in our religious creed," Clinton concluded, "yet we have no reason to question the purity of their motives, or to impeach their good conduct." The case against the priest was dismissed and, there being now no testimony against Phillips and his wife, they were discharged, too.[3] Bradley and Brinkerhoff, sadly for them, were already in jail.

As the players in this drama intended, the "trivial" case had indeed turned out to have great "importance," establishing the legal foundation for the secrecy of the confessional. A second case in New York in 1817 confirmed it, and in 1828 the state legislature reinforced it with an explicit statute. Since then, virtually every other state in the nation has adopted similar legislation, protecting (in the words of the New York law) clergy of any denomination "in the course of discipline enjoined by the rules or practices of such denomination."[4] The seal had always been an indispensable element of confession for Catholics, crucial to its effectiveness, and others recognized this, too. During the proceedings, Riker had appealed to simple common sense: "If we could legally and constitutionally compel the clergyman" to reveal what he had heard, "who would afterwards go to confession?" Penitents knew that what they told their confessors would never leave the confines of the box—everything was *sub sigillo* (under seal)—and they took reassurance from that. For non-Catholics, however, this secrecy only deepened the mystery. Just what was going on in the confessional? If the penitent was receiving encouragement to live a better life, that was a worthy purpose. But what if the priest was somehow cooperating with or condoning the sinners' sins, minimizing their seriousness? Worse, what if the ready availability of forgiveness provided a kind of license for bad behavior, reassuring evildoers that they would be pardoned every time? And worse still, what if priests were using the confessional in furthering their own sins, specifically those of a sexual nature? The seal of confession was impossible to separate from the practice of the sacrament, but it also prompted an enduring curiosity and suspicion.

✠

THE SECRECY OF THE sacramental proceedings had its origin as an inevitable consequence of the shift from public to private penance in the ancient church. Once the purposeful, public shaming of sinners had been replaced by individual conversations between priests and penitents, it was vital to keep private whatever was said. As Riker would note in the Kohlmann trial, if penitents knew that what they confessed might later become public, they would not confess at all or, if they did, they would be inclined to something less than sincerity or completeness. The logic of the seal was self-evident, wrote Henry Charles Lea, compiler of a monumental three-volume *History of Auricular Confession and Indulgences in the Latin Church*, published in 1896. Lea, though the scion of an old Catholic family, had little sympathy for the church—"a spiritual autocracy," he called it—and he devoted his life to debunking its larger theological claims through the detailed examination of centuries of historical evidence. He produced a similarly comprehensive history (in four volumes) of the Spanish Inquisition and two volumes on priestly celibacy, together with other works. No matter how theologians tried to defend the seal on higher grounds, he said, its true motive was "the very human one that without it confession would be too odious to be successfully enforced"; it was all a case of "the most naked expediency." Lea's hostile tone notwithstanding, he had a point, and the scope of the seal had been "speedily enlarged" and accepted. The church council of 1215 that mandated annual confession for all Catholics confirmed it, hoping to reassure the laity by prescribing penalties for any priest who breached secrecy, including dismissal from the priesthood and lifelong confinement in a monastery.[5]

Monasteries were not as readily available in Kohlmann's day as they had been in the thirteenth century, but he was correct in arguing that, if he had revealed what he knew in the Phillips case, he would have forfeited his ministry. For later generations of American priests, too, the absolute nature of the seal was always understood as a given. The theology textbooks could not have been clearer on the subject. Just as there were no venial sins against the sixth commandment, so "there can be no slight violation of the seal," Jone's *Moral Theology* said flatly in the 1920s. "*No exception* is ever made, not even to save one's life or for the common welfare." Any breaking of the seal was always a mortal sin for a priest. Another text agreed, spelling out a long list of possible violations, both direct and indirect: the details of any specific sins, whether mortal or venial, and the circumstances surrounding them; the nature of the penance that had been assigned, particularly if it was harsh enough to signal mortal sins; whether absolution had been granted or not; even the fact that a particular person had gone to confession "if it suggested that the confession was necessary." (This last was also a sign of mortal sin.) When preaching, a priest could not use, however anonymously, something he had learned about in the confessional, "even if he knows through confession that certain sins are common locally." Not even the death of the penitent released a confessor from the obligation to safeguard what Kohlmann had called "all and every part and circumstance of what is communicated." It was priests, not penitents, who were bound by the seal. In most cases, of course, the latter had every reason to keep quiet about their sins once outside the box, and priests, as we have seen, tried to discourage their parishioners from gossiping among themselves about who the more lenient confessors were. But in certain circumstances, the seal might indeed apply to the laity as much as to the clergy. Anyone who overheard someone else's confession while waiting in line, for instance, was bound to secrecy and sinned greatly by talking about it.[6]

A good deal of time was spent in the seminary classroom reinforcing the seriousness of this message for future priests. Employing a metaphor from secular affairs, one seminarian wrote in his class notes that "there is a quasi-contract between penitent + confessor that [the] confessor will never reveal information." Echoing the insistence of his teacher, the student went on: "No purpose, no matter how good, excuses violation of the seal!" Once ordained and working in a parish, the clergy might be reminded periodically of what they had been told on the subject. A priest from the bishop's office in Los Angeles provided a typical summary in the pages of *The Priest* magazine in 1956, itemizing some of the familiar violations of the seal. He even thought that use of the common phrase "big fish," denoting someone who had been away from confession for a long time, was risky. Long gaps between confessions might well suggest that mortal sins were involved, and that came too close to crossing the line, even if the fish went unidentified. Another priest told the newly ordained that respect for the seal was "too elementary to need mention," but he mentioned it anyway, adding that any indication by a confessor that he recognized a penitent (by voice, by the sins committed, or otherwise) was a kind of violation, too. The Californian put it as clearly as he could: "Mum's the word."[7]

Most priests readily adopted these standards as their own. One thought that his own days of seminary formation had prepared him well to keep things to himself, perhaps in subtle and unexpected ways. As part of its routine schedule, his seminary (like others) observed a "grand silence" from nine o'clock at night until five-thirty the next morning; no one was permitted to speak aloud for any reason. "So when someone asks me how I can hear all those confessions and not divulge anything," he said later in life, "I recall seven long years of having to be still for eight hours every night." True, for many of those hours he had been asleep, but the habit of maintaining silence had been reinforced daily. The volume of confessions also helped obscure particular details—when it came to "confession stories," one cleric said wearily, "brother priests have heard them all"—and the trivial nature of much of what was confessed was easily forgotten, leaving little to talk about after the fact. Especially difficult cases might require a confessor to seek the advice of other, more knowledgeable or experienced priests, and that was permissible so long as the third party was not told (or could not deduce) the identity of the penitent involved. The *Messenger of the Sacred Heart* calmed a lay reader's worries by saying that, whenever a priest had to do this, he was careful to mask "any circumstances which would reveal the identity of the person confessing." Lost to history are any conversations around the rectory dinner table or advice sought and given in private consultations between older pastors and younger curates; it is difficult to imagine that informal occasions such as those never arose. Even John Ford had allowed for a priest's rethinking what he had said in the confessional, with or without assistance from a colleague, perhaps resulting in correction or emendation in the future with a particular penitent. And Jone had agreed that a confessor could "consult someone more experienced," though it was best in such cases to let the penitent know beforehand that he was going to do so, with appropriate assurances of anonymity. On the whole, however, "the priest must always do the safe thing (i.e., favor the seal)."[8]

Reminders to laypeople of the absolute secrecy of the confessional were commonplace in American Catholic culture,

and many stories circulated about heroic priests who had
defended it. The life of Saint John Nepomucene, a fourteenth-
century bishop in Bohemia, was offered frequently as an
exemplar. He had been martyred by his king for refusing to
divulge evidence of the queen's infidelity, having learned of it
in confession, and his story helped prove an important point.
Every year, the syndicated Catholic News Service distributed an account of his life that could be picked up by diocesan newspapers when his feast day (May 16) came around.
The tale even had a remarkable coda. Three centuries after
his death, reported the news release for 1931, the saint's
tomb was opened and his tongue—and apparently only his
tongue—"was found to be still incorrupt." The moral of the
story was obvious: God had guarded the tongue in death just
as the man himself had done in life, an additional spiritual
reward for faithfulness. There were other accounts of priestly
bravery. In the 1890s, a Canadian priest was praised for refusing to give testimony in a minor civil case (an employment
dispute), and he was jailed briefly until freed by an appeals
court. During the Second World War, the *St. Louis Register*,
newspaper of the archdiocese there, lauded a German prelate
for resisting the Nazis, risking death by his silence. After the
war, the same paper followed the case of a priest in Yugo-
slavia who went willingly to prison rather than tell his com-
munist captors what they wanted to know. School children,
no less than adults, were reminded of how absolute the seal
was. In 1957, *Treasure Chest*, a biweekly comic book of stories,
puzzles, and lessons for use in parochial grade schools, ran a
dramatic story of two refugees who slipped through the Iron
Curtain. They told a Protestant American serviceman that
they wanted to go to confession immediately, having been
denied it for so long, and they explained the basics of the
sacrament to him. A flashback panel showed a priest, hands
bound behind his back and surrounded by three vaguely

The seal of confession explained to school children, *Treasure Chest*, 1957.
"Passports to Paradise: The Sacrament of Penance," *Treasure Chest of Fun
and Fact* (January 9, 1957), pages 17–22.
Credit: American Catholic History Research Center, Catholic University of America

Soviet-looking guards, refusing to tell a judge what he had
learned in confession. The message was consistent: penitents
need have no fear that their confessors would ever speak of
their sins to anyone else, no matter how strong the pressure
to do so. "Never was it known that the secrecy of the confessional was violated," the *Catholic Telegraph* of Cincinnati had
said in reporting the Canadian case.[9]

As much as laypeople heard about the seal of confession,
however, sometimes the danger of breaking it might come
from them. What should he do, one priest asked the *Homiletic and Pastoral Review* in 1964, if a parishioner approached
him outside the confessional to talk further about something
that had come up during the sacrament? That might seem to
constitute a kind of release from secrecy, but the magazine
still recommended prudence, suggesting "Are you sure you
want to talk about this here/now?" as the proper response.

It was better if the two simply returned to the confessional to continue the discussion, since the seal would obviously be in effect there. "Whenever the seal is exposed even to the slightest danger," the *Review* concluded, "whenever there is a risk of engendering a distaste for the sacrament on the part of the faithful, extreme caution is the watchword. Sacramental secrecy is such an awesome responsibility" that it was "almost impossible" to be too careful in guarding it. The reply confirmed the point that Lea and others had made over the years. "Engendering a distaste" for confession was a problem all its own, one that the seal was designed to forestall, and priests could readily understand the connection. They knew that their parishioners, even as they were confessing regularly and in such large numbers, generally had at least some level of "distaste" for it. In fact, according to many writers, they were supposed to have a distaste for it, a revulsion that might keep them from sinning in the future. But the church had to be careful not to give them reasons to act on those feelings. "I must not make confession odious," the seminarian in Boston had written in his notes. That word—odious—showed up repeatedly in priestly discussions of the seal. Anything that provided parishioners with an excuse not to go to confession had to be avoided.[10]

All the same, actual practice did not always conform perfectly to the clear demands of the textbooks or the clerical advice manuals. Among themselves, priests might occasionally shade the boundaries of the seal. Like any professional group, the Catholic clergy had their own assumptions and unwritten rules, their own means for sharing common experiences. Though the phrase was discouraged, for example, the use of "big fish" was so nearly universal as to indicate that confessors might not adhere to the most exacting of interpretations. On its face, this was a harmless observation about a return to the sacrament after a lapse, but the jocular metaphor could also have an air of self-congratulation about it. Mission preachers used it regularly in reports to their superiors as a way of conveying how successful they had been at any given stop on their travels, and they made that point with other words too. "Such good cases!" a missionary enthused on one occasion, noting with pride the many men, young and old, in one town who were "squabbling to get at us in the box."[11] It was the same for parish priests. Anyone who could "land," as Father James Walsh had done, a "17 year fish" had grounds for believing that he was doing a good job. Even if he was not boasting about it or claiming too much credit—God was involved, he would have been sure—he could still find satisfaction in the pious practice of his parishioners, and that helped reaffirm him in his work.

The clear line around the seal might blur in other ways, too. In his diary, Walsh even set down a dialog with an unidentified penitent, humorously noting how long it took to get a straight answer to his simple question of when she had last been to confession. "The last time" was the woman's first answer, "when the priest came" the second, "the time of the mission" third, and finally "I don't know." Following her into the box soon after, "a city employee" said in the course of his confession that he let "his drinking wife" squander his wages; she managed the household finances, the man explained, because he "does not know one bill from another."[12] These accounts did not identify penitents by name and so may not have been direct violations of the seal—though a city worker with a thirsty wife could well have been known (or guessed at) by their fellow parishioners. Still, the personal details came close. Walsh's diary entries were intended only for his own eyes, of course, but did he also tell these stories aloud to priest friends in relaxed settings? His fellow clerics might very well have "heard them all," but there could still be a kind of collective release in repeating them to one another, regardless of what their old seminary professors had told them.

Proving a negative is not possible, and thus the Cincinnati newspaper could not have been certain that "never was it known" for a priest in America to have violated the seal of the confessional. Even so, for laypeople the seal was a reinforcement of the one aspect of confession they almost universally liked: its privacy. "Somehow," one woman said in 1971, "the anonymity of the black box can be a great comfort," its "therapeutic value" enhanced precisely because there was no recognition or eye contact. Twenty years before, another woman had expressed a similar sentiment, saying that she didn't mind talking to her priest face-to-face about a practical matter—making the arrangements for a wedding or a baptism, for instance—but "I'd rather ask about personal matters in the confessional."[13] Under normal circumstances, penitents spoke to their confessors alone, in the dark, and with a physical barrier between them. Their oral exchange was entirely private as it was happening, and the church's insistence on the seal guaranteed that this privacy would be maintained after the fact. There was no possibility that the things they had done, things of which they might well have been ashamed or embarrassed, would ever come to light. A great comfort, indeed.

✠

BUT ALSO, POTENTIALLY, A danger. Confession always covered a multitude of sins, but it might also cover *for* a multitude of sins. The one that concerned church leaders most was "solicitation." Moral theology textbooks, even those published in English, usually reverted to Latin when coming to this subject, but a reference encyclopedia from the 1910s defined the problem for a lay readership: "making use of the Sacrament of Penance, directly or indirectly, for the purpose of drawing others into sins of lust." Church law on the subject was "very severe," and pope after pope had "denounced this crime vehemently and decreed punishments for its commission." The possible forms the offense might take were spelled out with the precision customary in any Catholic consideration of sin. A priest enticing a person into sin with himself or with a third party; doing so immediately before, during, or immediately after confession; whether in the confessional box itself or somewhere else; whether by words or letters "or signs or other expressive actions"—any or all of these could constitute elements of the crime. A "completed sin against chastity" was not required, Jone's *Moral Theology* added delicately; the proposal alone was enough. The soliciting priest could not absolve his target of any other sins mentioned during the corrupted confession and of course could not absolve from the sin itself if the penitent gave in and became his "accomplice." In fact, the church shifted onto the victim (of either sex, though usually presumed to be female) the onus of what to do about it all. Since it was implausible to expect the offending cleric to turn himself in, those who had been solicited in the confessional had the duty to denounce him to the proper authority (the local bishop in most cases) within one month of the crime or—a slight concession—within a month of learning that they had that responsibility. The soliciting priest was not bound to inform his target of "the obligation of denunciation," one seminary professor told his students, but if the victim failed to do so, "excommunication is incurred *ipso facto*." Accusers did not have to reveal whether they had consented to the shameful proposition, and they could frame their complaint in such a way as to avoid "serious damage to self or family." They needed, of course, to tell the truth. The church wanted to be "severe on delinquent confessors," but it was "equally careful to protect innocent priests from calumnious charges," and thus a false accusation was so great a sin that it could be pardoned only by the pope himself. An allegation once proved, however, carried penalties that would permanently bar the priest from saying Mass or otherwise exercising his ministry, and it would strip him of his "benefices, dignities, and offices."[14]

All this was neither theoretical nor speculative. The church had had long experience with solicitation. Throughout the Middle Ages, sexual immorality among the clergy was widely known and almost as widely presumed. An investigation by the Inquisition (which was responsible for rooting out the problem, together with its duty of prosecuting Jews, Muslims, Protestants, and other heretics) found that in a diocese in Spain at least one-third of all local priests were living in sin, an offense called concubinage. That was probably a common rate elsewhere as well, and in some places it was almost certainly higher. Priests who did not already have long-term partners (effectively wives) could readily find them, and ironically the mandate for annual confession by all Catholics may have increased that likelihood. "It cannot be a matter of surprise," said Henry Charles Lea in his customary arched tone, "that the seduction of women in the confessional," while always possible, "could not but increase when the whole population was driven annually to the confessional." Luther had seized on the open secret as a key argument in his larger program of challenging the special role of the clergy, emphasizing instead "the priesthood of all believers," and the church had to respond. Efforts at the Council of Trent in the sixteenth century to improve the quality of the priesthood, through better education and closer supervision by bishops, were designed in part to diminish the abuse. The requirement that confessions, particularly those of women, always be heard in the distinct space of specially designed confessional boxes was also a contribution to this goal. If there were at least some kind of physical partition between confessor and penitent, the worst forms of solicitation might be kept in check.[15]

Centuries later, the insistence of American bishops that all parish churches have confessionals, placed conspicuously, was a latter-day expression of the same concern. As we have seen, this had not always been possible for the earliest missionaries, who heard confessions wherever they could as they rode their circuits, and the need to improvise persisted for a long time in out-of-the-way places. In rural Michigan at the turn of the twentieth century, one priest sat in "the little check room at the end of the hall" in a public building, with his back turned to the penitents, including "eighty men," who took advantage of his arrival in the vicinity. In the 1920s, a Jesuit was driven around the towns outside Portland, Oregon, by a layman— his "chauffeur, cook and general assistant"—in a "chapel car," listening to penitents in a tent set up wherever he found them, "whether it was on a mountain crag or a hay stack." (A good many of the confessions, he reported, began with the words, "It has been a long time, Father"—itself, perhaps, a near violation of the seal.) All concerned could recognize these as departures from the usual, compelled by circumstance, and some effort went into trying to replicate the experience of what would by then have been considered a "normal" confession in a church. The priest in Michigan had come up with an ingenious arrangement at another of his stops. "Confessions were heard in the McNulty [family] living room," he recalled in his memoirs of one occasion, shortly before Christmas, in a village outside Port Huron. "The confessional was a wicker rocking chair," positioned so as to serve as a kind of screen between himself and the twenty people who came into the room, one after another, to confess their sins. They knelt on the floor facing the chair's seat and spoke through the ad hoc grille of wicker latticework on its back, while he sat in a chair on the other side, his face turned away.[16]

As the church's infrastructure spread throughout the country, however, the enclosed confessional box in a parish church

was the standard location for the sacrament, helping to provide the intended sense of separation and privacy. Bystanders
could see their fellow parishioners going in and out, and the
clockwork regularity of it offered a kind of tacit reassurance
that nothing improper was going on. A particularly determined priest might be able to solicit an accomplice in two
minutes or less, but it would be difficult. Even so, suspicions
persisted, especially among non-Catholics. The personal conversations carried on in the confessional between priests and
women, particularly young women, seemed an invitation to
ill effects, both for the individuals involved and by extension
for society at large. By the middle of the nineteenth century,
American Protestants had built a powerful cult of domesticity, centered on an idealized vision of the family home, in
which husbands and fathers protected and provided moral
guidance to their female relatives. Catholic priests were dangerous interlopers who challenged this emerging model by
offering an alternative source of authority, one that claimed
divine sanction, no less. Surely, such power was easy to
abuse, it was thought, and the possibility that priests would
seduce their female penitents seemed inevitable. Even if they
did not go that far, were they routinely countermanding the
instructions of the male head of the household? If so, that
threatened to undermine all morality. When combined with
recurrent waves of hostile nativism that sought to restrict the
political and social influence of Catholic immigrants, these
attitudes only confirmed many Americans in their belief that
the Roman church constituted a clear and present danger and
that the confessional was the place where much of the damage was likely to be done.[17]

In such a context, stories about solicitation in the confessional had a life of their own. Lurid tales, alive since the
Reformation, about priests who corrupted young women
could be reworked for modern audiences, growing more

scandalous with time and repetition; often, the absence of any actual proof was taken as the best proof of all. Henry Lea recognized but resisted the temptation to exaggerate. He disapproved of "the most debased" literature, full of titillating details, and thought the historical record was actually worse. "The divorce of morals from religion [was] complete" in his view, with the real trumping the imagined. In the popular literature of the nineteenth century, however, thinly veiled pornography (tame by modern standards) was readily available, and no accounts were more successful than "escaped nun" tales, which combined several fears into one. Convents were themselves closed, secretive, and mysterious places, and thus they redoubled the danger. The confession of anyone, in private to a priest, was risky enough, but it was even worse if the encounter were taking place inside such a forbidding institution, doubly sealed off from the scrutiny of the world. Moreover, when these accounts presented themselves as true memoirs of women who had managed to escape the clutches of the church, they had even more impact. Nothing enhances the appeal of a damsel-in-distress story like a happy ending. Defining a new literary genre, the earliest bestsellers were those produced by Rebecca Reed (a real person) and Maria Monk (an obvious pseudonym, though someone using that name also took to the lecture circuit), both of whom purported to describe dangers they had personally encountered and, in the end, eluded. Reed's *Six Months in a Convent* (1835) and Monk's *Awful Disclosures of the Hotel Dieu Nunnery* (1836) provided all the "proof" that those already skeptical of Catholics and Catholic practices might need.[18]

Reed had actually spent a brief period as a novice in a convent of Ursuline sisters outside Boston in 1831 and 1832, though she did not dwell on the abuses of confession during her stay. She preferred instead to describe the debasing cruelties routinely inflicted by superiors of the order for minor infractions of the rules of the house: having to lie prostrate on the floor all night, being subject to arbitrary and changing commands, kissing the feet of the mother superior. By contrast, the team of evangelical ministers who ghost-wrote the text with Monk's name on it gave freer rein to their imagination, hoping to enflame their readers. Supposedly set in a convent in Montreal, the book even contained a fanciful floor plan, showing kitchens and dining rooms but also such ominously designated spaces as a "priests' gaming and feasting room" and one chamber that had a trap door into the cellar; just enough rooms were marked "unknown" to enhance the aura of mystery. The general arc of the story was designed to shock: priests from a nearby seminary snuck into the supposedly cloistered convent, had their way with the sisters and their female pupils, and buried the babies born of these encounters in the cellar—the trap door had its uses—often covering them with lime so as to accelerate deterioration of the bodies. The book was so popular, selling more copies than anything else before the Civil War except *Uncle Tom's Cabin*, that it was quickly brought out again in a new edition, which doubled the size of the original by including an appendix, a "sequel to the narrative," a "general review of the whole subject," and a supplement. Readers could not get enough.[19]

In cataloging the sins she had supposedly witnessed in the convent, Monk wasted little time in getting around to confession, recounting abuses there as early as the opening pages of chapter two. In her very first weeks in the convent, our heroine, age ten, encountered a girl who told her about "the conduct of a priest with her at confession." It was "of so criminal and shameful a nature, I could hardly believe it, and yet I had so much confidence that she spoke the truth, that I could not discredit it." Soon enough, she herself was having the same experience. "The priests became more and more bold, and were at length indecent in their questions and even in their conduct when I confessed to them." Monk's writers were shrewd enough to know that readers' speculations were more potent than any specifics, and so modesty quickly intervened to cut the account short. "It is not my intention to speak of it very particularly because it is impossible to do so without saying things both shameful and demoralizing." It was always better to say less than more, allowing imagination to fill in the rest of the story, so the same approach was applied in a later account of confession. "I shall not tell what was transacted at such times, under the pretext of confessing and receiving absolution from sin; far more guilt was often incurred than pardoned." And again, "I cannot persuade myself to speak plainly on such a subject, as I must offend the pious ear. I can only say that suspicion cannot do any injustice to the priests, because their sins cannot be exaggerated."[20] Even among those non-Catholics who, then and later, could dismiss these accounts as overwrought, an enduring suspicion about confession had been reinforced.

Others helped nurture the same images, which became a recurring theme in anti-Catholic polemic, and by the end of the century the testimony of a former priest seemed to confirm the worst. Charles Chiniquy had been born in Quebec and was ordained in 1833. He earned a reputation as a powerful preacher in the temperance cause, but he was ejected from both a religious order and from the diocese of Montreal for what were vaguely identified as "irregularities." He moved to Kankakee, Illinois, to work with French Canadian immigrants there, but quickly fell out with the bishop of Chicago, who stripped him of his ministry. By then, it was clear what the irregularities had been, and he eventually married his longtime housekeeper. He formed his own "Christian Catholic Church," loosely affiliated with the Presbyterians, and took to publishing and lecturing (in the United States,

Canada, Europe, and even Australia) to spread the message of Catholic moral corruption. His *Fifty Years in the Church of Rome* (1888) described his "Voyage through the Desert" of Catholicism "to the Promised Land" of Protestant enlightenment, but even more popular was an earlier work, *The Priest, The Woman, and the Confessional* (1875).[21]

The title alone may say everything one needs to know about the book. Readers, he said, were right to pity a "Brahmin" woman in India, "who, deceived by her priests, burns herself on the corpse of her husband to appease the wrath of her wooden gods." The same pity should be extended to the Catholic woman who, "not less deceived by her priests, suffers a torture far more cruel and ignominious in the confessional-box, to appease the wrath of her wafer-god"—the last phrase a bonus swipe at the Catholic doctrine of the Eucharist. The worst crime for Chiniquy came in the questions priests routinely put to their otherwise virtuous penitents, "questions which the most depraved woman would never consent to hear from her vilest seducer," questions whose true purpose was to provide vicarious sexual excitement to the priest himself, thereby rendering the confessional a "modern Sodom." For proof of this, he recounted a supposed conversation with another priest, who on his deathbed admitted to Chiniquy that he had heard the confessions of more than 1,500 women, married and unmarried, of whom "he had destroyed or scandalized at least 1,000 by his questioning them on most depraved things, for the simple pleasure of gratifying his own corrupted heart."[22] Only a certain kind of reader would stick with this sort of narrative for all three hundred pages of the book. But it was Chiniquy's status as a former insider, akin that of an escaped nun but more believable because he had been a priest, which gave his account its lasting appeal. For those who had never personally experienced confession, it could all seem too real.

For Catholics, however, the tales told by Monk, Chiniquy, and others were the very kind of "calumnious charges" about confession that the church hoped to head off. Any suggestion that such things were true had to be swiftly and categorically dismissed. The hysterical tone, fevered episodes, and prurient prose rendered such charges easy to laugh off. Worse, the argument ran, those who spread stories like these were bigots, pure and simple, their motives venal. The true goals of "ex-priest Chiniquy," one church publication was still saying of him as late as the 1960s, were merely to cover his own moral shortcomings and "to raise money for a livelihood." His claim to have been a personal friend of Abraham Lincoln and his theory that Jesuits had been responsible for the president's assassination made him that much more risible. But this kind of response was not just about the past; it might also be about the present, setting a pattern for how church leaders would deal with real cases of solicitation and sexual abuse as they arose. When facing any reports of actual solicitation in the confessional, the best approach was to give them no credence, to provide no grounds that would allow anyone to believe such things. In particular, as Lea had noted, "lapses of the flesh" among the clergy also had to be kept "from the knowledge of the faithful," a guard against making confession (the word again) "odious."[23] At the same time, the vigor with which all priests were warned against the crime of solicitation also constituted an enduring acknowledgment that it was always possible, that it might indeed happen. Documentation of abuse cases in America remained unavailable until very recently, when court proceedings that involved clerical sexual abuse of minors brought evidence to light. We will return to this subject in Chapter 8. In the meantime, the secrecy surrounding confession remained important in itself, and it had to be maintained, even in in extreme cases.

✠

ANTAGONISTIC SUSPICIONS ABOUT CONFESSIONAL secrecy
were the extreme expression of a more general curiosity, one
that was less excitable but nonetheless persistent, and twentieth century American popular culture found ways to speak
to this curiosity. While Catholic sensitivities were generally
respected in comedies or magazine cartoons (where confession was almost never depicted), the parallels between sin
and confession on the one hand and crime and punishment
on the other suggested a certain theatricality, so crime stories
could be irresistible outlets for explorations of the seal. Movies and television presentations were more benign than the
accounts of Monk and Chiniquy, but they had enough inherent dramatic tension to be broadly appealing. Nowhere was
this more apparent than in Alfred Hitchcock's 1953 thriller, *I
Confess*. Hitchcock had been raised as a Catholic—an "eccen-
tricity" in England, he noted—and he continued to identify
as such throughout his life, though he had only fitful religious
practice as an adult. (Even so, he had insisted that his wife
convert to Catholicism before their marriage, which lasted
half a century. Their daughter eventually married into the
family of a prominent American cardinal.) As a child, he had
received what was then a conventional religious education in
a succession of Catholic elementary and secondary schools,
an upbringing that emphasized dutiful practice and personal
rectitude. He had attended church with his Irish mother,
served as an altar boy, and experienced confession himself.
Knowing both the hold that faith could have on believers and
the potential for theatricality in all things Catholic, he could
make use of the requirements of the seal.[24]

I Confess is not one of Hitchcock's better known films,
though it appeared just as he was reaching the heights of
his popularity in America, released a year before the great

successes of *Rear Window* and *Dial M for Murder*. The film is set
in Quebec City, which allows for the background presence
of Catholic symbols and characters: habited nuns and priests
strolling the streets, crucifixes in courtrooms and the provincial parliament building, churches and religious statuary. The
plot is complicated, as most Hitchcock stories are. A German
refugee named Keller, taken in as the handyman for a parish
church, kills a local lawyer while disguised in a clerical cas-
sock, a simple case of robbery gone bad. Returning to the
church, he is met by one of the priests there, Father Michael
Logan (played by the matinee idol Montgomery Clift), who
notices his agitated condition and offers to help. Keller con-
fesses the murder to Logan, knowing that the priest will not
be able to reveal to anyone what he hears. In the course of the
ensuing police investigation, conducted relentlessly by the
longtime character actor Karl Malden, Logan himself comes
to be suspected of the crime. Flashbacks reveal that, prior to
his becoming a priest, Logan had had an affair with a woman
who is now the wife of a prominent member of parliament,
and the dead lawyer had been blackmailing her with threats
to ruin them both. Logan's desire to prevent exposure of all
this seems like motive enough and, when he refuses to speak
of his whereabouts (with his former lover) at the time of the
murder, he is put on trial. He is never tempted to expose the
real culprit, however, not even when judge, jury, and the public at large all think he is guilty. But the evidence is deemed
insufficient and so he is acquitted. In the ensuing turmoil,
Keller panics, flees, kills two more people (including his wife),
and is finally shot dead by the police. Logan kneels over the
dying man and imparts a final absolution as the movie ends.[25]

 The rules governing the seal of confession are on display
throughout, and Hitchcock abides by them. Viewers never
actually see the full sacramental confession: once Keller
begins his admission of guilt to Father Logan, the camera cuts

immediately to a scene in which he is relating the full details
to his wife later on. We never know what the priest has said
to him in the confessional, what penance was assigned, what
conditions, if any, there may have been for absolution—
indeed, whether absolution had ever actually been granted.
Did Logan, for example, withhold forgiveness until Keller
should turn himself in? But the seal is well enough known to
both Catholics and non-Catholics to provide the essential
drama. Even in his own defense—"not even to save one's
life," as Jone's *Moral Theology* had insisted—Logan cannot
breach the seal. Several times, Keller reminds him (and the
audience) of this, and for his part the priest signifies that his
silence will be, as expected, unbroken. When Keller tries to
speak of the matter again in the rectory, Logan tells him, "I
don't know what you're talking about," rigorously following
the admonition that anything said in the confessional should
not afterwards be discussed outside it, even if the penitent
wanted to. When the police detective presses Logan for what
he might know of the case, the priest tries to be polite, but
says, "I wish I could discuss it, but I can't" and "It is impossible for me to answer." Nor can the embarrassing details of his
long-ago affair, when laid out in court, shake his resolve.
During the jury's deliberations, one of its members says he is
sure that there is more to this story, but he accepts that Logan
cannot testify; it is the absence of hard proof that Logan
wielded the murder weapon that forces the verdict of not
guilty. As Keller is dying, he accuses Logan of having violated
his confidence: "a little shame, and that's all it takes to make
you talk?" A stoic silence is the priest's only response, and the
audience knows that the accusation is untrue. Logan has not
talked. The seal of the confessional has been reaffirmed and
upheld and, since the real killer is dead, a kind of justice has
been achieved—or, at least, the injustice of convicting the
wrong man has been averted.

For television producers no less than acclaimed film directors, the confessional was an attractive setting because of its
dramatic possibilities, including the question of when and
under what circumstances the seal actually applied. Not
every conversation with every priest about every subject was
covered by the requirement for secrecy. Determining when
or whether any given encounter really was a confession, and
therefore bound by the seal, could be tricky. The theologians
had never worried about this; they knew what a confession
was and laid it out in clear-cut language. Like all Catholic sacraments, it was understood as having both matter and form.
Matter consisted of the sins, particularly the mortal sins, submitted to the traditional three stages of contrition, confession,
and satisfaction; form consisted of the ritual actions and verbal formulas by which this matter was expressed and enacted.
When the penitent itemized sins and professed sorrow for
them; when the priest assigned a penance and said the words
of absolution; when both penitent and confessor did all this
with the intention of confessing and forgiving sins—that was
a confession. The exchange usually took place in the distinct
space of the confessional box, but as we have seen this was
not, strictly speaking, necessary. Confessions with the requisite matter and form that were done elsewhere—on the frontier, on the battlefield, in the tent of a "chapel car," through
the back of a wicker rocking chair—were still confessions.
The requirements for determining what was a confession
were clear. It was for this reason that priests were urged to
return to the box if a penitent wanted to talk further about an
issue first raised there. Anything said after that would clearly
be a confession, covered by the seal, removing all doubt.[26]

As part of a television crime show, however, a case could
have more twists and turns, details that would be worthy of
exploration by *The Casuist*. In one episode of the long-run-
ning series *Law & Order*, for instance, a teenager admits to an

uncle that he has participated in a thrill-killing, a conversation that the police have managed to record. The prosecutor, a self-identified lapsed Catholic, wants to introduce the tape at trial, even as he expresses some misgivings about doing so. But the uncle, dressed at the time in ordinary street clothes, is later revealed to be a Jesuit priest, who insists that the boy's admission meets the requirements for confession and that it cannot therefore by introduced as evidence. The audience hears his recorded voice telling his nephew-penitent, "You have to take responsibility," and later hears an abbreviated form of absolution: "God forgives you." The judge in the case agrees that this indeed constitutes a confession, and the recording is not admitted. No court, he scolds the prosecutor, has ever breached the seal. (The boy subsequently feels remorse and enters his own legal confession, an act that prompts conviction of his fellow killer.) In another episode of the same series, discovering whether absolution had been granted after an admission of guilt is essential to determining whether a confession had really taken place. When the priest in this case is forced to admit that the penitent never actually asked for forgiveness, the issue is apparently settled, and the accused accepts a plea bargain. Even then, the priest fears that he has crossed the bright line around the seal; as the episode ends, he leaves the courtroom, walks away, and dramatically removes his clerical collar.[27] Working the seal of confession into an hour-long presentation might take some creativity on the part of the writers, but it could be done.

The complex questions of the legal standing of the seal and what it did and did not cover might be truncated for television viewers, but those questions continue to play out in actual legal proceedings. Our discussion returns to New York for a case that illustrates the larger point. Father Louis Gigante was assigned to a church in the Bronx, where he was also a well-known community leader, even serving as a member of the New York City Council. In the summer of 1977, he was called before a grand jury investigating corruption in the department of correction. He was asked about conversations he had had with correction officials and with a jailed member of organized crime. In particular, prosecutors wanted to know whether he had had any role in arranging favorable treatment for the inmate. (Quite favorable: "catered meals with the proper wines while in jail," according to a newspaper report.) Gigante refused to testify altogether, citing the confessional seal and saying, "I will never violate my priestly confidentiality." At first, lower courts upheld his refusal, one of them noting that "it is difficult to say whether a conversation or part of one might be characterized as a confession." Through appeals, the case dragged on for a year and a half, with the state's highest court finally ruling that "it is only confidential communications made to a clergyman in his spiritual capacity which the law endeavors to protect." When the Supreme Court of the United States let this ruling stand, Gigante was sentenced to ten days in jail for contempt of court, released three days early for good behavior.[28] Other courts in other jurisdictions have reached similar conclusions.

"In his spiritual capacity": that was the deciding factor in this case, and apparently the best standard to apply more generally. Was a communication between pastor and parishioner conducted in a "spiritual capacity" or not? The rule that Anthony Kohlmann himself had articulated was held to be appropriate. If he had learned of the Keating robbery "as a private individual"—that is, as an ordinary person in ordinary circumstances—Kohlmann said he would recognize his duty as a citizen to cooperate with the law and to testify. But knowledge that came in a spiritual capacity was different and had to be treated as such. For Catholics, there were ways of determining what truly was a confession, but the rule could be applied to the clergy of other denominations as well. Since the Kohlmann episode, a body of case law has developed in America that tries to specify these rules. Like all case law, it is fluid and subject to change over time as different sets of facts present themselves. Recently, the investigation and exposure of clergy sexual abuse has prompted reconsideration of the absolute nature of the seal. Should priests be designated as "mandated reporters," for instance, required to report cases of abuse when they learn of them in confession? The traditional standards would have looked askance at such a requirement as violations of the seal, but other, higher societal values have begun to demand something else.

6

Psychology

IN THE MIDDLE DECADES of the twentieth century, few sources gauged American life and culture—high-brow, middle-brow, any-brow—better than *Life* magazine. In 1936, the publishing magnate Henry Luce, born in China to Christian missionaries, had bought an earlier publication with that title and converted it into a glossy, large-format record of current events. A weekly until 1972, it would survive on a monthly or occasional basis until the year 2000. With a circulation in the millions, its pages chronicled the doings of movie stars and politicians, but it was more than that. A short story by Ernest Hemingway might run in one issue, accounts of battles in Europe or Korea in the next. Gripping realistic photographs by such pioneers of the genre as Margaret Bourke-White and Dorothea Lange were among its principal attractions. Full-page advertisements for automobiles and household appliances were joined by smaller ones for hair coloring products and over-the-counter medicines. It could have deep and lasting influence. When Luce himself published an essay in 1941 entitled "The American Century," he set forth a vision that would become a common one in the postwar era: the United States had the duty to lead the world, the duty to make the world more like itself.[1] No matter the topic, if *Life* said something was important, it was important.

Thus, when the magazine gave extended space in five successive issues in January and February 1957 to developments in modern psychology, readers could be assured that they were learning something they ought to know. The editors had recruited Ernest Havemann, a PhD student from Washington University in St. Louis who gave up his studies for journalism, to prepare a series on "The Age of Psychology." With the advice and assistance of the head of the psychology department at the Yale Medical School and of the author (from Johns Hopkins University) of what had become the standard college textbook on the subject, Havemann guided readers through the field as it had developed since the work of Sigmund Freud at the end of the previous century. The foundational ideas and terminology—the unconscious, the id and the ego, the libido, repression and sublimation—were explained in layman's terms; the work that psychiatrists and psychologists did—not merely individual treatment but also the use of aptitude and personality tests, together with their applications in the military and in business—was described in a positive light. Popular misconceptions about the subject—that it was all about sex, for instance—were corrected. The "typical analyst" was no libertine, but a representative of "good middle-class orthodoxy, . . . a solid and even stolid citizen, devoted to his family and to his dog." Freud always had a dog, sometimes two, one installment pointed out reassuringly. Dissenters from the Freudian canon such as Alfred Adler and Carl Jung were accorded their due. The field had moved "out of the mental hospital and into the community," Havemann concluded, and, "for better or worse, this is the age of psychology as much as it is the age of chemistry and the atom bomb."[2]

The *Life* series paid only slight attention to the implications of psychology for religion. It acknowledged Freud's categorical dismissal of faith as an expression of compulsive neurosis, but a "rapprochement" now seemed underway. (A few years earlier, another of Luce's magazines, the equally influential *Time*, had run a cover story on Karl Menninger, the pioneering American psychiatrist and founder of the clinic in Kansas that bore the family name, pointing out that he was a Presbyterian; what could be more normal than that?) At least half the Protestant seminaries in the country now offered coursework in psychology and counseling, Havemann noted, and books popularizing psychological concepts drew on and incorporated religious ideas. Norman Vincent Peale, the minister of Manhattan's Marble Collegiate Church, had achieved wide success, first with his *Guide to Confident Living* (1948) and then with the bestselling *Power of Positive Thinking* (1952), while Joshua Loth Liebman, rabbi of Temple Israel in Boston, was not far behind in sales with his *Peace of Mind* (1946). Catholics still tended to be a bit dubious about the subject, but those suspicions "seem to be on the wane." Pope Pius XII had endorsed psychoanalysis in 1953, so long as any treatment recognized "the existence of the human soul and of the need to abide by the moral precepts of the Church." On the whole, "churches have tried to meet the psychologists and psychoanalysts half way."[3]

One priest who remained skeptical was Fulton Sheen. Originally from downstate Illinois, Sheen had attended seminaries there, where he was singled out for higher studies, eventually earning a doctorate in philosophy at Louvain in Belgium. From his position on the faculty at Catholic University in Washington, he became a regular in the 1930s on the syndicated radio program, *The Catholic Hour*. Later, he easily made the transition to the new medium of television with his own show, *Life is Worth Living*, earning spectacular ratings that drove the comedian Milton Berle (who shared his time slot on another network) off the air. Sheen had a dramatic voice and manner, with a practiced and well-cadenced

delivery. By the end of the Second World War, he may well
have been the most famous Catholic priest in America. What
he had to say on almost any subject was news simply because
he was the one who had said it. In March of 1947, he said
what he had to say about psychology. From the pulpit of
Saint Patrick's Cathedral in New York, he denounced the
entire corpus of Freudian thought as equal parts "materialism, hedonism, infantilism, and eroticism," every bit as dangerous to American values as Marxism. Psychoanalysis was
"a form of escapism" whose practitioners (specializing in the
treatment of comely young women and the well-to-do, he
sneered) produced only "victims," gulled into thinking that
they could be helped by it. Perhaps worst of all, those who visited psychiatrists were overlooking a more obvious and more
readily available means for achieving "peace of soul"(also the
title of his 1949 book that would compete with Liebman and
Peale on the bookstore shelves). Catholics had had the better answer all along. The most effective way to address one's
personal problems was to be found not on the psychiatrist's
couch, but in confession, the true "key to happiness in the
modern world."[4]

Sheen's attack repeated critiques that had been circulat-
ing among Catholics for some time. He was merely rehashing
an old argument in more colorful language. To begin with,
this line of reasoning went, Freud and his disciples made no
room for the personal soul, sure that there was no such thing.
That was simply unacceptable. The idea of the unconscious
as the true motivation for human behavior was just as bad,
undercutting the conviction that good deeds and bad deeds
were freely chosen, and that individuals had to take responsibility for the choices they made. The Catholic notion of sin
was grounded in the belief that wrongful behaviors could
be clearly identified, regretted, and, with effort, changed.
Talking one's problems out with someone else might help the

process along, but it was better to do that with a person who brought to the task not merely human empathy and professional credentials but also divine assistance. Even so, by the time of Sheen's denunciation, attitudes had begun to soften. Catholics were coming to more open and even appreciative assessments of the subject. Three years later, a less well-known priest-professor from Catholic University, addressing an audience of social workers and health care professionals, would be saying publicly that "psychiatry may offer considerable assistance" in addressing individual and societal problems.[5] Larger cultural attitudes were steadily encouraging the "rapprochement" that Havemann detected, and soon enough what went on in the confessional would itself come to be understood, at least in part, in psychological terms. The toll this took on the traditional Catholic world view was subtle but enormous, transforming the outlook of Catholics, lay and clerical alike, and preparing the way for a steep decline in the practice of confession.

✠

LONG BEFORE FREUD HAD begun his first observations of hysterical patients, Catholics had their own notions of psychology, derived, like much of the rest of their intellectual framework, from the thought of Thomas Aquinas. What he had said in the thirteenth century still applied in the twentieth, where it could serve as a bulwark against the steady encroachments of "modernism," defined by one pope as "the synthesis of all heresies." In this understanding, psychology was a branch of philosophy, one that focused on the nature of the human person, which was believed to have certain essential, unchanging characteristics. Among these was the power to decide what to do in any given situation. "With free will and a conscience," wrote a Jesuit in *America* magazine, capturing the Catholic position in a single sentence, "we are responsible and rational creatures." Each of his carefully selected words was full of meaning. The will was free, and humans could therefore choose one course of action rather than another. We had both the ability and the obligation to form our inner conscience properly, distinguishing good and evil, so that we would choose correctly. Once we had done so, we were responsible for the choice we had made, accepting the consequences if we had gone in the wrong direction. Finally, all this was a rational process: we had the capacity to weigh the merits of our behavior, carefully and dispassionately, and to act accordingly. We might on occasion make a bad choice, but after reflection and with guidance we were able to recognize it as such and, it was hoped, to amend our actions in the future. All of this seemed challenged by modern psychology. "Sometimes," wrote John Ford and Gerald Kelly in a 1958 survey of moral theology, "the psychiatrists and psychologists with whom we discuss these problems do not understand how absolutely basic free will is."[6] How, for example, could sinners determine whether they had given "full consent of the will" to a mortal sin if the will had no such power?

The apparent determinism of the Freudian system seemed its most glaring error, taking the question of responsibility off the table. If wrongful actions happened outside the control of deliberate human intention, those who performed such actions could scarcely be held accountable for what they did. "The psycho-analytic [*sic*] theory with its unconscious and its complexes is avowedly deterministic," said a writer in the *Ecclesiastical Review*, a journal for priests and seminary professors. "Liberty is an illusion; we think we push, but we are pushed by the unconscious. Men are puppets, moved in their actions by the strings of an irresponsible unconscious." Just as bad was any assertion that the libido played the crucial role in the formation of this all-controlling unconscious, acting as the unseen puppet master. "To regard everything between heaven and earth as a sexual symbol, to explain all human activity from the most common to the most sublime, whether normal or abnormal, as an expression of sex" was not only wrong, it was "repulsive." *Integrity* magazine, a short-lived publication of the 1940s and 1950s produced by and for Catholic laypeople, tried to laugh off the whole idea with a jaunty limerick: "A man with an upsurging 'id' / Sought relief from the life that he hid. / 'Oh go right ahead,' / The psychologist said, / 'You've just done what your libido bid.'" More serious writers acknowledged that certain deep-seated anxieties—in 1911, the *Catholic Encyclopedia* had called them "dreads"—might have some such origins, and those could "only be properly treated through the mind." But nearly as important in any treatment would be some simple, well-regulated habits. "Long hours in the open air and good hours of sleep," together with regular exercise and a healthy diet, were the best prescription for such cases.[7]

Freudians might protest that these critiques misstated their views, but serious Catholic reservations about the content and validity of psychological theories were often reinforced by more prejudicial and ad hominem remarks. Few occasions were lost to remind American readers in particular that the modern discipline was of indisputably foreign origin. To some writers, Freud was simply "the Viennese psychiatrist," but others were more pointed in identifying him repeatedly as "a Jewish physician of Vienna." In an era when interfaith tensions were sometimes raw—certainly between Catholics and Protestants, and especially between Catholics and Jews— such a phrase needed very little decoding. The same applied to analysts and other psychiatric practitioners, who were characterized as disproportionately Jewish. (There was some basis for this, the growing ranks of American clinicians having been augmented by refugees from Hitler's Europe.) As late as 1960, one Catholic writer was saying that, if a priest found it necessary to recommend that a troubled parishioner consult a psychiatrist—he remained skeptical that this was a good idea, putting the phrase "mental health" in scare quotes—special care was needed: "only the psychiatrist who subscribes wholeheartedly to the teachings of Christianity can be trusted with the soul of a Christian patient." It was obvious who was left out in that calculus. More generally, another writer thought, too many "champion[s] of Freud" were just plain weird, "folk of the Greenwich Village type, that strange race ever on the search for new gods."[8] Best for Catholics to keep their distance.

An even more cynical assertion in the case against psychology was that its practitioners were all in it just for the money. Sheen's claim that "most psychoanalysts cater only to the rich" was a facile charge for him to make and for others to repeat. Among immigrants and second-generation Catholics, many of them struggling to climb into the middle class and to stay there, it may have had particular resonance. Here the contrast with confession could not have been more plain. Why would someone pay to talk to someone else about personal problems or to seek advice, when those same services were available for free in churches everywhere for several hours every Saturday afternoon and evening? To underline the point, *Integrity* turned again to light verse with a sardonic "Ode to a Psychiatrist": "Come to me, all men with fears, / And I will give thee solace, / I'll bring peace of mind, my dears, / For just a thousand dollars." That might be caricature but, explained one Redemptorist priest in only slightly less mocking terms, an analyst "is a man who sets up his confessional in an office building downtown, puts in a supply of soft couches and establishes a fee for each confession that he hears." Confessional boxes might not be as comfortable, but they were still better, and they cost nothing.[9]

Catholic derision could not hold back the growing impact of the "age of psychology," however, and over time a number of priests and others promoted a reconciliation between their faith and the emerging modern discipline. A small circle associated with Catholic University took the lead and, by training their own students and launching them on careers, they helped form a new generation of Catholic psychologists. The university, opened in 1889, had hopes of becoming an intellectual powerhouse overnight, offering the finest theological education for the clergy while also achieving distinction in secular subjects. Father Edward Pace, originally from Florida with graduate degrees earned in Germany and Rome, set up a rudimentary psychological laboratory on campus in 1891, from which he supervised studies of sound and other sensory stimuli. He was soon joined on the faculty by his former student, a Benedictine monk named Thomas Verner Moore, who had completed a dissertation on perception and reaction times. Given the common hostility to Freudian theory, it is not surprising that much of their work focused on experimentation and data collection. Both saw the importance of keeping up with professional developments in the field — Pace was a charter member of the American Psychological Association, founded in 1892 — and neither ever doubted that their pursuit of the new science was compatible with their Catholicism. Moore focused increasingly on clinical applications, opening an outpatient facility in a Washington, DC, hospital, later affiliated with the university and focused on work with children. Other church-affiliated universities gradually became interested as well. Many of them still confined psychology coursework to their philosophy departments, but some places established more substantive programs, offering both undergraduate and graduate degrees. St. Louis, Loyola (Chicago), and Fordham Universities formed professional psychology departments, and the movement spread to other Catholic campuses once the Second World War was over. Catholics studied the subject at secular and public universities as well. In the 1930s, Sister Annette Walters, a member of the Sisters of Saint Joseph, earned a PhD in psychology at the University of Minnesota, where she was a student of the behaviorist B. F. Skinner. (They became lifelong friends; she called him "Fred.")[10]

By then, Catholics were emerging as a small but cohesive presence in the field. In 1936, the Chicago Society of Catholic Psychologists formed, with an initial membership of teachers and clinicians numbering more than one hundred. Its stated goal was to promote "a close integration of theoretical and applied psychology with the principles of Scholastic philosophy and the Catholic Church," and early meetings featured papers on such topics as special problems in child psychology and in the psychology of prison inmates. The growing interest was not merely localized, and the Chicago group helped spawn a larger, national organization. During the annual meeting of the American Psychological Association (APA) in 1947, attendees took steps to form an American Catholic Psychological Association (ACPA). The guiding force for this was William Bier, a Brooklyn-born Jesuit at Fordham who had been a student of Moore's at Catholic University, having completed a dissertation on the use of the Minnesota Multiphasic Personality Inventory in religious settings. The ACPA roster grew quickly to more than two hundred nationwide, and membership doubled in the 1960s. By then, it was publishing a regular newsletter and a twice-yearly scholarly journal, the *Catholic Psychological Record*, which contained reports of clinical studies, together with book reviews and lists of recently completed dissertations of interest. In order to uphold strict academic standards, every member of ACPA also had to be a member of the larger APA, which had become the premier professional association in the country. This policy effectively excluded those who were interested only in "philosophical" psychology, now more clearly defined as outside the discipline's mainstream. At its own annual meetings, the Catholic group focused on three major goals: promotion of the teaching of psychology in Catholic colleges and universities; placement services (facilitated by the newsletter) and support for informal professional networks of Catholic psychologists; and psychological testing for applicants to religious life as priests and sisters.[11]

The last of these was a particular interest of Bier's, laid out in two essays that he published in 1953 and 1954, heralding an important shift in broader attitudes toward psychology on the part of church. The decision of any individual Catholic to become a priest, a religious sister, or a brother was always a personal one, and the church understood it as a "vocation," the response to a calling that came ultimately from God. Determining the validity of this call—did it really come from God, or was it the product of human motives?— was largely a matter of prayer. Vocations had to be tested by those in authority to determine whether the applicant was genuinely attracted to religious service, not merely someone who was fleeing life in the world; once again, prayer was central to that process. But, Bier wrote, "human motivation, we know now, is a much more complex affair than was previously suspected. Our motives are seldom simple, and seldom single." It was here that psychology, perhaps even the once questionable concept of the unconscious, could help. While it would be "excessive" to reject all conscious motives "and to see in them nothing but disguises for hidden tendencies," a broad cultural consensus had formed around the conviction that "conscious motives are sometimes deceptive, and that the dominant motives for our actions are not always the ones which consciously move us." Sorting out an applicant's promptings was necessary, and this was not really an outlandish idea. After all, "a certain level of physical well-being is required" of those entering religious life, attested by "a doctor's certificate of good health"; an assessment of mental health was needed too, since "mental health is no less necessary." Certain neuroses—by then, Bier could use the word without apology in a Catholic publication for a Catholic audience—would be impediments to a successful career as a priest or sister, and it was clearly better to identify those sooner rather than later, before admission rather than after. Seminary faculty and the superiors of religious orders could use the tools of psychology in deciding whether to accept applicants who thought they had a vocation. Testing alone did not provide a definitive yes–no answer in any particular case, but "psychological testing has a function to play."[12]

Because some form of psychological evaluation of applicants became universal within only a few years of Bier's proposals, it is difficult today to appreciate how controversial these ideas were at the time and how radical the change would be. Traditionally, the power to admit candidates had rested almost exclusively in the hands of seminary rectors and the superiors of male and female religious orders. They were reluctant to give up that power or to share it, particularly with someone who had no formal standing in the church. "Superiors say 'no!'" exclaimed one respondent to a survey on the subject, while another had had conversations with a superior who said that he "wants a test *he* can interpret"; yet another "would wish to know [the] interpreter" before according any weight to an assessment. Bier recognized these obstacles. It might be good, he conceded, if the testing of applicants to an order were done by a member of that order, who knew its general religious culture, but it was more important that the process be overseen by "a competently trained psychologist," someone who could administer the tests properly and interpret the results professionally. As other commentators noted, there were also practical problems to be worked out and procedures to be articulated. Test subjects had the right to a certain degree of "psychic privacy," for instance, and psychologists therefore had to be as careful with them as they were with any patient regarding the information they gathered and shared. Anything an applicant said that crossed the line into what was called a manifestation of conscience—essentially the sort of thing a person might discuss in confession—had to be avoided. This sometimes led to a reluctance on the part of examiners to explore questions of sex and sexuality, a general hesitancy that may in particular have allowed future sexual abusers to get through the process more successfully than they otherwise might have.[13] This failing would become apparent as revelations of abuse multiplied fifty years later.

The church never adopted uniform procedures—church administrative practice gave every diocese and every religious order virtual independence from every other—nor did it draft a formal, collective policy. But a revolution in attitude was occurring quietly and quickly, and by the middle 1960s the psychological evaluation of candidates had, without much notice, become the norm. What "we know now," as Bier had casually put it, could not be ignored. Religious superiors, said a clinical psychologist from New York who had worked with many groups of priests and sisters, "are convinced that psychological assessment is indispensable to an effective program of selection and education, and they are engaging professional services to this end." In 1965, a clinician from Pittsburgh agreed, and he even worried that some superiors were becoming "overly confident in the value of the psychologists' services, . . . unrealistically hoping for quick solutions to their problems." The specific tools that were employed varied from place to place. Some used the Minnesota personality test that Bier had studied, but a full gamut of instruments— personal data questionnaires, sentence completion exercises,

Rorschach tests—was put to use. No one screening device was dispositive, another psychologist said, "but when used with prudence and joined with other sources of information" the results were "helpful in determining the suitability of candidates for the religious life." Without widespread discussion or coordination, superiors and seminary rectors everywhere concluded that it was foolish, and probably irresponsible, not to incorporate psychological information into their decisions and into the supervision of those under their direction. In an encyclical letter in 1967, Pope Paul VI had explicitly called for drawing on "the assistance and aid of a doctor or a competent psychologist" in the vocational process; by then, he was merely endorsing what had already become routine practice, at least in the United States.[14]

In short order, virtually every new Catholic priest, sister, and brother had had personal experience with psychological evaluation of some kind, having gone through it themselves as part of their formation. Some candidates might try to resist, clinging to the older suspicions, but if they did there would be consequences. The seminary applicant described in one published case study, from which names and other personal identifiers had been removed, resented having to take any tests at all and was uncooperative throughout. By turns he was surly and sarcastic, at one point snapping at the psychologist (who hadn't asked), "Yes, I love my father." Such a disposition "hardly augurs well" for success as a priest, the evaluator concluded, and the seminary rector agreed; the young man was not admitted. A woman applying to a community of sisters had a better outcome. She was young and still needed some additional personality development, another psychologist thought, but she had "gained insight and improved significantly in the past few years"; she was admitted as a "suitable candidate."[15] In neither case was the psychological evaluation the only factor in the decision, just as those who promoted testing had insisted. But the process of weighing the sincerity of any religious vocation was now incomplete if it did not include psychological information.

A parallel development was the incorporation into priestly and religious training of what was called clinical pastoral education, usually abbreviated to CPE. Deep immersion in theology was obviously the foundation for a priest's work, but how could he translate or apply any of that in the lives of the ordinary laypeople who would be his parishioners? Spouses in a rocky marriage, for example, would probably not benefit very much from a simple rehearsal of the theology of it all. How could a future priest learn what to say or what to do when faced with such a situation? Since the early years of the twentieth century, Protestant seminaries and divinity schools had been giving their prospective ministers some practical professional experiences while they were still students. Placed for a time in general or psychiatric hospitals, they encountered real patients and then, with the help of doctors, therapists, and ministers, they later analyzed those encounters, trying to understand the dynamics that had been at work in order to improve their interpersonal skills. The system was based on "verbatims," word-by-word accounts (written out after the fact) of everything that had transpired: what the patient said, what the chaplain said, what the patient said next, even the silences and nonverbal gestures. These verbatims were then scrutinized in group sessions with both supervisors and the other students. The critiques could be instructive, but they could also be sharp, pointing out failures and missed opportunities as readily as successes.[16]

By the 1960s, Catholic seminaries and religious orders were adopting these same methods, relying more or less explicitly on the "client-centered therapy" of the psychologist Carl Rogers, which emphasized attentive listening as the most important skill. Catholic seminarians were now placed alongside their Protestant peers in structured CPE settings, sometimes for ten weeks during the summer, sometimes in more extended "field" years prior to ordination. For many, this was their first experience of any kind of group dynamics or sensitivity training; for some, it constituted a form of group therapy, probably another first. In one instance, conducted by Jesuits, the program included a semester of weekly small group work of more than an hour, followed right after by a second hour of examining what had just happened—all before the students received their initial CPE assignment. In another case, a professor at the University of Notre Dame outlined a multiyear, "scaled" program for progressively more responsible placements, the seminarian "immersing himself more deeply in the pastoral ministry" as time went on.[17] How directly all this influenced their later work of counseling parishioners in any given case is impossible to reconstruct. But these priests learned early in their training to define their ministry, and to judge its effectiveness, in ways that accommodated and took advantage of the things "we know now" from psychology.

The larger effects of these changes were profound, helping to demystify the field and to prompt acceptance of some of its fundamental perspectives and methods. Only a few years before, journals like the *Ecclesiastical Review* had been warning that modern psychology was "destructive of the liberty of the will and consequently of all morality," and *The Priest* was putting the words "mental health" in scare quotes. Offhand denunciations of psychology as just so much godless "materialism, hedonism, infantilism, and eroticism" had derived much of their force from the absence of actual acquaintance and knowledge. Now, those attitudes could no longer stand; the *Review* was publishing essays on how priests and psychiatrists could collaborate, and even on the mental problems (from simple depression to outright schizophrenia) that priests and sisters might themselves experience and what superiors should do about them. Moreover, exposure to psychology did not end with admission to a seminary or a religious order; its use would continue into ministry. CPE had cemented that expectation, and the modern discipline could no longer be ignored. In 1964, one writer simply assumed that every priest and every seminarian had taken a "regular university course" in psychology to prepare them for their work. For those who were older, already out of school and needing to make up lost ground, he provided an annotated reading list, covering personality theory, developmental psychology, and other subjects. This was admittedly a "do-it-yourself" course and a poor substitute for the real thing, but it could familiarize priests with at least "some of the leading attempts by psychologists to explain 'what makes men [and women] tick.'"[18]

Changing attitudes among clergy and religious leaders were equally reflected among laypeople, who came to incorporate psychology into their everyday outlooks in ways they had not previously done. The "age of psychology" had dawned for them just as it had for everyone else. The establishment of psychology departments in Catholic colleges and universities, one of the early goals of the ACPA, helped lay the foundation. Enrollment in Catholic colleges soared in the 1950s and 1960s, and those students had steady exposure to coursework in modern psychology. At Newton College of the Sacred Heart, a small Catholic women's college in Massachusetts, for example, every student was required to take at least one psychology course during her academic career, chosen from a list of nineteen possible classes; this would provide a basis for "understanding human activity," the college catalog said. At the Jesuits' Boston College, located just two miles away, some initial reluctance "in the minds of a few" older members of the faculty, particularly those in philosophy and theology, had been overcome, according to the department chairman (himself a priest). The number of students in psychology courses rose steadily; by the 1970s, that department was regularly placing in the top five at the school in the number of undergraduate majors, usually behind only such stalwarts as English, history, and pre-med biology. The faculty added a master's program, while also cooperating with the college's school of education in establishing a graduate degree in counseling psychology for elementary and high school teachers.[19]

Beyond the confines of the academic world, American Catholics, like their fellow citizens, became accustomed to taking advantage of what psychology had to offer, and they were increasingly likely to have experienced various forms of counseling and therapy. They had come to appreciate what a practitioner in the field could do, often in contrast to what was available from the clergy. Recognizing credentials played an important role in the shift. "My priest never had the training that my psychiatrist has," one woman had said. "My psychiatrist opens me up," she went on; "my priest never allowed me to do that." Another woman agreed. "The priest is far from the profession[al] standards available today in marriage counselors, psychiatrists, school counselors, clinical psychologists, etc.," she said, and that led her more and more to seek help from the one source and not the other.[20] The Catholic approach to psychology had turned decisively in a positive direction, with both clergy and laity now expressing their confidence in its usefulness.

✠

THIS SHIFT WOULD HAVE far-reaching consequences for the American Catholic practice of confession, but the opening to psychology also had a more immediate use in addressing a specific problem that had troubled confessors and penitents for a long time: the problem of scrupulosity. Years of instruction about the varieties of sin and the multiple distinctions

between kinds of sin led some Catholics to give too much scrutiny to their behavior as they prepared for confession. They
found it difficult to bring their examination of conscience to
an end, thereby (they feared) rendering theirs a "bad" rather
than a "good" confession and leaving them unforgiven. Were
they forgetting something, for instance, and thus failing to
achieve the completeness they had been told was essential?
Did they confess to having committed a sin six times when
it was really seven—or maybe five? They worried that, in
choosing their words, they were confessing mortal sins as if
they were venial sins and so misleading the priest, a form of
lying in the confessional that was of course itself seriously sinful. Some were concerned that their purpose of amendment
was not firm enough, missing the mark required to indicate
true sorrow. Others fretted that they had not performed the
assigned penance fully or properly; this, too, would invali-
date the sacrament, they were convinced, and would have
to be mentioned in their next confession, redoubling their
guilt in the meantime. The church's demand that they be serious and thorough in confession led scrupulous Catholics—
often scorned by the clergy as "scroops"—to think that they
could never quite fulfill the church's high expectations. They
accepted the requirement for confession, but they thought
they could never measure up.

   Scrupulous penitents could twist themselves into closed
loops, unable to escape, and concerns of this kind showed up
regularly among those who sought reassurance by writing to
Catholic periodicals for answers to their questions. Someone
asked the *Messenger of the Sacred Heart* in 1933 whether it was
a mortal sin all its own "not to go to Confession as soon as
possible when one has committed a mortal sin." The reply
came that immediacy was not required, though "considering
the great risk of dying in sin and the danger of fatal accidents
in modern life, it is certainly prudent to obtain absolution as

soon as possible." Another reader told the *Messenger* that "it takes me hours to examine my conscience," and as a result trips to the confessional were rare: confession was something "I keep putting off" for fear of insufficient preparation. This might be a case, the magazine responded, where the devil had troubled "a fervent person" with "endless scruples so as to deter him from the Sacraments." In 1957, "E. M.," a correspondent to *Sign* magazine, admitted to having engaged in confession "shopping," though in an unusual way—looking for a confessor who was not less but rather more exacting than others, one who encouraged and tolerated extended examinations. The magazine disapproved of this, calling it "misguided self-direction." Another writer to *Sign* had confessed an unspecified mortal sin six years before, "but now wonder whether I did fully"; did it need to be confessed again? Here, the answer was characteristically nuanced. If the "sacramental declaration" had been made "according to your knowledge at the time," that was sufficient.[21]

It was up to the priest on the other side of the confessional grille to try to break penitents such as these of their counterproductive habits. The scrupulous might think of themselves as devout, committed to following the church's rules to the letter, but "there is nothing holy or saintly about scrupulosity," a seminary professor told his students. Such people, he thought, had the wrong idea of God, who was not merely "a judge, ready to pounce on them the moment they deviate" from the straight and narrow. Another instructor of future priests was even more pointed: some "people want to feel guilty and if [a] priest removed their guilt they would feel guilty about not feeling guilty." Finding solutions with the scrupulous was not easy, but several approaches were recommended. A priest "should not hesitate to forbid [a] penitent to examine his conscience more than one time a day," the seminarian in Boston wrote in Noldin's manual, and other writers said that the examination should be limited to the more normal "five minutes or less." Requests from penitents for what was called general confession—a review of one's entire life, a practice that was rare among laypeople—should usually be denied. If a penitent showed signs of a tendency toward over-preparation, the priest should simply exercise his authority to keep it in check. "Scrupulous people," wrote a future Paulist priest in his class notes for moral theology in the early 1960s, "if they talk too long, stop them." The confessor "will want to keep the confession *short*." Sometimes, stern priestly commands were the only solution. "When the proper authority tells a scrupulous person not to mention matters over and over again," said the *Messenger of the Sacred Heart*, "this authority and sacred assurance should be reverenced and obeyed." A priest's instructions should be followed "exactly," a Jesuit from Ireland told an American audience. "If you do that," he went on, addressing himself to troubled penitents, "you are being humble and obedient, and that, in your present state, is what God wants of you most." When a priest told a "scroop" to move along, the *Messenger* said on another occasion, "it is clear that the voice of the confessor is God's will."[22]

Discouraging penitents from looking on God only as a kind of hanging judge might have been commendable, but much of the way that priests traditionally talked about confession, steadily expanding the number of mortal sins, had encouraged just such thinking. Scrupulosity should be combatted wherever it appeared, all agreed, but what priests and seminary professors (not to mention the sisters who taught in parochial schools) said about sin and confession could push some Catholics forcefully in that direction. The voice of God, as expressed through a confessor, might be sending a mixed message. The common imagery of the confessional as a courtroom reinforced the idea that the penitent, who was there in role of "both accuser and defendant," had to accept the punishments that were due. Even though priests were told that they should also act as spiritual fathers, teachers, and physicians in confession, laypeople often saw them primarily in their law-enforcement capacity, and sometimes priests emphasized this too. When presiding at Mass, one said in the pages of *The Priest* magazine in 1951, he was a "co-offerer with Christ" in the holy sacrifice, but in the confessional he was a "co-jailer with Christ." It was a startling metaphor—Jesus as prison warden—but one he liked so much that he repeated it. Just as confusing were recommendations to laypeople about "uncertain sins." If a penitent was "uncertain whether a particular act is sinful or not, it is always sinful to perform such an act," one authority said, since doing so in the face of uncertainty demonstrated a willingness to do the wrong, rather than the right, thing. Equally problematic were concerns about the distinction between real sins and mere temptations to sin. The scrupulous might want to confess the latter, even if they never gave in. One person—gender unspecified, but age given as thirty-nine—posed a dilemma to the question box of a diocesan newspaper: "My confessor's husky voice appeals to me. I worry that this is a sin." This was clearly an example of scrupulosity, the paper thought, but some penitents could still worry.[23] Wasn't it safer, a scroop might think, to confess more rather than less, just in case?

By the 1950s, many priests were concluding that the scrupulous were best understood in psychological, rather than theological, terms. One of the first to argue the benefits of this approach was Verner Moore, the pioneering psychologist from Catholic University. Scrupulosity was "fairly common," he thought, "a habitual mental disorder" that might show up anywhere and in anyone, though he considered it more common among women than men. However and in whomever it was manifest, the tendency was often rooted in childhood, the result of parents and teachers who, perhaps with innocent enough motives, had simply scared their charges when it came to sin: "More or less neurotic children may suffer for years from phobias that had their origin in someone's foolish attempt to frighten them into being good." (As with Bier and other Catholic writers of the time, the psychological language, used now without hesitation, is worth noting.) In other cases, the underlying condition might be a kind of "psychic exhibitionism," in which "the penitent finds pleasure in going over his sins, in being looked at, and in getting attention." Many came to agree with Moore's diagnoses. Scruples were "part of the total personality profile," a priest-clinician wrote, "and not simply an isolated moral phenomenon." One of the first textbooks on pastoral counseling for Catholic priests, co-written in 1959 by a psychologist and a theologian, said flatly that scrupulosity was "an emotional problem" and had to be treated as such, even commending Alcoholics Anonymous for its ability to change destructive behaviors. Such lessons could be applied in the confessional. "When the confessor feels that he has before him a very sick person," the authors concluded, "suffering from an obviously advanced obsessive-compulsive malady, his only recourse is to refer him, if possible, to a good psychiatrist." In fact, identifying "the psychiatrists and psychologists in his area" should be one of a priest's first tasks when assigned to a new parish, they said, and the religion of the practitioner was no longer the primary qualification. "In the expression 'good Catholic psychiatrist or psychologist,'" another writer agreed, "the emphasis should be on the 'good' rather than on the 'Catholic.'"[24]

The example of Alcoholics Anonymous was very suggestive, and by the 1960s a nationwide movement had taken shape around the idea of Scrupulous Anonymous. The impetus came from priests of the Redemptorist order, tending as always toward leniency and understanding in the confessional. They had begun publishing a monthly devotional magazine in 1911, called *Liguorian* in honor of their order's founder (Saint Alphonsus Liguori), and in the 1940s they moved the operation to a rural town (renamed Liguori) south of St. Louis, where they expanded the publication to produce pamphlets and other educational material for local churches. In 1963, Thomas Tobin, one of the editors, had published an essay in the magazine entitled "The Tangled Torment of Scrupulosity." Using expressly psychological terms—personality types, repressed feelings in the unconscious, "ambivalent love-hate relationship in the parent image," depth therapy—Tobin offered a framework for understanding the problem. "The scrupulous person knows full well what is right and what is wrong, though he cannot tell himself what to do. His fear or anxiety prevents him. . . . He is obsessed with the thought of sin and guilt," he wrote. Addressing this "great anguish" was the only lasting remedy, and that involved more than simple priestly commands to stop.[25]

The response to the article was immediate. More than one hundred people wrote in, asking whether there was some sort of group that could help them with their problem. No actual organization was formed, but in March 1964, the magazine spun off a distinct monthly newsletter, four pages in length, called *Scrupulous Anonymous*, bearing the motto "Help to Help Yourself." Subscriptions skyrocketed: over 4,500 within a year and 8,300 by 1968. The goal was to provide the understanding that would bring the scrupulous to the point where they could accomplish their own cure. "The fact that others have their scruples under control is encouragement that you can do the same," the first issue said, and readers were asked to write in (identifying themselves, as in the AA model, only by their first names) with accounts of what had worked for them. The overwhelming majority of subscribers were women—about 75 percent of those who responded to a survey in 1965—though men contributed too. Carol from

California, for instance, said that the best starting point was to "like yourself"—to "like the nature God has given you." Specific steps, she said, many of them designed to distract from thinking too much about sin, were also important: charitable work, creative outlets like painting, even casual association with "people you know to be good Catholics" and following their example. Advice on how parents could prevent their children from succumbing to scrupulosity abounded: "no nagging" (Adelaide from New York); "maintain a calm, worry-free atmosphere" (Donald in Ontario); just "let them be children" (Mrs. A. C. from New Jersey). The magazine did not copy the Alcoholics Anonymous model exactly; there were no meetings or twelve-step programs. But it did offer "Ten Commandments for the Scrupulous," which laid out such rules as not revisiting sins that had been confessed previously, not repeating penances out of fear that the words of the prayers had not been said distinctly enough, not (after all) confessing doubtful sins.[26] The working assumption was that these elementary forms of behavior modification, self-administered, could have a cumulative effect and would, eventually, prompt healing. There were no measures of the success of any of these efforts, but the magazine is still published today, indicating both the persistence of the problem and a faith in psychology as a means to address it.

✠

THE APPLICATION OF PSYCHOLOGICAL insights and methods to confession went beyond the particular problems of the scrupulous. Thinking of the sacrament in psychological categories, and not merely in the categories of the theology textbooks, had a broader impact on both confessors and penitents. Most priests tried to insist that, despite some surface similarities, going to confession and talking with an analyst or psychologist were nonetheless different. Psychology helped

people deal with something that happened to them, "a certain kind of involuntary *misfortune*," a writer in *Commonweal*
explained, whereas confession was concerned with "wilful
[*sic*] *misdeeds*," things that people did. A "psychoneurosis" was
a sickness, and thus it was "usually contrary to the sufferer's
will both in itself and in its symptoms and manifestations." A
sin, by contrast, was "an evil human act," done deliberately;
"confession presupposes the power to sin and the power to
turn away from sin." John Sheerin, the popular devotional
writer, concurred on the importance of these distinctions: "We
can be very happy that psychiatry is making great strides," he
said, adding melodramatically that psychiatrists were "bat-
tling day and night against the scourge of mental disease."
But sin was still the human reality it had always been, and a
psychologist "cannot possibly do what the priest can do: he
cannot forgive sins." Two extremes had to be avoided, *Sign*
told a reader in 1962: one "says confession is a sort of pre-sci-
entific form of psychoanalysis," the other that analysis "is a
kind of secularized form of confession." That was too simplis-
tic. Each approach, operating in its own sphere, was valid.
Religion and psychology, *Sign* concluded, had achieved "a
state of peaceful coexistence," with every sign of developing
further into "active and mutual co-operation."[27]

At the same time, many commentators had begun to
remark on the specifically psychological profit that came
from confession; its spiritual benefits were accompanied by
psychic benefits. A "well-intentioned confessor" ignored the
"psychopathological aspect" of the process at his peril, said
a French priest writing for an American lay audience, and
doing so was almost certain to leave penitents with "neurotic
obsessions." He scoffed at those who said, "'Psychotherapy?
I don't believe in it'—as if one could 'believe' in penicillin,
or in an appendectomy." The writer in *Commonweal* agreed:
"Frequent and honest self-examination, and the necessity of

formulating its findings in the confessional" could promote "mental hygiene and prophylaxis," whatever else they did for the soul. The authors of *Psychiatry and Catholicism*, the textbook used in most Catholic colleges, thought so too. The sacrament was neither purposely nor purely a therapeutic exercise, they said, but confession had undeniable "psycho-therapeutic aftereffects, for it not only rids the penitent of his sins but greatly contributes in most cases to his feeling of security by ridding him of his feelings of guilt." It had even become possible to describe confession in explicitly Freudian terms. "Affective discharge—abreaction—is in the main what causes a sense of release" that some people felt after confession, one study reported. Not every penitent experienced such a catharsis, of course, and we may well wonder how many of the hundreds who lined up in their parish churches month after month for routine confessing had the dramatic "discharge of psychic tension" that another study identified. By attending to that possibility, however, confessors could have more success in identifying "specific remedies which will help the individual to change and improve," said the experts in pastoral counseling. "The psychologist and the religionist have much to learn from one another." The woman we met in Chapter 4 who reported that confession could be a "joyous" experience; the man there who said that confessing boosted his feeling that "I'm worth something"; the priest who marveled at "all the wonderful things that have happened in the confessional"; all of them were open to the psychological benefits of what they were doing.[28]

But the "peaceful coexistence" of confession and psychology masked a deeper conflict and a more unequal struggle. Just as some early Catholic critics had feared, a clear sense of sin might be challenged, or even entirely abandoned, once psychology had been let through the mental door. Faith in "the therapeutic" had "triumphed" throughout the Western world, one social scientist observed in 1966, rendering the very idea of sin "all but incomprehensible" to contemporaries. It was "therapists, not priests," another said later, who now seemed to offer the path to a "modern equivalent of salvation." A more popular version of these scholarly arguments, one that remained sympathetic to traditional ideas, was stated forcefully in 1973 by Karl Menninger, the devout Presbyterian psychiatrist whom *Time* magazine had profiled. His best-selling *Whatever Became of Sin?* analyzed the "new social morality" that had emerged over the course of the twentieth century, as psychological concepts achieved wide acceptance. His basic observation was undeniable: not many people spoke openly of sin any more. Things that society had once considered sins, he said, were now reclassified as crimes or as diseases, offences "translatable into psychological terms and 'explained' by psychological theories." But that, he thought, let too many people off the moral hook, since "only the neurotics need to be treated and the criminals punished. The rest may stand around and read the newspapers. Or look at television." Without renouncing his lifetime of work in psychiatry, Menninger hoped to reinvigorate a distinct idea of sin. He even amended the traditional list of seven deadly sins, adding those of "collective irresponsibility" such as war, environmental degradation, corporate greed, consumer wastefulness, and cruelty to animals. Clergy of all denominations still had a role to play in denouncing such sins. "How?" he asked, answering himself with a resolute: "Preach!"[29] Whether that would prove a sufficient counterweight to the "new social morality" was a good question, but he had nonetheless confirmed a fundamental change in modern life. Sin had lost much of its saliency.

The timing of Menninger's book and the public discussion it prompted was significant. A decade of war and domestic turmoil had undercut old certainties, and the consequences of those upheavals were only just beginning to become apparent. The mental world of all Americans had been changing along the lines he and others described, and the world of American Catholics had changed even more, both materially and spiritually. Catholics had been climbing the social, economic, and educational ladders for several generations by then, and increasing numbers of them were enjoying a sense of security, belonging, and self-confidence unknown to their parents and grandparents. Moreover, their church was itself going through what many openly called a revolution. New expressions of older theological concepts abounded, and devotional exercises that had been common for centuries were being remade, seemingly overnight. The simple experience of going to Mass, for instance, was dramatically different in 1970 from what it had been in 1960—or, for that matter, in 1965. The revolution was also evident in confession. After decades at the center of American Catholic religious practice, confession was heading toward a dramatic collapse.

7

Collapse

HIGHLAND PARK, MICHIGAN, A city of not quite three square
miles, is almost completely surrounded by Detroit. Its only
other border, just a few blocks long, is with Hamtramck,
equally small. Though encircled, the two municipal islands
have stoutly maintained their independence, resisting all efforts by the metropolis to swallow them up. For a long time,
Highland Park had good reasons for keeping to itself, principal of which was its strong tax base. Politicos in Detroit
always coveted that, but the city's leaders were careful to
safeguard it as their own. Where the value came from was no
mystery. Henry Ford had opened a manufacturing plant there
in 1909, and a few years later it instituted the assembly-line
production that would revolutionize the industry and put the
ownership of automobiles within reach for most Americans.
Like attracts like, and in 1925 the Chrysler Corporation was
founded in town, making its headquarters there for the next
seventy years. The steady jobs brought in workers, and the
little city's population hit a peak in the 1930s at more than
fifty thousand. Many of those autoworkers were Catholics—
Poles and other East Europeans especially, but other ethnicities as well. They were served by two parishes in Highland
Park, with three more in Hamtramck.[1]

The crown jewel among the churches was Saint Benedict's in Highland Park, an impressive brick structure at the corner of Church Avenue and John R Street, the oddly named thoroughfare honoring John R. Williams, Detroit's first mayor. Opened in 1915, the parish was the centerpiece of a close-knit neighborhood, and by the 1940s, it was presided over by the formidable Monsignor Vincent Hankerd. He hailed from a kind of Michigan Catholic nobility, descended from one of the oldest Irish families in the state, and he had an equally prominent (biological) sister who was the superior of the Immaculate Heart of Mary Sisters, based in the town of Monroe, south of Detroit. Monsignor Hankerd had three younger priests to assist him at Saint Ben's, and they helped supervise the many devotional and social organizations for parishioners, young and old. The thriving parish had both an elementary and a high school, with a combined enrollment of more than eight hundred pupils, overseen by the Sisters of Saint Joseph; schools at the three parishes in Hamtramck taught a total of three thousand kids. But at Saint Ben's as at most Catholic parishes, it was the regular round of religious services that constituted the core of its activity: Sunday Mass, every hour on the hour, and times set aside weekly for confessions. Into the 1950s, Saturday morning from eleven until noon was for children, particularly those who had not already been brought to confession during the week by the sisters in the school. In the afternoon, the three curates—like most pastors, Hankerd usually left the confessional duties to them—were in their boxes from three to six, and they came back again from seven thirty to nine thirty.[2] The routines of parish life, for both priests and people, focused as much on Saturday afternoon and evening as on Sunday morning.

Today, Saint Benedict's parish in Highland Park is no more. Decades of social change eroded it slowly but steadily.

During and after the Second World War, increasing numbers of African Americans (not Catholics, for the most part), eager for jobs in the factories, began to replace the older population, often facing a hostile welcome from the white ethnics who lived on the surrounding streets. Violent urban unrest in the 1960s helped accelerate the white flight and the economic decline. The automobile companies left town, too. Ford started downsizing in the 1950s and closed up shop in 1973, relocating elsewhere; Chrysler moved to the suburbs in 1993. The archdiocese of Detroit faced declining church attendance everywhere in the region and was left with too much infrastructure for too few people. Churches once full now had rows of empty pews, but the heating bill still had to be paid and the roof sometimes leaked. Contraction was the only recourse, and parishes were shuttered or consolidated. Saint Ben's closed its schools in 2005, and in 2013 it merged with two other churches to form a single parish called Saint Moses the Black, named for a fourth-century robber who converted, gave up his life of crime, and joined an Egyptian monastery. (The Saint Ben's church building survived, becoming home to Soul Harvest Ministries, a Black Pentecostal congregation.) There was one priest in residence at the new parish, located across the city line in Detroit and now serving a growing population of Black Catholics. There was just one Mass on Sunday morning and weekday masses only four days week. And what of confessions? The six hours on Saturdays from the earlier era were replaced by only one. Any parishioner who wanted to confess could do so on Sunday morning at nine o'clock, before Mass began at ten; only a handful, if that many, could be accommodated in such a narrow window.[3] The days when a priest might spend hours hearing "only 88" confessions at a single sitting, as Patrick Healy had done in New York a century before, were gone.

The dramatic decline in the number of American Catholics who went to confession regularly, or in fact at all, was not unique to Highland Park, Michigan. By the time Saint Benedict's closed, that decline had been underway for decades, and it could be seen in the times that parishes designated for confessions. The laws of supply and demand—or, perhaps, the laws of demand and supply—had once led churches to expand the available hours, the need for confessors fueled by the streams of penitents. Those same dynamics have now led churches everywhere to cut back. A single hour, as at Saint Moses, would probably be more than enough. National surveys confirmed the trend. One, conducted in 1975, found that the number of Catholics who went to confession once a month—long encouraged as a standard—had gone down over the previous decade from 38 percent to 17 percent, while the number who said they confessed "never" or "practically never" had gone up from 18 to 38 percent. Another study, ten years later, concentrated on people it identified as "Core Catholics," those who participated most actively in the life of their local parish, with leadership roles in its organizations and services. Twenty-six percent of them never went to confession, and another 35 percent said they did so maybe— maybe—once a year; only 6 percent confessed monthly. "It is clear," the study's authors had to conclude, "that frequent Confession is no longer part of the religious consciousness of Core Catholics." A later survey found that 58 percent of parishioners told interviewers that a person could be a "good Catholic" without regular confession, and in yet another less than one-third of Catholics said yes when asked if confession was essential to their "vision of what the Catholic faith is." A national association of priests and laypeople working to promote church participation of all kinds was even more blunt. It coolly rated a variety of parish activities on a descending scale from "Beginning to Die" to "Dying" to "Close to Dead," and at the top of the Close to Dead list was confession.[4] Seldom does history offer an example of a practice undertaken for so long by so many that collapsed so quickly. The question is why.

✠

EVEN AS EARLIER GENERATIONS of Catholics were confessing in large numbers, laity and clergy alike had been accumulating a list of recurring dissatisfactions. For some, the main problem was the speed of it all. Many people, of course, were grateful that their potentially embarrassing encounter would usually last for only about two minutes, but for others the rapid turnover felt minimizing and inappropriate. "Some priests seem too anxious to get on to the next [person], like supermarket checkers," one woman said. For their part, confessors were not unsympathetic to this complaint. "A priest will always give his penitents as much time as they need," a Jesuit wrote, "but when a big crowd is waiting" there was an obvious incentive to keep the line moving; parishioners who dawdled could be "an annoyance." The very success of the clergy at urging frequent confession had generated problems of its own, swelling the numbers but creating a new set of expectations. "How people glare at the penitent who's taken a long time and kept them waiting," another woman told a reporter. A priest who gave his penitents "time to discuss their problems" at length, she went on, "far from being appreciated by the parishioners is avoided. 'I wouldn't go to Father So-and-So; he takes too long,'" she imagined them saying. It was hard not to notice the contrast between the gravity of the sacramental work the church told them they were doing and the haste with which it was done. Yet another woman reported that she once "had hardly time enough to get down on my knees before the Father started giving me absolution," and a friend had had a similar experience. "I even had them shut the grille once," he said, "before I had time to explain that I hadn't finished." The rush made another man feel that he was simply being ignored: "the priest didn't even listen," he said afterward. Those who confessed rarely, a woman added, "would be more likely to come again" if the confessor "did not give the impression of being too busy."[5]

In addition to the pace, other sorts of priestly behavior could also rankle penitents, a complaint that went well beyond those confessors who asked too many pointed questions. In 1966, a layman wrote to *Sign* magazine saying, "I know that no priest will turn against me" in any of the other sacraments, "but I know that I can do or say something in the confessional that could cause a priest to turn against me forever," particularly if he admitted to certain kinds of sins. (He did not say so, but he may have been thinking of contraception.) This had the effect of transforming confession into a "sacrament of fear," he thought, hardly the ideal. Just a year earlier, a writer in the *Homiletic and Pastoral Review* recognized the same problem, suggesting that the courtroom metaphors applied to confession had been counterproductive. This priest did not go so far as to consider Jesus a "jailer," but he was uncomfortable with his own role as a judge when hearing confessions. Too often, that job description gave way to acting like a "prosecuting attorney [who] interrupts. He cajoles. He cries out: 'Answer only yes or no.' What better recipe have we than this to make confession something odious?" The writer had faithfully picked up the vocabulary of his seminary professors in not wanting to make confession "odious." Other priests also acknowledged such complaints, with more than one attributing the decline in the number of confessions to "the poor performance of some priests in the confessional," especially the "mechanical way in which some dispense the sacrament." The consequences had seemed obvious to the reluctant judge.

Too much judging, he feared, had a cascading effect, "driving people from the once a week to the once a month and from once a month to once a year and from the yearly to the hardly ever or never."[6]

Gender dynamics also played a significant role in heightening discontent. Since priests were by definition all men, male penitents might not have noticed, but when a woman went to confession she was always talking to someone of the opposite sex. As contemporary feminism gained traction—*The Feminine Mystique* was published in 1963—the writer Sally Cunneen found growing unease. Of the more than six hundred women she surveyed in 1968, only 16 percent described their communication with priests (including but not limited to confession) as excellent or good, while 65 percent of them rated it fair or poor. When asked how confession was "relevant to your attempts and failures to live as a Christian," 58 percent of the women responded "inadequately or not at all." Individual experience confirmed the stark data. "I've often thought," one woman told a researcher, "that if the person in the confessional were a woman, I might have been more honest, especially when my problems were of a sexual nature." Another woman, who admitted that it had been years since her last confession, doubted that the sacrament "will ever be meaningful for many of us" until women could be confessors as well as penitents. She added that her own best experience of "confessing"—she deliberately put the word in quotation marks—had come in conversation with "a special nun—very special." Some men had the same reactions. "If we must continue having private confession," one begged, "please, please, please let women be ordained so I could confess to a more sensitive, feeling person!"[7]

Compounding all these reactions was a growing realization that much of what was confessed was trivial. The same sins, most of them likely venial, confessed the same way every time, could easily become an unreflective exercise in merely going through the motions. "We could teach a parakeet or a myna bird to say the words" of most confessions, one priest observed sarcastically. Shifting analogies, he thought that too many people saw the sacrament as "some kind of slot-machine deal. You know, pop in certain words and formulas and out pops absolution and an easy penance." If penitents' confessions were purely "mechanical," another cleric thought, the "conditioning of years and years of mechanical confessors" was partly to blame. Increasingly, some laypeople began to resist putting themselves in that position. "One reason I stopped going to Confession," a woman from New York candidly told a national magazine in 1971, was that "the priests I encountered seemed so much more concerned with how often I was late for Mass than with my relationship with my children, my husband, or my neighbors." She accepted that her confessor sometimes had to play the part of a judge, but when he did, she thought, he was presiding only in "traffic court." Penitents who tried to focus on more substantial matters might get rebuffed. A woman from New Jersey recalled that she had once brought up problems "that bothered me (for ex.—not enough prayer time), and have had priests chuckle—like 'you came to confession for this?'" The same feelings were shared by a woman in Illinois. She was no great sinner, she said, and "the last time I went to confession, I was made to feel I was wasting the priest's time. I haven't gone since."[8]

Triviality may have been as common as it was because many on both sides of the confessional grille recognized that patterns of confession established in childhood persisted into adulthood. Confession was not, a prayer guide from 1966 said, "a magic washing away of sin" or (as another priest put it) "a speedy dunking in a spiritual detergent," but Catholics too often acted as though it was, just as they had when they were children. It was hard to break habits that had been ingrained early in life—the "list of sins programmed since grade school," one woman remembered—and to embrace instead what a layman identified as "the adulthood of a mature laity." Priests encountered this all the time, a Franciscan agreed, noting that he routinely listened to sins "so trivial or irrelevant" that it was impossible to imagine a penitent could muster any genuine sorrow for them, let alone worry about avoiding them in the future. A common attitude was "I don't know what else to say," as one person put it, and that had led, in another priest's experience, to hearing a grown man confess that he had "talked in church." Repeating formulaic phrases from years of earlier confessions was easier than confronting "un-Christian behavior" that called for true remorse, such as being "unkind, angry, [and] self-centered."[9] Here, too, the clergy's long efforts to promote regular confessions, particularly "devotional" confessions, may have been too successful. Advising penitents who otherwise lacked serious new sins to come to confession anyway, repeating some already-forgiven offenses from a previous occasion, almost inevitably led to thoughtless repetition. If anyone was at a loss for "what else to say," it was simplest just to say again what they had been saying over and over since they were kids.

These persistent problems with the sacrament as it was practiced might have continued to fester, but by the 1960s American Catholics were claiming a right to act on their dissatisfactions. The women who, after bad experiences of confession, "haven't gone since" were not alone in asserting their independence; they were part of the larger group who had come to think that one could be a "good Catholic" without confession, just as the surveys would document. This new sense of freedom to act as they chose, even if it was contrary to an explicit demand of the church, had many sources, some of them grounded in the changed circumstances of Catholics in America. For a generation or two by then, many Catholics had been moving from the crowded city neighborhoods of "ghetto Catholicism" into leafier suburbs, asserting an autonomy which they thought (rightly or wrongly) earlier generations in their families had lacked. They were increasingly the products of extended years of schooling, and much of "the tenor of parish and Catholic community life," one pastor admitted, "offers little" to such people. They had expanded mental outlooks. "I and countless other middle-class thinking Catholics" needed answers to moral problems that "we can believe in," said a man from New Hampshire to *Sign* in 1969. It obviously meant something very important to this man to view himself not only as "middle-class" but also as "thinking." Both characteristics demanded respect. It was not enough for priests to set standards of behavior; laypeople had to be convinced and had to accept and believe in those standards. Surrounded by many tangible signs of progress, more and more Catholics were seeing themselves (in the words of another man) as "adults, with all that term implies."[10] Moreover, the church itself now seemed to be giving those adults permission to embrace this sense of themselves and to adjust the terms under which they would practice their Catholicism. The catalyst was the Second Vatican Council.

That gathering of bishops from around the world, held in Rome over several months in the fall of four successive years between 1962 and 1965, had come as a surprise. Worldwide or "ecumenical" councils were rare in the Catholic church. The last one had been convened almost a century before, and the one before that had been another three hundred years earlier. Most observers expected little from this one, a mere restatement of traditional teachings and perhaps a modest effort at rapprochement with the Orthodox churches of the east, separated from Rome since the eleventh century. But once assembled in Saint Peter's Basilica, the bishops set aside the anodyne documents prepared in advance by the Vatican bureaucracy and proceeded to draft their own, all intended to help the church speak more effectively to the contemporary world. The resulting sixteen official statements covered every aspect of church life. They examined questions of deep theology (the Bible and other sources of God's revelation, for instance, together with the role of the Virgin Mary) and the relationship between Catholics and members of other religious traditions, particularly Jews and Muslims. Internal church structures were reevaluated, endorsing the idea of a less monarchical, more "collegial" form of governance, in which the pope consulted with and relied upon the advice of local bishops. For ordinary Catholics, the most apparent changes would be those pertaining to the liturgy of the Mass and the other sacraments. Specific recommendations were few, left to be worked out later, but the overriding goal was to encourage Catholics to "take part knowingly, actively, and fruitfully" in all church ceremonies. Among other things, this opened the door to the use of vernacular languages rather than Latin.[11]

Across America, small groups of Catholics met to discuss the work of the council as it was underway, reading its documents together as they were issued, one after another. At a church outside Denver, for instance, the pastor encouraged formation of "little parishes," informal gatherings in family homes using the work of Vatican II (as the council was familiarly called) to deepen their personal faith. Published in translation in inexpensive paperback editions, the council's texts also became a focus of study in the religion and theology classrooms of Catholic high schools and colleges. Nothing approaching a majority of American Catholics undertook this kind of intense scrutiny, but everyone was aware that changes were afoot and that new ways of being a Catholic were emerging. Above all, an expansive "spirit" of the council was spreading quickly, regardless of what any particular document had said. The church's rules were still the rules (though they might be subject to modification over time), but the development of an individual Catholic's own inner spiritual life was more important. The idea of participation by laypeople in the work of the church—done "knowingly, actively"—was embraced by those very people. The routines of religious practice were still necessary, but they were far from sufficient. The council had even proposed a new central metaphor for the church. Abandoning earlier, more theologically opaque descriptions, it instructed parishioners to think of the church not primarily as an institution, but as the "People of God," a democratic imagery that appealed to Americans in particular. The church was no longer—or not only—the pope, the bishops, the priests, and the sisters; it was them.[12]

This "spirit of Vatican II," however ill-defined its boundaries, was nevertheless real, and it had far-reaching consequences for how American Catholics understood and practiced their religion. To begin with, the deliberations of the council, widely reported in the press, had demonstrated that church leaders did not always agree with one another. It was legitimate for them to debate and then to amend the formulations and truths of faith. Older ways of doing things, appropriate once, might not convey the intended meaning any longer, and they could (and should) be altered to highlight what was truly important. The Mass, for centuries a religious spectacle in a foreign language that laypeople simply watched as it unfolded, was now conducted in the language of the congregation so that they could join in, aloud, with its prayers. In 1966, the requirement that Catholics abstain from eating meat on Fridays, a simple self-denial that may have been the most recognizable social marker of their faith, was abruptly abandoned. And if the hierarchy could debate changes such as these, the laity could engage in their own reconsiderations. Just following the rules was not enough anymore. "Being a devout Catholic was much easier," one man said as the changes began to multiply, "practicing full Christianity"—as he now understood he must strive to do—"is much more difficult." The spirit of the council, one historian has said, gave laypeople "the language with which to assert their rights as the People of God" and "supported a critical perspective on the Church's pronouncements." Above all, it had turned them into "a deciding people," free to choose how to practice "full Christianity," how to find the ways that had the most meaning for them.[13]

A deciding people could decide many things, and some simply decided that they would not be practicing Catholics anymore. There was no formal procedure by which a person could "resign" as a Catholic, but survey after survey showed that noticeable numbers of people were effectively doing just that. This was already happening throughout western Europe, where rates of regular religious observance, even in nominally Catholic countries, were plummeting into the single digits. For a long time in America, "falling away" from the church had been strongly stigmatized, socially and otherwise; now, it seemed a freely available option. Saying "I was raised Catholic"—not "I am Catholic"—became common as a self-descriptor. What scholars of religion call "disaffiliation" began in earnest in the aftermath of the council and picked up speed as the twentieth century came to an end, particularly among Americans younger than age thirty-five. Almost a third of the respondents to one survey said they had been brought up as Catholics, but barely one-quarter still identified as such. For people such as these, abandonment of confession was merely one aspect of a larger abandonment of religious identity.[14]

More important to understand are those Catholics who were, as another study said of them, "defecting in place."

They still considered themselves to be Catholics, still participated (occasionally or even regularly) in the church's rituals,
still sent their children to Catholic schools, from kindergarten
through college. But they were now doing all that on renego-
tiated terms. In some cases, they explicitly rejected specific
church teachings — on clerical celibacy, on the ordination of
women, on homosexuality — but they nonetheless considered
themselves to be Catholics. And in particular, these "defecting" Catholics were deciding that they would no longer go
to confession. The documents of the council had not considered such a possibility, with confession meriting only a few
scattered sentences. The sacrament's general purposes had
been restated, and pastors were encouraged to do what most
of them were already doing in making it readily available to
parishioners. Beyond that, the council was vague, expressing
only a hope that "the rite and formulas" would be "revised so
that they give more luminous expression to both the nature
and effect of the sacrament." Those revisions would come,
though as we shall see they had minimal impact in arrest-
ing the decline. Meanwhile, if laypeople were put off by the
speed of most confessions, if they were treated in gruff or perfunctory ways, if they finally noticed that they were applying
childish standards to the complexities of adult life, if women
in particular were getting nothing from the experience — if,
in short, confession had become meaningless and unsatisfying, they could just stop doing it.[15] The church still told them
that they should confess, but it was now also telling them that
older practices which did not promote spiritual development
might have to be left behind.

Moreover, they might even have to rethink the "matter" of
confession, the sins for which they were expected to feel and
express their sorrow. If eating meat on Friday was no longer
a sin — it had been a mortal sin, in fact — were there other sins
that were now permissible? As late as 1952, one examination

of conscience was warning laypeople against the sin of asserting their own moral autonomy, sternly urging penitents to
ask themselves, "Have I . . . considered myself capable of
handling my own [spiritual] affairs?"[16] Now, the church was
asking them to do exactly that. Nowhere would this issue
be more clearly joined than with the persistent question of
contraception.

✠

CHURCH TEACHING ON THE subject had the virtue of consis-
tency. Ever since the papal encyclical of 1930 had restated
it forcefully, any possibility of modification for Catholics
seemed out of the question, even as Protestants and others
were rethinking the entire issue. "The Church is so completely
committed to the doctrine that contraception is intrinsically
and gravely immoral," wrote John Ford and Gerald Kelly in
an overview of contemporary moral theology in 1963, "that
no substantial change in this teaching is possible. It is *irrevocable.*" At about the same time, a Redemptorist asked rhetorically whether the church "will ever have a change of mind in
the matter? Less chance than the zebra having a baby squir-
rel." Writers for lay audiences could be even more waspish.
Birth control, said a publication of the Knights of Columbus,
"actually means no birth and no control." Those who practiced it were committing the deadly sin of lust, and they were
probably prompted by ignoble, worldly motives. "They want
to have a good time while they are young," a priest from Minnesota suggested, or they just want to be "fashionable." Married couples who used birth control inevitably "degenerate,"
another priest was sure, "into lukewarm and bad Christians."
In particular, they either stayed away from confession so as to
avoid interrogation and possible scolding, or they refused to
mention this "intrinsically and gravely immoral" sin, thereby
rendering their confessions sacrilegious.[17]

Since the end of the Second World War, however, pressures had been building that challenged this clarity. Babies boomed after the war, particularly in Catholic families, but at the same time Catholics could not ignore evolving attitudes in the rest of American society; many began to share them. The long campaign for birth control reform had lost much of its earlier eugenic aura, and state laws on the subject were in flux, helped along by the United States Supreme Court, which began to define a broad zone of constitutionally protected privacy. The Federal Council of Churches, representing most mainline Protestant denominations, endorsed the use of birth control in marriage, giving new respectability to open discussion of a previously off-limits subject. Planned Parenthood, organized in 1942, emphasized the positive role that contraception could play in responsible parenting and family life, allowing couples at least to space their children, no matter how many they eventually decided to have. By the end of the 1950s, concern for "overpopulation" was growing in some quarters, and the nation's birthrate, though still strong, began to fall off. Development of the rhythm method, which was judged more "natural" than other forms of birth regulation, seemed to offer the promise of dependability. Catholic writers were initially suspicious of this, but it quickly won favor and became the only officially acceptable way, other than complete continence, for Catholic couples to limit the size of their families. In addressing an Italian association of midwives in 1951, even the pope spoke of it approvingly, the first time any pope had said something positive about birth limitation; he followed this up with a second endorsement only a month later. By the time the oral contraceptive pill was authorized for sale in 1960, change was well underway.[18] The irrevocable doctrine was being subjected to sustained questioning.

Together with their fellow citizens, Catholics began to rethink the issue and specifically to wonder about how to address it in the confessional—indeed, whether to address it there at all. One woman explained to Sally Cunneen that, while she still attended Mass regularly with her family, she no longer took communion. She was embarrassed by this, worrying about what her neighbors would think, but she felt it was necessary because she had stopped going to confession. "I cannot in all honesty confess and be sorry" for using birth control, she said. A correspondent reported to *Sign* the experience of a recent epiphany on the subject: "All of a sudden, I see no sin involved in this practice." Other Catholics adopted a kind of passive-aggressive approach. One of the things that "turned me against confession," a woman told *U.S. Catholic* magazine, was a priest who asked her point-blank if she and her husband were practicing contraception, even though she herself had not mentioned it. "At the time I had a good answer," she said with self-assertive pride: "I was pregnant." Another woman resolved to stop going to confession after an unsatisfying encounter in the box. She was pregnant for the sixth time, she said, and she wanted to talk to a young curate whom she thought would be compassionate. He seemed like a "wonderful and holy" priest, and she hoped he might give her advice and perhaps some encouragement in clearing her conscience. Instead, he launched into a sentimental discourse on the beauty of large families, telling her how "lucky" she was. "He meant to be kind but his glibness repelled me," she said. "I never talked to a priest about it again."[19]

Other priests were more understanding, and some tried to find ways to be helpful. John Ford and other theologians had insisted that confessors should always be firm, even to the point of denying absolution to "recidivists," and that any priest reluctant to do so was "gravely negligent"; recall Ford's warning to seminarians that "word gets around" about those who went soft. But priests with real-life parishioners could not simply ignore the experiences—and often the anguish—of their people, and many of them recognized a shift in attitudes about contraception. Clergy and laity had both been taught that laypeople had the duty to form their own conscience, on this as on all moral questions. A proper understanding of church teaching played a crucial role in that process, of course, but Catholics who came to a different conclusion after serious reflection were bound to follow their own conscience, even if it was technically "erroneous." The parishioner who "all of a sudden" saw no sin in birth control could not be expected to act as if he did, and just reading the moral theology rule book to a penitent was increasingly unlikely to produce any good effect. "We didn't harangue on birth control," said one Chicago priest, ordained in 1969, "because we sensed people didn't believe it." (Long after the fact, he admitted: "I don't.") When a penitent did seek help in the confessional, a priest might have to be creative. A pastor in Detroit later described his general inclination by recounting an exchange that may or may not have been drawn from real life. A parishioner had reluctantly confessed to using contraception even though she did not think she should have to; she had no intention of stopping. "Are you sorry about this?" the priest asked. "No, I'm not sorry," was the forthright reply. He followed up with, "Are you sorry that you're not sorry?" "Well, yeah, I can say that." "Well, that's good enough. Say an act of contrition and let's get on with it."[20] How often priests adopted this kind of approach cannot be known. Many, like the Chicagoan, simply stopped talking about the matter altogether, a silence that gave tacit endorsement to a similar silence from their parishioners.

As Ford had suspected and feared and in the end probably knew, word did get around. Informal networks were transmitting word-of-mouth knowledge about which priests in which parishes were sympathetic, particularly when it came to using the pill rather than rhythm. (If priests and bishops had to take the regular rectal temperatures on which rhythm depended, said a mother of six acerbically, "Catholic marrieds would not still be waiting for an answer on contraception.") One approach "I *hear* about," a woman from Massachusetts reported, "is that some priests do not agree with other priests or church teachings on such matters as the pill, contraception, etc." She may in fact have had direct personal experience of this and was only covering her tracks by claiming to have learned of it secondhand. But active searching by parishioners for the right kind of confessor became something of an open secret. "It is a scandal to shop around for a pill priest," another woman said, but she did it anyway. After a confessor had denied yet another woman absolution, she concluded to herself, "I'll find a more lenient priest. I want to be a good Catholic, but the Church gives us no choice."[21]

Those in authority liked to think that this was not going on. "It has been reported," one priest said in a pamphlet he modestly titled *All the Answers about Marriage and Birth Control*, "that some women, in conversation with other women," were telling their friends how to find a lenient confessor. Such cases were "rare," he asserted hopefully, and the official line continued to hold. In 1965, one priest asked the editors of the *American Ecclesiastical Review* whether he could recommend use of the pill to a parishioner, particularly to help her regularize an unpredictable menstrual cycle. Since some writers had begun to say that this was permissible, he thought the question was open, thereby allowing him to approve the otherwise problematic course of action. The stern reply came quickly: anyone who argued for the lawfulness of the pill was "defying the authoritative decision of the Vicar of Christ." If parishioners claimed to have received such permission from a confessor, another writer said, it was either a "misunderstanding of what the priest did tell them, or a process of rationalization in an effort to find an excuse." Still, it happened.

"A year ago," someone from the Bronx told *Sign* in 1968, "I received permission from my confessor to use contraceptive pills. It was a very relaxed and wonderful year."[22]

Any uncertainty was laid to rest (or at least that was the intention) when Pope Paul VI issued an encyclical letter, *Humanae Vitae* (Of Human Life). The subject of contraception had been taken off the agenda of the Vatican Council, lest it derail that body's other work, and was assigned instead to a separate theological commission, initially made up only of priests but later expanded by adding a number of married couples. Its work, conducted behind closed doors and extended over several years of study, helped create a vacuum that allowed Catholics to think that the church's teaching might not be so irrevocable after all. By 1967, reports were leaking out that change was coming and that a strong consensus—one press account said the vote had been 52 to 4, though this was never confirmed—had coalesced around the idea that the teaching should be revised. A majority report argued that, while every Catholic marriage should be open to the possibility of children, not every sexual act in marriage had to be. Moreover, the experience of countless husbands and wives showed that the rhythm method was simply too unreliable, an unwanted source of anxiety and tension; without explicitly endorsing use of the pill, the report raised the possibility that it was morally acceptable. Dissenting from this view was none other than John Ford, who had been attached to the commission because of his preeminence as a moral theologian. He and a colleague drafted a minority report, emphasizing the potential damage that any alteration in the supposedly unchangeable teaching might do to church authority generally. If the church could have been so wrong on such an important matter as this, how could Catholics rely on what it had to say about the morality or immorality of anything else? Both reports went to the pope, who sided with

Ford's position in the document that the Vatican released at
the end of July 1968.[23]

Reaction was immediate and particularly outspoken in
America. The language of the pope's letter had been nuanced,
emphasizing the ideals of marriage; it never expressly
denounced contraception as mortal sin, though it did declare
it contrary to the natural law. Still, the underlying message
was unambiguous: the pope had maintained the prohibition
on what was generally called "artificial" birth control. Catholics who used the pill or some means other than rhythm had
sinned, and they were obligated to seek forgiveness for it in
confession. Few laypeople actually read the encyclical, but
most had no doubt that they would ignore it. "You know as
well as I, Your Grace," a woman from New York wrote to one
bishop, "that only the most infinitesimal number of Catholics
have discarded their pills because of this." A married couple
was resolved to continue both their use of contraception and
their refusal to confess it: "How can persons of integrity confess as a sin something which their consciences tell them is
not an offense to God?" A woman, about to be married, who
had participated in prenuptial counseling in her parish, was
likewise unmoved by the papal statement. "As for myself,"
she said, "my mind has been made up for a while, and my
views, after all this, have not changed, and I have no reason
to believe that they will." Even a nun saw the matter clearly:
"I do not believe that a person can be asked to sacrifice his
own conscience for the beliefs of one man," a religious sister
in Baltimore wrote to her archbishop.[24] Here was something
entirely new: a formal papal encyclical reduced—by a nun, of
all people—to "the beliefs of one man."

Many members of the clergy were similarly unpersuaded.
A week after the encyclical was published, one priest in Washington, DC, read from his pulpit, as instructed, a letter from
the city's archbishop, Cardinal Patrick O'Boyle, reaffirming

the papal declaration. ("The confessor must clearly state what the teaching of the Church is," O'Boyle had said in a companion letter for the clergy alone. "In other words, he must teach that objectively contraception is wrong.") But then, the priest also read aloud from statements that had been published by bishops in Britain, France, Germany, and elsewhere which stressed the right of Catholics to follow their own consciences in the matter. O'Boyle quickly learned of this artful defiance, and he suspended the priest, ordering him to move out of the parish rectory immediately. Thirty-nine Washington priests were eventually relieved of their duties for similar dissents, prompting objections and support from clergy and laity around the country, including a rally of more than three thousand people around the Washington Monument. "For stating what is common practice," wrote a pastor from New Jersey, alluding to confessors who overlooked contraception or sanctioned use of the pill, "these priests have suffered various and severe indignities." No American bishop expressed any public dissent, but at least one acted on his private opposition. James Shannon, an auxiliary bishop of Minneapolis-St. Paul who was thought to be a rising star in the hierarchy, immediately stopped hearing confessions himself, saying that he could no longer enforce on laypeople a teaching in which he did not believe. He later resigned as bishop, left the priesthood, and married.[25]

What was at stake in all of this was not merely the question of what was sinful and what was not. It was also a matter of who got to decide what was sinful and how church teaching would be presented and received. Laypeople needed clear and convincing reasoning, not mere assertions of authority — "reasons we can believe in," as the man from New Hampshire had said. "Thinking Catholics" now required "an intellectual argument why certain actions under certain conditions are unlikely to lead to the attainment of the true purpose of marriage," a man from New York wrote to Cardinal O'Boyle; this was "not as easy as issuing a categorical order. . . . *When will the Church start a sincere effort to appeal to the faithful as rational beings rather than just a herd of followers who are told what to do?*" One priest wrote another bishop that he had never experienced "such perplexity in knowing what to do or say when appealed to for advice" on birth control; he was unable to explain the pope's action to parishioners because, he said, "I have not been able to come up with a satisfactory explanation to myself." He was not alone. A national survey of parish clergy, taken in the aftermath of the encyclical, found decidedly lukewarm acceptance of it. Only 13 percent upheld the traditional injunction that those who confessed to practicing artificial contraception should be denied absolution absent a promise to stop. At the same time, almost half of all priests thought that they should simply accept the "formed conscience of the penitent."[26] The view of Catholics who had concluded, whether suddenly or not, that there was no sin involved should be accepted at face value. Sin was being redefined.

✠

POPULAR REJECTION OF THE teaching of *Humanae Vitae* did not, on its own, prompt a wholesale rethinking of the nature of sin by American Catholics. But it was of a piece with a broader reconsideration already underway. Starting in the 1950s, some of the leading theologians in the Catholic world began to abandon the tradition embodied in the manuals and textbooks, which had been intended to provide clear guidance to priests for a lifetime of hearing confessions. Two Germans, Bernard Häring (a Redemptorist) and Karl Rahner (a Jesuit) led the way in this shift in attitude. "Moral theology proclaims eternal truth," Häring said, "but in each age the manner varies to meet the needs of the times." Their works were read in translation, and they exerted a powerful influence in American seminaries and rectories, with their stress on the centrality of a person's basic moral and religious orientation. Wrongful deeds could not simply be overlooked, but the church's true goal was to promote a more encompassing disposition that would govern one's entire life and behavior. Encouraging Catholics to work at developing what one of their American disciples called a "fundamental option to choose God" was a surer path than what Häring had minimized as "exclusive stress on the counting and adding" of specific sins. Yes, people might sometimes do the wrong thing; these thinkers never rejected the notion that original sin had left humankind with enduring inner weaknesses. But if Christians' basic orientation was toward sustaining their connection to God and to other people, they were doing what was expected of them. For this reason, it was less useful to "speak of *sins* in the plural," another American concluded in 1971, reviewing recent theological developments; better to focus on "*sin* in the singular" and to struggle to counteract it.[27]

The message of the theologians quickly filtered down to priests and local parishes. A priest from Florida laid out some of his own "second thoughts on sin" in an essay for fellow pastors, rejecting what many had come to call the "act-dominated concept of sin." Reading a number of biblical texts in a new way had led him to conclude that sin, particularly mortal sin, had its origin in a "total, final, anti-God position" and that this was in fact extremely uncommon; "total orientation away from God" was "well-nigh impossible in the ordinary course of events." A Jesuit seminarian had the same view, thinking now of sin generically, less likely to be found in "specific acts" than "hanging like a smog of bad atmosphere" around human life and activity, the product of an "environment of disorder and loneliness." A more senior theologian, working with a bishop in 1972 to draft a new statement on sin and confession, agreed. "Mortal sin is rare," he said flatly, an assertion at odds with such earlier views as those of the "comprehensive" examination of conscience from thirty years before that had identified 220 mortal sins and only 147 venial sins. In 1970, one parish priest had even asked the *Homiletic and Pastoral Review*, "Why do we say that some actions are 'wrong' while others are 'right'?" It is practically inconceivable that previous generations of Catholic clergy would have been troubled by such a question, but by then the *Review's* editors were taking it seriously. "The distinction between right and wrong has no definable origin," their long, inconclusive answer began, since the difference between the two had just seemed obvious. This reply, from a supposedly authoritative source, would have been equally unimaginable in an earlier era. None of the authors of the theology manuals would have been in doubt as to the origins, or the reality, of right and wrong.[28]

As they absorbed the new thinking themselves, parish priests began to convey similar messages to their congregations, which seemed ready to receive them. Most people were "happy to embrace a new concept of sin," an observer commented, though for at least one layman the transition was rocky: "I find that many confessors are as confused as I am as to what constitutes a sin," he said. In the past, added a woman from New Jersey in response to a journalist's inquiry, "we have been too caught up with kind, number, times [of sins]. The spirit of the law was sacrificed for the letter of the law." A woman from Virginia agreed: "sin is not necessarily to miss Mass on Sunday, but instead to be uncharitable to friends, relatives, and the sick." An individual's judgments about right and wrong now mattered at least as much as official teachings. It used to be simple, said one participant in a conversation recorded by Sally Cunneen, to determine what was sinful and what was not. "If you use the measuring stick that's in the textbook, then there's no doubt," the woman said, but "I just don't feel guilty" about much of that. Her friend countered that "it doesn't *matter* how you feel," but this elicited a quick, psychologically inflected response: "I think it's more important what I *feel* than what the book says." To be sure, some parishioners adjusted to the new moral outlook with difficulty. The parents of a child preparing for first communion in 1967 were "amazed," they told *Sign*, to hear their parish priest say that "no one was to go to confession" unless they had very specific mortal sins to account for. This was probably unlikely, he went on, especially for grade school kids; those with lesser concerns should stay away, a policy that seemed too stark for the magazine's editors. But other sources were more disposed to leave the decision to "thinking" lay Catholics. "A sense of sinfulness is aroused more successfully by self-reproaches," said the *Messenger of the Sacred Heart*, adding sarcastically that stern denunciations of "sins that we hate most because we are not guilty of them" no longer had much effect.[29]

Besides, more serious sins, previously overlooked and greater than any one person, were now getting the attention they deserved. Karl Menninger's enunciation of such offenses as war and harming the environment had won an appreciative audience, including many Catholics. "Sin is a social, as well as a personal, reality," one woman wrote, "sins of injustice, poverty, and prejudice," with effects on the entire community. "Sin is not only an offense against God," another writer said, "it is also a refusal to help build up our [human] family. Sin is not a private affair." Earlier preaching on the subject had left too much out, many came to conclude, and this new vision found clearer evidence of sinfulness in the daily news. "Contemporary man," one priest said, "is more liable to think of war before he thinks of masturbation as an example of sin." None of the traditional texts had "said much that was useful about the moral decisions of a conscientious

objector," according to a source from 1975, "or about a housewife carrying non-union lettuce out of the supermarket past
farm worker pickets or about the parents who are determined
that their children are not going to be bussed out of South
Boston." Examinations of conscience were being rewritten
to accommodate these emerging understandings. Once, the
questions proposed for identifying violations of the first commandment, for instance, requiring worship of the one true
God, had focused on such issues as Catholics participating in
Protestant services. Now, there were more philosophical concerns: "Are there false gods I worship by giving them greater
attention and deeper trust than I give to God?" The first
false deity mentioned was "money," and sins of materialism
showed up elsewhere as well. The biblical injunction against
stealing was likewise extended into new territory: "Do I share
my possessions with the less fortunate? Do I do my best to
help the victims of oppression, misfortune, and poverty?"[30]

On its own terms, this enlarged way of looking at human
behavior represented a positive development. Individual
actions often had social consequences, and it was good to
remind people of that. The older categories had been too limited. "Mortal and venial sin are a frightfully inadequate way
to describe human acts and the presence of evil in our world,"
said one Jesuit. Too much emphasis on sexual sins in particular had been misplaced, according to another priest. "Justice is more fundamental than chastity," he said. At the same
time, these insights had an undermining effect on confession.
Auricular confession had always depended on penitents' ability to identify specific wrongful deeds that they themselves
had done, to describe these in a few words, and to express
their sorrow. It might very well be a step forward to encourage them to think of sin as an enveloping "smog," whose
destructive effects were subtle. But how could individuals
take their own personal share of responsibility for smog? It

was helpful for the church to encourage its members to think about promoting justice for migrant farm workers and opposing racial segregation in schools. But should a "housewife" really confess to buying the wrong kind of lettuce? "This new sense of the ambiguity of evil," wrote the editors of *Commonweal*, the lay Catholic magazine, "does not fit the popular understanding of confession." The church was now telling lay people to think about the deeper moral consequences of what they did, but that did not match up with the ways it asked them to articulate those insights in the confessional. A man from Wisconsin embodied the problem. He never went to confession any more, he said, and the degree to which he had adopted the new moral analysis was the reason. "In my childhood," he said in 1982, "everything was a sin. I now believe that the only sins are those we commit against our neighbor." Apparently thinking of then-current events, he added a political codicil: "and those we allow our government to commit against our neighboring countries."[31] It would be a rare penitent indeed who could find the words to assume any kind of personal accountability for that in the confessional.

If there were new ways of thinking about sin, there were also new ways for individuals to come to terms with the consequences of their actions, and these drew freely on contemporary culture. Menninger had noted of some of them. The entire postwar period had seen "a multiplication of methods for dealing with troubled people," he said: "psychoanalysis and other psychotherapies, diets and plastic surgery, Zen and yoga, sensitivity groups, and encounter groups"—all offering "cures for ills of the body, mind, and spirit." While these mostly left ministers out of the picture, the clergy might in fact employ some of them profitably. Catholic priests began to recognize their usefulness, evidenced in particular by their adoption of the language of "forgiving yourself." Since "it is *our own selves* first of all that we injure or destroy by sin," said one, penitents should perhaps begin their remorse there. "Until we learn to deal with and forgive the enemy within," said another priest, "we may not have much success," either at confessing or at embracing God's forgiveness. He proposed several methods for accomplishing the task, including journal-keeping (a way of "accepting . . . my feelings") and sharing one's "dark or shadowed side" with a close friend who was not a priest. Even in extreme cases, self-forgiveness was crucial. Coming close to breaching the confessional seal, one priest reproduced a dialogue he had had with a couple who were sure that they were being punished because, after their marriage, "we spent several years in sin"—almost certainly an allusion to the practice of contraception. They later confessed to this and they had stopped, but they were still ill at ease. "What is happening to you," the priest told them, "is that you, who have been forgiven by God, . . . have neither the courage nor the love to forgive yourselves. Yes, God has forgiven you; but you won't forgive you."[32]

Here again, the impact of this kind of talk on confession was profound. If it was essential that penitents forgive themselves, what exactly was the role of the forgiveness imparted by the priest? Proponents of the new idea saw the two as complementary, reconciling traditional religious practice with the insights of the modern social sciences. But the once clear lines were blurring. Some priests, of course, recognized the implications, and they mocked the whole idea. Most people needed little prompting to forgive themselves, said one, "but that does not mean that God is granting them the forgiveness" they really needed. Self-forgiveness was at best irrelevant, at worst a matter of sinners who were simply "heap[ing] excuse upon excuse" and "backing up their right to sin."[33] If penitents had once been encouraged to think of themselves as both defendant and prosecutor in the confessional courtroom, now they were apparently a sympathetic jury as well.

This reinforced the ambiguity that *Commonweal* had observed. Sacramental confession might still be a good thing, but there were other ways, possibly better, to confront one's failings. The need to go to confession, on anything like a regular basis or maybe at all, was further undercut.

At the same time, practical changes in parish routines after Vatican II also worked against the urgency of going to confession, including the approval of what were called anticipation masses. Though these had been allowed earlier, they had remained rare, but as of 1969 Catholics were told that they could fulfill their obligation for Sunday Mass by attending the service any time after four o'clock on Saturday. This was presented as analogous to the Jewish tradition, in which the Sabbath was understood to begin with sundown the night before. Parishes everywhere readjusted their schedules to accommodate these new "Sunday" liturgies, which proved immediately popular, particularly with older churchgoers. One parish outside Boston, for instance, began offering Saturday anticipation masses at five o'clock and again at seven. But it also posted hours for confession on Saturdays from four to five thirty and again from seven to eight thirty; in effect, the schedule was getting in its own way. The hours for confession, in place for decades, were now times for Mass. Similarly, use of the vernacular as the language of the service had a real, if unconscious, effect on the decline of confession. At the beginning of Mass, the congregation now recited aloud the "Confiteor" prayer that had formerly been said only by the priest and in Latin; it included the phrase "I have sinned exceedingly in thought, word, and deed." This may not have been the detailed itemization of offenses used in the confessional, but it came to seem sufficient, particularly since at the end of the prayer parishioners heard the priest say to them: "May Almighty God have mercy on you, forgive you your sins, and bring you to life everlasting." Was more

[handwritten marginal notes: "couples to reconcile important general confession" and "this is more important than is made out"]

forgiveness needed than that? Finally, postconciliar emphasis on the centrality of the Eucharist led many Catholics to
conclude that receiving communion was the most effective
way to reconcile themselves to God. Going to communion
at Mass without having gone to confession beforehand was
not only "permissible," *Sign* magazine told its readers, "it was
and should be the most usual and normal procedure." The
Eucharist, said one theological adviser to bishops, was "the
primary [emphasis in original] celebration of reconciliation,"
and laypeople heard that message too. A nun commented that
laypeople were now "aware that the Eucharist forgives sins,"
and a layman agreed, concluding, "If the heart is contrite, . . .
forgiveness is in the eucharist [*sic*]."[34] With such a combination of changes, theological as well as practical, the decline of
confession could only continue.

✠

PERHAPS, SOME BISHOPS THOUGHT, modifying confession
so as to give what the council called "more luminous expression" to the sacrament might reinvigorate it, and they exper-
imented with modest changes. In particular, many began
to question the age at which children got their initial introduction to the sacrament. Two priest-psychologists were
not telling most pastors anything new when they wrote in
1966 that "the confusion and attitudes of pre-adolescence
persist into adulthood." Any priest who had heard someone
like the grown man who confessed to "talking in church" or
the woman who repeated her "list of sins programmed since
grade school" had encountered the problem. Moreover, the
idea that second-graders were capable of committing mortal
sins that had to be confessed now seemed laughable. Would
"an All-just and All-merciful God and Father (Who loves
them more than their parents could possibly understand),"
the two writers asked incredulously, really "send them to

hell for all eternity?" Would it not make more sense to put off a child's first confession until after the first reception of the Eucharist? About half the nation's bishops promoted postponement, one saying that it would counteract habits of self-accusation and "breast-beating" that children picked up only too readily. In 1969, Cardinal John Dearden in Detroit directed the parishes in his jurisdiction to delay first confession until a child was in the fourth grade, two years after first communion, and the response was overwhelmingly positive. One pastor in Birmingham, Michigan, asked the parents of the fourth graders in a first confession class what they thought of the change, and they voted twenty-three to zero in favor of it. "Children have much better understanding at this age," one of them said. Others hoped that the new timing would spare their kids some of their own bad memories of confession: "fear & reluctance followed by . . . much guilt," a parent recalled. The Detroit experience was not unique. "It's a pretty pokey diocese that does not do it" the new way, one observer concluded.[35]

He spoke too soon. Apparently prompted by fear that confessional habits would not take hold if children got too late a start at them, Rome expressed its disapproval. Two separate departments in the Vatican weighed in to put a stop to the new approach, and in a joint letter in early 1977 they reaffirmed confession before first communion as a norm to be strictly enforced. "Grave disturbance was created by some opinions based on psychological and pedagogical reasons," they wrote—the tone of contempt seems obvious—and the "traditional doctrine of the church was almost overturned." Any attempt to invert the order was unacceptable. The American hierarchy protested, asking to hold off resumption of the old practice, but their request was denied. The youngest children might not have a very sophisticated understanding of sin, a later statement from Rome conceded, but it was still important "to educate them, from a tender age, to the true christian [*sic*] spirit of penance" and "to the just sense of sin."³⁶ American bishops and pastors were unhappy with this resolution of the case, but they obediently followed instructions.

More comprehensive efforts to revise the practice of confession had been underway since the final sessions of Vatican II in December 1965. With the glacial speed that was characteristic of almost anything that had to pass through multiple layers of church bureaucracy—"appalling cautiousness," one American complained—a document describing a "new rite" for confession was finally published in 1974, and it was approved for use in the United States two years later. The change most immediately apparent was one of terminology. The theological name of the sacrament had long been Penance, a term that emphasized the wrong that had been done through sin and the individual Catholic's acceptance of appropriate punishment. There was nothing wrong with that idea, but it was deemed incomplete. While usage of "penance" never entirely disappeared, the sacrament would now be known officially as Reconciliation, a word that one participant in the revising process thought had "happier" connotations. The stress was not on the rupture caused by sin, but rather on the sinner's reconciliation with God, the larger community, and self. The change was greeted with optimism in many quarters. "There may well be fewer confessions," one priest wrote, but they would be "better ones."³⁷

The new rite authorized several different ways in which the sacrament could proceed. One was to be applied only in extreme cases of imminent death, the others intended for normal use. The first of these was continuation of the familiar practice in the confessional box, and this option remained popular with those parishioners who were still going to confession. "Being over seventy," a woman from Maine said, "I go out of my way to find a priest who still sits in his darkened box." (Even at that, she admitted that it had been "a few months" since her last confession and that she probably went less than once a year.) Now added to this, however, was the possibility of conducting confession as an open conversation, carried on face to face. This was intended to be less formulaic, "more in keeping with wholesome contemporary trends," said the *Homiletic and Pastoral Review*. It was "more personal, more human, more like the way Jesus himself proclaimed the forgiveness of sins," a priest said, creating, in the words of another, "a greater sense of ease and informality." Those were, of course, values that earlier generations of confessors had not worried about; for them, confession was not supposed to be easy. No one could be required to confess openly, but anyone who wanted "a more personal experience" could choose to do so. Parish priests liked it, believing that it fostered a better interpersonal dynamic, and in many churches physical space was reallocated to provide for a separate "reconciliation room," outfitted with chairs, in which the more informal conversations could proceed. Seventy-nine percent of clergy in one survey preferred face-to-face confessions, but a majority (58 percent) of lay penitents were sticking with anonymity if they confessed at all. "I feel so traumatized by years of the 'old rite,'" said a man from New York, "that I cannot relate to the 'new,'" and the expanded option had not brought him back to confession. Nor did it have any substantial effect. Sixty-five percent of the priests in the same survey reported that they were hearing twenty or fewer confessions per week.[38]

The new rite also provided for the creation of communal penance services. These were rituals in which parishioners gathered in their church, most commonly on a weekday evening, to listen to a scripture reading and a brief exhortation. After that, they had the opportunity, if they wanted it, to confess individually, either face to face or in one of the boxes, though they did not have to do so. The "great value" of this approach, a theologian thought, was in "placing emphasis on the [community dimensions of sin and reconciliation,"]while still preserving the practice of private confession and absolution. In the first year after approval of these services, nearly two-thirds of all parishes in the country had had at least one, and most priests seemed to like them. "The service can indeed bring you grace and peace and forgiveness," said one, "so try it." Not many laypeople did. Even "core Catholics," those mainstays of local church life surveyed in the 1980s, seemed uninterested: fully half of them had never attended such a service. The new ritual was an odd hybrid, a Jesuit pointed out, difficult to understand because it "combines what are really two separate approaches, one communal, the other more privately oriented." In short order, *Commonweal* observed, the popularity of these liturgies had "already begun to fade."[39]

The final possibility made available in the new rite proved more controversial and, though it was never formally rescinded, it had a very short life. This was a communal penance service that did not include individual confession, but in which absolution was given to all in attendance, though with the admonition that anyone aware of having committed a mortal sin should confess privately later. In extraordinary circumstances (such as soldiers going into battle, as we have seen), priests had long been permitted to grant "general absolution" to a large number of people at once. The new text raised the prospect that this might be done in less dramatic cases, and one American bishop tested this approach. Bishop Carroll Dozier of Memphis, Tennessee, organized two such services in December of 1976, just a few months after the new rite was published. Following preparation in local churches and a public advertising campaign (including television and radio spots, together with newspaper ads), about twelve thousand people filled an arena in Memphis for a "Day of Reconciliation"; a week later, a smaller crowd of two thousand attended a similar service in the city of Jackson, about ninety miles to the east. In both instances, the program began with Bible readings and a short sermon. Then, two lay readers posed a series of questions, each one followed by a brief silence to allow for what was in effect a guided examination of individual conscience. The questions touched on matters both personal—"Have we kept guard over our tongue so that no pain is caused to any of our neighbors?"—and social—"Do we give of our abundance to those in need?" After this, the bishop imparted the general absolution to everyone present, and the Eucharist was distributed. The ceremony ended not with a rousing hymn but with an invitation that people in the stands turn and talk with one another as an expression of "a forgiving and reconciled community." Dozier was very pleased with the results, "the greatest spiritual event in the history of Memphis," he said expansively. He hoped that such services would become regular events, in his own and in other dioceses, appealing in particular to "religiously inactive Catholics."[40]

The Vatican's disapproval of Dozier's program came swiftly, conveyed in an open letter, addressed to the entire American hierarchy and distributed the following spring. The ceremonies, it said, had caused "grave confusion" about the use of general absolution, "imparted in circumstances which did not correspond" to those intended. Beyond that, Dozier himself had overstepped his authority, Rome thought. "General absolution is not something that [a local bishop] is free to employ according to his personal judgment," the document concluded. The dismissive sniping at "personal judgment" was a nice touch, though the rite had explicitly assigned to individual bishops the responsibility for deciding when and whether such services were appropriate. Dozier angrily interpreted the reaction as a deliberate "public reprimand of me," and he was not alone in thinking so. "The idea was to humiliate"

him in front of other American bishops, said a columnist in
the lay-run weekly newspaper *National Catholic Reporter*, and
"to stop anyone else from duplicating the Memphis rites."
If that had been the intention, it worked. Plans for similar
services elsewhere were quickly abandoned, and a national
organization of clergy and laity advising bishops on the liturgical reforms of Vatican II scrapped its plans to publish a
guidebook for how to conduct general absolution services.
The issue had suddenly become "delicate," they realized,
"in the light of developments since . . . the Memphis experience." Renewed Roman condemnation seemed inevitable,
particularly "if we show the pastoral positive effectiveness"
of such services; better "to wait for a more opportune time,"
which never came. The final option set forth in the new rite
thus became a dead letter. In future years, theologians would
continue to debate the matter of general absolution, but no
other laypeople would have the experience of the crowds in
Tennessee.[41]

In the end, the effort that had gone into preparing the new
rite did little to restore the confessional habits of American
Catholics, and any hopes that expansion of the available
options might revitalize practice were disappointed. Penance/
Reconciliation had become, as one priest put it, "a ghost sacrament." By the end of the century, after nearly fifty years of
declining numbers of penitents, study after study had proved
the point. Confession was, one of them concluded, "no longer part of the religious consciousness" of otherwise regular
practitioners of their faith. There might be minor variations
among different subsets of Catholics. Older parishioners,
particularly those who had been born before Vatican II, confessed more frequently than their children or grandchildren,
but even most of them did not confess any more: only 28 percent did so, according to a study done in 1999. Slightly higher
percentages of Hispanics than non-Hispanics told another

researcher that they had gone to confession sometime in the previous two years, but the number for both groups was well below half. A cross-section of young adults showed little inclination to continue the practice. In 1997, they placed private confession in thirteenth position when asked to rank nineteen elements (including Mass attendance and charity toward the poor) as "essential" to being a Catholic; two-thirds of them rated confession either as "important but not essential" or simply "not important."[42] Younger children were still taught how to confess, and they were periodically brought to confession by their religion teachers. In the past, this had prepared them for a lifetime of confessing on their own, but by a wide margin that outcome was now uncommon.

And in the meantime, those early experiences of confession were revealed to have exposed them to a new danger, the danger that some of them would become the victims of sexual abuse by their priests.

8

Revelations

IF THE HISTORY OF confession in America were only a narrative that described the establishment and growth of the practice, its decades of flourishing, and then at last its abandonment by Catholics, that history would end here. The arc of the story would be noteworthy for the steady ascent, but mostly for the swift descent, the speed with which the end came for something that had been so deeply embedded for so long in a rich religious culture. Once, believers had taken for granted that they would fulfill this obligation of church membership faithfully. They would periodically interrupt their normal activities, pause to scrutinize their recent behavior, identify the things they had done that they should not have done, confess those offenses to their spiritual guides, and then receive God's forgiveness through them. Now, believers, even the active and fervent among them, take equally for granted that they will do all those things seldom or never, that private confession is a thing of their past.

Confession did not disappear completely. Some Catholics, though manifestly a minority of them, still confess occasionally; a very few do so regularly. Parish churches still post the times when the local clergy will make themselves available for this purpose, times measured now in minutes rather than in hours. But the possibility of confessing remains. Moreover, since Penance/Reconciliation is one of the seven official sacraments of the church, those who are new to the faith, whether young or old, are introduced to it and instructed in how to go about it. Most will probably not sustain the practice much beyond their initial exposure, but this preparation at least raises the possibility that they can discuss their failings and problems with a confessor when they feel moved to do so.

While it promises comforts, however, the sacrament may also be hazardous, since we know now that confession has played a significant role in sexual abuse perpetrated by priests on children, adolescents, and adults of both sexes. Abuse itself was not new. Widescale awareness of it was by the early twenty-first century, thanks to revelations of evidence that had been accumulating for decades. The history of confession is not reducible to the history of abuse in confession, but abuse is an unavoidable part of that story.

✠

THE CLOSE PERSONAL EXCHANGES that can take place between priest and penitent have always been open to evil possibilities. The earliest formal condemnation of priests who took advantage of their position for sexual ends seems to have come from a church council in Spain in the fourth century and, as we have seen, efforts to curb solicitation in confession gained new vigor in the aftermath of the Reformation. The standards regularly reaffirmed by the theology textbooks were a tacit acknowledgement that this serious offense might recur at any time. How common violations were in the deep past is difficult to specify, and even attempting to compile statistics is of limited value. A single transgression, ever, by anyone, particularly when it involves a child, obviously merits unequivocal condemnation.[1]

The church's incentive to keep evidence of abuse secret was plain, grounded in the longstanding fears of making

confession "odious" and of undermining the laity's defer-
ence to the authority of their priests. The extravagance of
the accusations by Maria Monk, Father Chiniquy, and others had seemed to render any suggestion that there was an
actual problem easy to write off as just so much frenzied
anti-Catholic bigotry. Still, American bishops occasionally
confronted the necessity of having to deal with errant clergy,
and in doing so their hope was to attract as little attention as
possible. Direct evidence of abuse cases in the United States
in the nineteenth century is vanishingly rare, with only scattered surviving fragments. In Boston in 1889, for instance,
the archbishop drafted what was in effect a one-page memo
to his files when he learned that, at one church, "several
young men and boys" had accused their pastor "of sin with
them." The details were left unstated, but to a modern reader
they are clear enough. The priest was immediately removed
from his parish and sent to a monastery in England for the
rest of his life, the archbishop regularly forwarding money
for his upkeep there. Meanwhile, the prelate had decided that
"things would be arranged so that he could leave on account
of his health," and this was the public story that was invented
to cover the man's quiet departure from the city. Six months
later, the newspaper of the local Irish Catholic community
finally printed a short notice that he was "in the South for the
benefit of his health." His name never appeared in the newspapers again.[2]

Nearly a century later, knowledge of clergy sexual abuse,
particularly of minor children, could no longer be kept under
wraps. A full history of the phenomenon remains to be written, but its general outlines are clear. Cases that could at first
be dismissed as exceptional began to coalesce into a more
systemic and sinister pattern. In 1984, a priest in Louisiana
named Gilbert Gauthe was sentenced to twenty years in
prison for abusing more than thirty children in his various

parish assignments. His guilty plea was a public event, and a few years later a pioneering book-length treatment, Jason Berry's *Lead Us Not into Temptation*, laid out the evidence against Gauthe and, just as important, the long effort that had gone into covering up his crimes. The National Conference of Catholic Bishops discussed the problem formally for the first time, and a set of guidelines was drafted for individual bishops to follow as needed, but these were never officially adopted, made mandatory, or uniformly applied. Next, in 1992, came the case of James Porter in Fall River, Massachusetts, who had left the priesthood, married, and later admitted to abusing forty children, including those of former parishioners as well as some of his own. Asked once how many total victims he may have had, he answered with a chillingly offhand, "Oh, jeez, I don't know," guessing that the number might have been as high as one hundred. He would die in jail. More high-level discussions, mostly inconclusive, followed, but the dam of broad public awareness finally broke in 2002, when the *Boston Globe* exposed Father John Geoghan and other local priests who were repeat offenders. Stories from around the country quickly proliferated. Not only had abuse been common, but the way bishops everywhere had dealt with their supposedly one-of-a-kind cases was strikingly consistent. Usually, an offender was quietly transferred to another assignment—sometimes within his home territory, sometimes to the diocese of another bishop—most often without notice that there had ever been a problem. A perpetrator might first be sent to one of several counseling centers, run by other priests, in the hope that such treatment would result in a "cure," a term whose meaning was elusive; patterns of abuse were left largely unchanged. Many victims and their families were simply ignored, though some were given financial compensation, ostensibly for counseling but with the proviso that they remain silent about what had happened to them.[3]

The rapidly expanding crisis required a response from the institutional church. Meeting in Dallas, Texas, in the summer of 2002, the bishops conference adopted a "Charter for the Protection of Children and Young People," together with a set of "Essential Norms" to be applied in handling abuse. These required that, following a single credible accusation, a priest be removed from active ministry pending further investigation. A National Review Board was established, along with a permanent office of the American hierarchy, headed by a laywoman who was a former FBI agent, to compile information on abuse and to monitor compliance with the procedures. Abuse victims themselves—increasingly, they preferred the term "survivors"—had already been organizing on their own to keep up the pressure. Many states revised their statutes of limitations for crimes of abuse, whether by extending the period during which complaints could be filed or by opening temporary "windows" that allowed civil lawsuits (but not criminal prosecutions) for older abuse, otherwise no longer actionable. Both approaches were based on recognition that it often took years for survivors, particularly those who had suffered as children, to be able to talk about what they had endured and thus to seek legal recourse. Some states amended their laws concerning mandatory reporting, the requirement that those who learned of crimes reveal what they knew to police and other civil authorities, though these laws usually excluded information that had been gathered specifically during confession. Finally, a growing number of dioceses agreed to comprehensive financial settlements with survivors and their families, settlements that eventually grew to the billions of dollars. As early as 2004, three dioceses—Portland, Oregon; Tucson, Arizona; and Spokane, Washington—had filed for bankruptcy, and many more would do so later.[4]

The demand for action from the public, Catholic and non-Catholic alike, also prompted the bishops to commission a thorough study of the abuse of minors by priests. A team of scholars from the John Jay College of Criminal Justice in New York was retained and, after a year of data collection, the researchers produced a nearly three-hundred-page report that painted a detailed picture. Of the 110,000 priests who had been active in the United States between 1950 and 2002, about 4 percent could be identified as abusers of children, roughly the same ratio as that found in the population at large. There was very little regional variation; abuse had shown up everywhere. Half the victims had been between the ages of eleven and fourteen; some were older, but about one quarter of them were younger than ten. Most of the perpetrators were in early middle-age when they started abusing, and reported cases had peaked in the 1970s. A slight majority of the abusers had only a single victim, but almost 45 percent of them had more than one; some—including Gauthe, Porter, Geoghan, and Paul Shanley, another Bostonian—had more than ten. In nearly two-thirds of cases, the abuse had extended over a period longer than a year, and 17 percent of victims had one or more siblings who were also abused. The finding in the report that attracted the most attention was that 81 percent of the victims of American priests were boys, a contrast to the general population, in which girls were more likely to be abused, many of them by their own fathers or other relatives. Later investigations, in the United States and elsewhere, would show that the number of abused girls and young women was in fact higher. Even though many of its other measurements would also be revised by subsequent research, the Jay report remained significant as the first effort to describe the dimensions of the problem.[5]

The details of the abuse were also exposed in the report. An offending priest usually began by "grooming" his victims beforehand, establishing an apparent friendship that the perpetrator could subsequently turn to his advantage. The abuse might occur almost anywhere and at any time, including during visits to the victim's home. It might take place in the parish rectory, in a priest's private vacation or family home, or in a hotel room as the two traveled together for seemingly innocent purposes. The abuser's car, the parish school, and even the church itself might be a site of abuse. The report unblinkingly itemized what had happened between abuser and victim. Fondling and sexual touching, whether outside or inside the clothing of either or both of them, were common, and so was masturbation, whether individual or mutual. In some cases, the priest had provided pornographic materials to facilitate the abuse, and an underage victim might be given alcohol or drugs. Oral sex was frequently involved too, and outright rape — the report used the clinical term "penile penetration" — occurred in about one quarter of all cases. Where the rape of a woman had resulted in pregnancy, the priest-perpetrator had sometimes encouraged or helped arrange for an abortion.[6] The picture could hardly have been more sordid, but it had to be confronted forthrightly.

The number of new cases had begun to fall off by the 1980s, but the identification of abuse from earlier decades, still demanding justice, kept public recognition of the problem alive in the period after the John Jay report. New financial settlements were concluded with survivors, and grand juries increasingly brought charges. Some priests were tried and convicted for older crimes, and that might depend on a close reading of legal technicalities. Shanley, for instance, had relocated to California (with the connivance of the archdiocese of Boston), and the "clock" on the statute of limitations had "stopped ticking" while he was out of state. Discovered there and extradited back to Massachusetts, he was tried in 2005 and served twelve years in jail, later moving to a supervised halfway house until his death. Others, beyond the reach of the statutes, were dismissed from the priesthood — "laicized" was the technical church term for what was more commonly known as defrocking. This was a cumbersome process, however, one that frequently got bogged down in technicalities at the Vatican, which had the final say in every instance. Some offenders resisted these efforts and were still priests at their death, the dismissal effort not yet completed. Several bishops were forced to resign for their response (or lack of response) to earlier cases and sometimes for abuses that they themselves had committed. The most dramatic such dismissal would be that of Cardinal Theodore McCarrick, the archbishop of Washington, DC, who had abused seminarians and the children of family friends. He was laicized in 2019 and later faced criminal charges; having descended by then into senile dementia, he was never tried.[7]

The mandates of the Dallas Charter were effective enough, as far as they went, in part by raising the general level of watchfulness. Since the bishop of every diocese could determine for himself how to implement the norms, however, enforcement could be uneven, and some church leaders acted more affirmatively than others. The retired FBI agent who had headed the national office drew up a "report card" on the entire effort, ten years out, and the grades were mixed, ranging from C+ (for guaranteeing an effective response to allegations) to B (implementing good investigatory procedures) to A- (taking steps to guard against future abuse).[8] The problem had festered for decades, and time would be needed to address it properly. However much church members, whether clergy or laity, wanted the immediate "crisis" to be declared over, the scandal persisted.

With every investigation, a vast archive of evidence grew, eventually amounting to millions of pages of original documents. Depositions, transcripts of interviews, letters and memos subpoenaed from diocesan files, police reports, records of ineffective treatment of offenders, and other materials kept multiplying. In 2003, a private organization called Bishop Accountability began to gather together this documentation, physically scattered around the country, and to make it accessible to a wider audience. Devoted to making public what had once been kept secret, it drew on the power of the internet to build and maintain a constantly expanding website. The site was searchable, and the public could now use it to reconstruct the actions of particular bishops and particular abusers.[9] The specifics it contains are dismaying—adjectives fail us—and we must always remind ourselves of both the innocence of victims and the humanity of survivors. But we cannot look away, and in particular we must pay attention to how some of the perpetrators used confession in the commission of their crimes.

☩

ABUSE OFTEN BEGAN WITH grooming, the priest forming a relationship with the victim that could be manipulated to ease a transition from mere acquaintance to something malign. Casual personal contact between clergy and laity had generally been uncommon. Priests had few friendships among laypeople, who, for their part, held the clergy in high but remote regard. A priest who went contrary to these expectations and built a reputation as an approachable, even "cool," guy could employ that image, if he wanted, to identify and attract targets. Paul Shanley was particularly good at this, establishing himself as a charismatic figure, especially with young people. He earned glowing newspaper coverage as a "street priest," working with runaways, gay adolescents, addicts, and other outcasts. "They flock around him as if he was the Pied Piper," one woman wrote enthusiastically to Boston's archbishop after a group from her suburban church had helped him conduct a free-form outdoor Mass. The *Boston Globe*, later pivotal in exposing abuse, praised him repeatedly for his work, while the *New York Times* quoted a mother who said that "it hurt thousands of people" when he was reassigned to traditional parish duties. Whatever good he may have done, his unusual ministry and charming personality also gave him ready access to potential victims, and he seldom passed up opportunities. Father Lawrence Murphy from Milwaukee likewise adopted an outgoing persona. He was a teacher and administrator at the Saint John's School for the Deaf in that city, starting in the 1950s. Students were attracted to him because, as one of them put it, he was "so friendly, and so nice and understanding" that they sought his company and his advice, unwittingly putting themselves in harm's way. While Murphy's actions also extended to his car, his office, and his mother's country home, his "understanding" nature made him a sought-after confessor, and he used confession for grooming and then as a location for abuse itself.[10]

In a sad twist, opportunities for misuse of the sacrament increased dramatically in the 1970s with the introduction of face-to-face confessions. The traditional box, with priest and penitent separated by a solid partition, had made physical contact during confession impossible; indeed, that had been its very purpose. But eliminating the presumption that the box was necessary and opening up more informal ways for a person to go to confession changed all this. When confessor and penitent could sit or stand or walk together, with nothing in between them, the dynamic was new. Touching, fondling, and more could now proceed unimpeded, made to seem merely the next logical stage of an intimate conversation. Michael DeScoise, a priest in Pueblo, Colorado, had masturbated a fourteen-year-old boy as the two walked together in a rural area "under the pretext of Sacramental Confession," according to a report of the state attorney general. Robert Burns, a priest from Ohio temporarily serving in Boston in the 1980s after completing—successfully, local church officials had been told—an abuse treatment program, took the same approach. He befriended a parish altar boy who also did odd jobs in the rectory, at first merely tickling and punching him in a good-natured way. "Then," a lawyer's summary recounted, "he began touching his genitals after a face-to-face confession when he was about age thirteen or fourteen," behavior that continued outside of confession as well; it soon escalated to include masturbation and oral sex. "He would tell Father Burns that he didn't want to do this and Father would stop, but then it would pick up again."[11]

The questioning of penitents in confession proved a convenient trigger for abuse. Notwithstanding the traditional warning that priests keep questions to a minimum, some used interrogation as a prelude to sexual assault. Hearing the face-to-face confession of an eighth-grader in the 1970s, James Cotter in Boston instructed the boy to talk about his sexual fantasies, telling him that he could "cure" him of his anxieties, particularly his anxiety about homosexuality. This he later did by engaging in mutual touching with the boy in a school bathroom and then encouraging him to masturbate in his presence. Abusers might also entice or force their penitents to perform sexual acts on them. Mark Haynes, a priest in a town northwest of Philadelphia, listened to an adolescent girl who confessed to performing oral sex on her boyfriend. He pressed for a detailed account of what she had done and then insisted that she repeat her actions on him before granting her absolution. Daniel O'Friel in Altoona, Pennsylvania, asked a teenage boy about the kinds of things he did with his girlfriend, a conversation that led to mutual masturbation— an "easy way to go to confession," O'Friel told him nonchalantly. Maria Monk's melodramatic accounts of priests who were "indecent in their questions and even in their conduct when I confessed to them" apparently had their counterparts in real life after all.[12]

Abusers could put their targets' sense of religious obligation to use. Since penitents were accustomed to following their confessors' instructions, a priest might even order
them to confess after what *he* had just done to *them*. Nicholas
Cudemo, another Philadelphia area priest, began molest-
ing a young girl from his parish in 1971. "He would tell the
11-year old that the only way for her to connect with God
was through him," said a later grand jury report. "Only after
confessing was she 'worthy of God's love,'" and he required
that she confess to him after he had raped her. (Exactly what
she was supposed to confess is unclear, probably that she
had had sex with someone.) Several years later, Cudemo
impregnated her, later driving her to an abortion clinic
even though he insisted that he was "very pro-life." Albert
Gondek, a priest in Wilmington, North Carolina, had a long
conversation with a thirty-year-old man at a parish penance
service, during which he thrust his hand between the man's
legs and fondled him. When the victim asked for the absolution that normally concluded a confession, Gondek gave it
to him. Cudemo and Gondek had learned—or should have
learned—in the seminary that a priest who solicited sex
from a penitent could not absolve his "accomplice," the curious and insulting word the moral theology textbooks applied
to the victim. Any such absolution was, said one text, simply
"invalid," automatically subjecting them to excommunication.[13] They did it anyway.

Some abusers were more scrupulous, at least when it came
to following the canonical rules. Instead of demanding confessions to themselves, they insisted that their victims confess to someone else, and sometimes they did so too. Father
William Lambert in South Dakota raped a thirteen-year-old
boy on more than a dozen occasions, and each time the two
of them went and confessed to another priest, though not
always the same one. A lawyer later inquired whether any

of the unnamed confessors had reported the crime and was told that the confessional seal precluded them from doing so. "They couldn't do that unless I asked them to," Lambert said, misrepresenting the applicable canon law, "and I didn't ask them." Some victims got little sympathy when, as the church's strictures on solicitation expected them to do, they reported their experience to a different confessor. A boy who had been molested by Theodore Feely at a parish in Rockford, Illinois, went to a nearby church and recounted the abuse. According to the victim's later lawsuit, that confessor "pulled him out of the confessional and told him he was making blasphemous statements." A victim in Lafayette, Indiana, had a similar experience. In 1982, he was abused by Father James Grear, and a week later he went to confession in a neighboring parish. As it happened, he remembered later, the person he confessed to was Raymond Gallagher, who was at the time the bishop of the diocese of Lafayette. A subsequent legal filing asserted that Gallagher calmly "instructed John Doe to forget about the abuse, to ask God to forgive him [apparently meaning Grear], and not to disclose the abuse to anyone else."[14] Many bishops in those years were ignoring or minimizing cases of abuse brought to them in their offices; this bishop was doing so in the confessional too.

This handful of examples by no means exhausts the cases of abuse in confession, the abuse *of* confession. They are hard to read about, and they have been difficult to write about. Hundreds of others could be advanced, and their omission here does not minimize either their gravity or the damage they inflicted. The priests in question were profoundly cynical, taking advantage of their authority and targeting the most vulnerable of the people they were supposed to be helping. Today, we seek relief from revulsion at these accounts by trying to remember that not all confessions led to these repellant outcomes.

Such thinking goes only so far. This misuse of the sacrament, repeatedly and with such seeming ease, shows the religious and emotional power that confession had, as well as the perils to which it could expose its practitioners. The intimacy and secrecy of the encounter, appropriate in their proper exercise, could easily be put to evil ends. A practice intended to relieve people of the weight of their sins had too often become the quintessential occasion of sin. And in that lay a final irony. To the extent that such abuse was possible and that it occurred repeatedly, the collapse of confession was maybe not such a bad thing after all. Survivors of abuse could certainly be forgiven—one uses the word advisedly—for wishing that they had never been introduced to it in the first place.   *this is v strong*

CONFESSION OFFERED ONE PARTICULAR occasion for abuse by Roman Catholic priests—they had other occasions as well—but the offense was not unique to them. Clergy of other denominations (Baptists and Mormons prominently among them) engaged in similar behavior, and so did scout masters, physicians, teachers, coaches, and parents. Notorious cases involved Larry Nassar, a doctor for the United States women's gymnastics team, and Dennis Hastert, a former high school wrestling coach who rose to become Speaker of the House of Representatives in Congress; both were exposed as abusers and spent time in jail—in Nassar's case, the remainder of his life. (Hastert pleaded guilty to financial irregularities in making payments to a survivor, the statute of limitations having expired with regard to the abuse itself.)[15] While personal pathologies can never be ignored in accounting for such violations of acceptable norms, to focus only on particular individuals is to overlook structural factors that may not be so readily apparent, factors of power and authority. Every abuser operated within a larger social or institutional setting, an array of facilitating circumstances and conditions that permitted the otherwise impermissible. Sexual abuse flourished in many contexts. Why did it flourish in the context of the Catholic priesthood?

As awareness of the problem first spread, many observers proposed simple answers to this question, answers which appeared, on their face, to be supported by common sense. Homosexuality was at the root of it all, some said. Since so many targets of priest perpetrators were male, this argument went, the problem must be that too many gay men, stereotypically but wrongly presumed prone to abuse, had been admitted into the priesthood. Weed them out and the problem would go away. While the percentage—estimates vary—of gays in the priesthood was higher than that in the population at large, such an explanation overlooked social science data showing that most abuse was committed by heterosexual men. Abusers were opportunistic "generalists," taking advantage of whatever victims were readily available to them, regardless of gender. Others identified clerical celibacy as the fundamental cause. According to this line of thinking, if Catholic priests were allowed to have normal sex lives through marriage they would not be disposed to engage in abusive behavior. Here again, general patterns belied the assertion. Married or otherwise "partnered" men were far more likely to be abusers than were celibates. Still other commentators blamed the reforms of the Second Vatican Council, contending that these had introduced moral confusion into the church, undermining the strictness and certainties of an earlier era. The worst of the abusers, however, together with most of their enabling bishops, had been ordained before the council's reforms; they were products of the older church, not the new one.[16] All these answers were too facile. Abusers may have been, as many called them, "bad apples," but something had allowed the apples to go bad in the first place—or had accelerated their deterioration. To identify what that was, better to focus on larger factors, including the common understandings, and even the theology, of the Catholic priesthood itself.

Catholics had traditionally looked on their priests differently from the way members of other religions viewed their ministers and leaders. Like Protestant clergy, priests were authorized to conduct the rites of their church and to offer spiritual and moral guidance to its members. Unlike Protestants, however, they did so from a position that rendered them distinct from the people they served. Priesthood was not merely the assumption of a particular role in the community but a fundamental change of identity. Priests were still recognizable as human males, but their true inner essence had been transformed at ordination into something else, a change with important consequences. They were understood to have been given the power not merely to preside at a communion service, for instance, but actually to make God present on the altar in the Eucharist, to be the agent through whom the bread and wine truly became Christ's body and blood. At Mass, one abusing priest had said in a remarkable statement of self-justification, he was responsible for "bringing the Creator of all things down to earth." No layperson could do that. A priest was nothing less than "another Christ"—not quite God himself, but something considerably more than the ordinary believer. Official church statements had reaffirmed this view repeatedly, from the Middle Ages into modern times. In 1937, for example, Pope Pius XI had spoken of the "ineffable greatness of the human priest" because of "the indelible character imprinted on his soul." An American guide to the ordination ceremony from the early 1960s had spoken of priests as holding the "second rank" in the church, below bishops (who were first) but above laypeople (who, though never mentioned, were apparently third). The very

idea that the church had "ranks" was deeply embedded, and
even the formal language used when a priest was defrocked
reinforced the rankings; in such a situation, the offender was
said to have been "reduced to the lay state." Such clear views
of who was "reduced" and who was not confirmed that priests
would always be, as one study concluded, "above and apart"
from other Catholics. Different rules applied to them because
of who and what they were.[17]

These distinctions, often characterized as "clericalism,"
were built into the structures of the church. Both clergy and
laity accepted them unthinkingly as the way things were
and had to be. For priests, a sense of their special position
had been inculcated from their very first days of seminary
study. Seminaries in America were organized and conducted,
as they had been in Europe for centuries, along essentially
monastic lines. Strict separation from outside influences was
thought crucial in the preparation of clergy; the seminary
was by design a little world of its own. Wherever possible,
it was located in a rural area, and contact with laypeople,
particularly women, was rare. Reading newspapers, listening to the radio, or watching television were forbidden. The
hours of the day were governed by an unvarying monastic
rule, with times for rising, prayer, study, simple recreation
(often consisting merely of long walks), meals, and bedtime.
All teaching was done by priests, with the curriculum focused
mainly on dogmatic theology (which prepared the students to
defend distinctive Catholic doctrines against the critiques of
Protestants and others) and on moral theology (which prepared them for their future work in the confessional). Toward
the end of their studies students would get some instruction
in preaching and in how to conduct the various rites of the
church.[18] Many of these regulations loosened over time, but
they had a lasting effect nonetheless. A priest's service to the
world was grounded in his standing apart from that world.

Seminaries were educational institutions with all the familiar trappings of schools (classes, exams, academic degrees), but their more important purpose was what was called "formation." Seminarians were not merely being educated in academic subjects; they were being formed into certain kinds of people. They were, as one historian wrote, being prepared to "absorb a sacramental character at ordination, much as softened wax is impressed with a seal." The real work of the seminary was to soften the wax, readying it for the seal that would imprint the "indelible character" the pope had spoken of. To accomplish this, seminary rules stressed spiritual ideals that future priests were to cultivate, but they also identified the more mundane ways in which those traits should be embodied. Commitment to a life of prayer came first, but no less important were the "virtues and qualities distinctive of a good priest," said the rule book for the seminary in Boston (the institution that produced Geoghan, Shanley, and other abusers). "The world looks to the priest for example and edification," it went on, and seminarians were therefore expected to develop and maintain the proper demeanor. Anything "out of harmony with the spirit of their vocation and the tastes it should inspire" had to be abandoned, replaced by a dignified way of carrying themselves that conveyed subliminal messages to everyone they met. No matter how rough and ready a priest's personal or family background might be, he was expected to cultivate the right kind of "tastes." There were to be "no crudities in posture and bearing," for example, but rather an air of self-contained reserve ("they must subdue voice and laughter"). Priests, a seminary professor in New York had said, constituted an "aristocracy of virtue," and they were expected to behave like aristocrats, maintaining connections among themselves while keeping their distance from the less worthy, from the lower "ranks." A sociological study of the American priesthood in the late 1960s showed how successful the church had been at inculcating these attitudes. It noted a tendency among the clergy "to associate themselves in their friendships and recreational patterns with other clergy," and overwhelming majorities (71 percent of priests, 92 percent of bishops) thought that this was how it should be.[19] Trained early to keep themselves apart from ordinary believers, priests sustained that remoteness throughout their lives and careers, and this only reinforced their position of superiority.

Such a separate and elevated status formed what a detailed study of clericalism has identified as "an invisible backdrop" to church life, one that affected laypeople no less than priests. While parishioners might begin to question some church teachings in principle (on the sinfulness of contraception, for instance), an individual priest's position was difficult for them to challenge, even in the aftermath of abuse. In the early 1980s, Thomas Forry, a Boston priest who also served as a military chaplain, began an affair with a local woman; she divorced her husband and moved in with him. At some point, however, he decided that he wanted to return to his work as a priest, and so he evicted her from the house they shared on Cape Cod. Homeless now, she wrote to the archbishop's office, asking for assistance in paying her rent. She did not want to cause any trouble, she reassured church officials, saying twice that, in spite of everything, Forry was "a good Priest." This may have been simple boilerplate, but it was boilerplate that she had learned and continued to use in spite of evidence to the contrary. Here was a measure of the extent to which laypeople internalized the notion that priests were different, that they were "good" even when they demonstrably were not. The family of Margaret Gallant offers an even more heartbreaking example. Seven young boys, members of her extended clan in Boston's working-class Jamaica Plain neighborhood, were abused by John Geoghan. When she later saw the priest treating local children to ice cream cones, she wrote in alarm to Boston's Cardinal Humberto Medeiros. Her concern was not merely the obvious one that Geoghan was on the prowl for new targets. She was also motivated by her desire to avoid any scandal that might be caused by this bad apple. She insisted that she was acting out of her "firm love for Holy Orders," the sacramental name for priestly ordination. "Our desire," she concluded, "is to protect the dignity of Holy Orders."[20] She herself had assumed some responsibility for guarding that "dignity," hoping that the reputation and standing of "good priests" not be tarnished by a bad one.

None of this should be taken as a matter of blaming the victims. The subordinate position of the laity and the dominant status of the clergy, both conditions reaffirmed in overt and subtle ways, were sadly on display. Laypeople did not need a sophisticated grasp of the theology of Holy Orders to know that the sacrament confirmed the gap between themselves and their pastors. Authority had come to priests because every one of them, regardless of personal characteristics, was "another Christ," and that put victims at a perpetual disadvantage. Think of the adolescent altar boy abused by Robert Burns. He could sometimes muster the courage to tell the priest that he wanted him to stop, and Burns would do so for a time; then, the abuse began again. Even leaving aside the differential in power that came with the disparity in their ages, the priest's standing allowed him to continue. Potential victims, particularly the young but adults as well, were less able to resist grooming and even violation because, it might be said, they knew somehow that they were *only* lay people; they were "reduced" in ways that the priest was not. The resonances that came with the title of priest were enough for the predator to get his way.

We begin to see why and how confession could be a facilitator of sexual abuse. Laypeople might sometimes try to shift the power imbalance that was built into the sacrament. They might rely on carefully crafted euphemisms in describing their sins; they might decide not to mention some of them, even though they knew that risked further sin. But once having confessed, they were used to doing what their priests told them. The penance a confessor assigned as punishment had to be fulfilled in order for the forgiveness of sins to be accomplished. It was not up to laypeople to question—let alone disobey—what they had been instructed to do. If a priest handed out a penance of saying five Hail Marys, that was the number that had to be said. And it was the number that was said. Such an order had come not from an ordinary human being, but from God, from "another Christ." The *Messenger of the Sacred Heart* had summed it up perfectly when it told a "scroop" in 1951 that "the voice of the confessor is God's will."[21] That rule applied to everyone, not merely the scrupulous, and it applied in both normal and unusual circumstances. Catholics had been trained to obedience. They had accepted that this was their duty, a duty that had to be fulfilled even in the horrifying circumstances of abuse.

Conclusion

THE BOY, GROWN NOW (he had to admit) to an old man, went back to the church. How long, he wondered, had it been since the last time he was there? His father's funeral, probably, more than twenty-five years before. He and his siblings had all moved away and had had no occasion to revisit the place that had once been a center of their young lives. He was pleased to see signs of health and even progress. The school—which they had not attended; they were public school kids—had been expanded, and connected to it was a new parish center for activities and organizations. The church itself seemed smaller than he remembered it, as most places do when we revisit the scenes of childhood as adults. It was in very good condition. There was sturdy, practical carpeting on the floor, replacing what had probably been (he didn't recall exactly) worn wood or simple linoleum. The heavy pews had been replaced with trimmer ones of a lighter wood, and they were not uncomfortable, with a little more leg room than formerly. The ornamental patterns on the walls looked to have been freshly repainted. The parish had recently marked its one hundred and fiftieth anniversary, he learned, and the building had probably been spruced up in anticipation of celebratory events. The stained glass windows were still in place. He had forgotten a couple of their scenes, but as soon as he saw them they came back to him: the Sermon on the Mount; Jesus with little children on his lap; the depiction of what may have been an Old Testament scene that he had never understood and still could not identify. The sun coming through them recreated the familiar patterns of light and shadow.

Two of the four original confessional boxes, those at the front of the nave, had been removed, replaced on one side by statuary and on the other by a table with copies of the weekly parish bulletin and other fliers and announcements. The two remaining confessionals at the rear were still there, but they had been rebuilt, reconfigured so that penitents could have the option of either a face-to-face interaction or the familiar anonymity. The advertised times for confession were Saturday afternoons from two thirty to three thirty. A priest, likely the pastor, arrived promptly, walked the length of the side aisle, and took his place in one of the boxes; the other one remained unused. A man, about forty years old, had been waiting for the priest, and he entered the box immediately. Three or four minutes later — it seemed wrong to time him precisely — he emerged, walked to the front of the church, knelt for a short while, and then left. A few minutes later, another man, roughly the same age, reenacted the scene. Over the course of the remaining hour, two women, somewhat older, also confessed with the same dispatch. By then, parishioners were beginning to arrive for the four o'clock Mass that would fulfill their Sunday obligation. None of them stopped to confess, merely taking their places and chatting quietly with their neighbors. The priest left the box at the appointed time and returned to the sacristy, no doubt to prepare to conduct the liturgy. The visitor went back outside into the bright, early autumn sunshine.

This scene, he knew, was entirely characteristic of what had happened to confession in America, a sharp contrast to his youthful experience. A few Catholics still made it a part of their religious practice, but by a long stretch most did not. True, the pattern admits of some variation. A priest friend who teaches at the University of Notre Dame has told me that students in the dormitory where he lives line up for confessions one evening every week and that he spends an hour or more hearing them, one after another and without a break. But the general picture remains unchanged. Another friend, pastor of a parish in a small town in rural Massachusetts, says that he no longer bothers to post regular hours for confessions. He canceled them altogether, as most parishes did, when the church was closed during the COVID-19 pandemic; confessions could be heard "by appointment," he announced, but no one made an appointment. These days, he goes over to the church on Saturday afternoon and putters around. If anyone comes in and signals a desire to confess, he will attend to them, but that almost never happens. Over nearly four years there, he estimates that he has heard perhaps a dozen confessions from his otherwise faithful congregation, not counting children brought in before first communion and confirmation. It may be different in other parts of the world, but in the United States (and in Europe and increasingly in Latin America) what had been rule—regular confession by Catholics—had become exception. This book has been an effort to chart and to explain that reversal.

Some people may miss the now lost world of full pews, dutiful parishioners, and long lines at the confessionals, but lost worlds do not usually come back, no matter how idealized in memory. Despite its many flaws, there was a solidarity in that world, a community formed through participation and collective activity that promoted a reassuring sense of belonging. It connected disparate individuals and families with one another and, they hoped, with the divine. The social distinctions that mattered elsewhere faded. Penitents waiting their turns to get into the box could see their neighbors—the well-off and those barely getting by, the highly educated and the drop-outs, the office workers and the factory workers, the old and the young—all sharing the experience. No one was better or worse than anyone else. Well, maybe in fact they were, but they were all equally acknowledging their inadequacies, accepting the appropriate correction and punishment, and expressing a desire to do better. Here was a visible sign that they were all—"the pope and the least member of the church," as Anthony Kohlmann had told his parishioners in New York—in something together. What that shared something was could be difficult to define precisely, but it was no less deeply felt for that. Scholars have tried to find words for it. Some call it a Catholic "imagination," while others emphasize the centrality of simple (or perhaps not so simple) "presence."[1] Its binding force was powerful, even for those who were sometimes only going through the motions without deep reflection. Catholics did not enjoy confessing, and they often struggled to achieve the relief and reassurance it was supposed to offer. But they could earn a badge of honor from the fact that confessing was embarrassing, even in the absence of eye contact. After all, as we have heard more than one Catholic say, religion ought sometimes to be hard, and confession provided a jolt "that keeps you on your toes." That they endured this little hardship together helped bind them to one another.

Few, however, will miss the fears that always accompanied confession. Fear, of course—the fear of eternal hell in particular—had its uses. It might keep people from sin in the first place or, if not, at least prompt them to frequent confession. Nor will many miss the nagging obsessions that often accompanied confession. For all its noble ideals, the sacrament as practiced by American Catholics was always susceptible to focusing on less, rather than more, important things. Even penitents who were not excessively scrupulous might concentrate too much on minor details. Had a child lied six times, or was it seven? (A friend has told me that she concluded early on that odd numbers sounded somehow inherently more believable than even numbers. After genuinely trying to remember how many times she had, for instance, pushed her sister, she would always round up—up, not down, so as to be safe—to the next odd number.) Had an adolescent entertained impure thoughts or acted on them nine times, or was it ten, or even more? Had a grown man, as one admitted, "talked in church"? Despite its scorn for "scroops" and their fixations, the church had consistently pushed Catholics toward that very pitfall. If there were 220 readily identifiable mortal sins and only 147 venial sins, as one supposed expert had determined, careful accounting was always a good idea, a hedge against further, and possibly worse, spiritual trouble. A seminary professor even warned the future confessors in his classroom that, if a penitent said "about" when counting sins, that might itself be sinful. Precision was demanded in so serious a business, but cataloging every last tree of individual conduct often obscured the forest of a genuinely upright life.

The broader vision that began to guide Catholic thinking in the latter half of the twentieth century was therefore welcome. The woman who recognized that sin was not merely "a private affair" but "a social, as well as a personal, reality" was expressing a truth that, possibly surprising to some at first, quickly came to seem so obvious as to barely need stating. To be fair, the church had never discounted the link between individual conduct and its larger social ramifications. Some things were undeniably wrong as personal failings, but they were also wrong because they harmed the general community or failed to build it up. Still, the emphasis in confession had always been on particular penitents and their specific offenses, whether significant (setting a bad example for children or driving drunk) or insignificant (saying "damn" or underestimating the amount of time spent at "servile work" on a Sunday). Now, like the priest who said that justice was more important than chastity, the church made an effort to adjust the moral focus. No one was ever free of the duty to "do good and avoid evil," as the adage insisted, but personal actions were often reflections of deeper, structural troubles, and those, too, had to be recognized, condemned, and resisted. Racism, sexism, consumerism, indifference to unfair economic conditions, environmental depredation, and other collective offenses—maybe even cruelty to animals—demanded correction too. Such attitudes and actions could not be left unexamined or written off as just the way things were. Individuals should scrutinize the extent to which they harbored any of these wrongs in their own hearts or had, whether deliberately or unwittingly, promoted them. If so, they had to repent at least as much as they did for their lesser sins.

The problem was that these insights were difficult for Catholics to express in confession as they had practiced it for generations. If theologians had to struggle to describe the complex ethical connections between the particular and the universal—the best that one of them could do was to equate sin with "smog," everywhere and nowhere at the same time—how were ordinary laypeople supposed to do that within the confines of their two minutes in the confessional box? Starting the car that morning may indeed have contributed in its own little way to harming the environment, but were drivers now to confess having done so, as they might confess to adultery or insurance fraud? And exactly how sinful was that lettuce the nameless "housewife" had bought, and what should she say about it to her confessor? Identifying the hidden consequences of seemingly insignificant actions was all very fine, and individuals did well to examine and reconsider their attitudes toward, for example, women or people of other races. Having done so, they might act or even vote differently; they might buy a different kind of lettuce. But none of that seemed either connected to or dependent upon confession. Preachers and religious teachers were offering their listeners more sophisticated categories of moral thinking, more mature, "adult" ways of reflecting on what they did. Finding the words to talk about any of that in confession was much harder. Face-to-face confession, less formulaic and more like a frank conversation with a trusted friend, might provide the opportunity for this. That option was never popular with laypeople, however, only a few of whom could overcome their reluctance to talk about their shortcomings, even with a priest, if they had to look him in the eye. No matter how much Catholics accepted the enlarged definitions of wrongful activity, confession no longer seemed like the place to discuss or to implement them.

At the same time, these positive new ways of considering moral and ethical questions had shortcomings of their own. Abandoning the concentration on petty sins was a healthy development, but it diminished the strong sense of personal responsibility that had been key to the older view. The "act-dominated" notion of sin was indeed limiting, and emphasis on the "fundamental option" was more comprehensive, offering a different, arguably better, standard of right and wrong. But where did that leave individuals in thinking about their own "acts"? Did those not matter anymore? After all, everything "we know now" about human motivation and behavior, thanks to modern psychology and otherwise, said that those were complicated things, and people might be neither fully conscious of what they were doing nor fully responsible for doing it. If everything could be understood and explained—explained away?—actions once deemed sinful could shrink in import. They might still be wrong, but just how wrong was unclear and maybe not wrong enough to be worth dwelling on. One could cut people off in traffic or spread gossip about a coworker and still maintain a fundamental orientation toward God. Yes, someone might think, I had driven aggressively for no reason, but I still loved my family and tried to raise the kids to be good people. Yes, I had given myself too-generous a benefit of the doubt in filling out this year's tax forms, but I went to church and volunteered at the food bank. In such a context, "forgiving myself" might be sufficient, no matter how firm or vague the "purpose of amendment" to be more courteous or more honest in the future. As scoffers at the idea had worried, many people were entirely too ready to forgive themselves.

Even as laypeople were facing the dilemmas presented by changing notions of sin, the church's authority to prescribe and enforce behavioral standards was eroding. The priest who had begun to wonder where the idea of right and wrong came from in the first place was surely a hesitant judge in the confessional courtroom, and he was not alone. But two more general shocks substantially reshaped the moral landscape for American Catholics. The first was manifested most clearly in the ongoing struggle over contraception and the papal attempt to quell that turmoil. It was probably a rare penitent who did not know that murder and bank robbery were sinful, but birth control was a subject on which opinions might vary, and those opinions were evolving. Moreover, it was a subject that hit home (literally) for ordinary parishioners, who were beginning to conclude that they knew more about marriage and family life than the clergy. Priests had once told laypeople that they were not competent to decide such matters on their own and should just do what they were told by clerical experts, by "someone trained to make judgments in moral matters," as one said. Increasingly, American Catholics were unpersuaded by such Father-knows-best strictures. When it came to deciding how many children a married couple would have and when to have them, these "thinking Catholics" had to have reasons "we can believe in." Though trained to be docile and accepting, they were getting used to the idea that they could trust their own conclusions. Whether doubts about the teaching on contraception had come on "all of a sudden," as with a penitent we met, or had grown slowly over a longer period, laypeople were asserting their right to define sin for themselves. What they thought and felt was more important than "what the book says," as one woman told another. On that basis, they might go shopping for what someone had bluntly called "a pill priest," or they might simply refrain from mentioning the subject at all. From there, it was a short step to staying away from confession altogether. The parishioner who could no longer "in all honesty" confess to using contraception because she did not think it wrong was speaking for many. The broader reconsideration of all sins was crystallized in this one case. Such thinking—and the actions that followed from it—profoundly altered the relationship between believers and church leaders. A genie was out of the bottle.

Trying to get that genie back in therefore had some urgency for prelates and theologians. John Ford and Gerald Kelly, whose final word about the church's stance on contraception had been an italicized "*irrevocable*," with "no substantial change" possible, were well aware of the larger dangers in so clear a disregard for so clear a teaching. Word was sure to "get around," and not only on this issue but on all kinds of other things as well. Altering an official position just because laypeople did not like it set a very dangerous precedent, and holding the doctrinal line was more important than ever. One of the opponents of change in the papal commission on birth control had seen the problem clearly. What about "the millions we have sent to hell" for using "artificial" contraception, he asked at one point, if the practice were declared to be not sinful after all?[2] Eating meat on Fridays could be taken off the list of mortal sins without much reaction; that was a little thing. But this was a far more serious business, and the worry was that parishioners were getting into the habit of ignoring what the church had to say. That tide had to be stemmed, and reaffirmation of tradition in *Humanae Vitae* was an opportunity to do so. But if the hope had been that this would settle not only the specific case but also shore up church authority generally, the result was precisely the opposite. No one, as a lay correspondent told a bishop, had thrown away their pills in the aftermath of the encyclical. Unsatisfied now with direct orders, people were demanding reasons they could believe in. In fact, nuns were joining laypeople in rejecting the "opinion of one man"—even if that man was the pope—leaving Catholics ever more clearly on their own in making decisions about right and wrong.

The second shock to the Catholic moral system did not, given its timing, contribute to the collapse of confession; that was already well underway. But it virtually guaranteed that confession, once it had all but disappeared, would have no renaissance. This was the scandal of clergy sexual abuse, widely exposed at the beginning of the twenty-first century. The facts of the cases still shock. Many priests were revealed to be abusers, and some of them were shown specifically to have used confession as an occasion or site for their crimes. Some bishops, too, were abusers, and even those who were not had repeatedly chosen to accommodate the priestly offenders, more eager to preserve their status and reputations than to help the innocents who had been attacked. The gulf between the way things were supposed to be and the way they really were could not have been deeper or more apparent. All these men were supposed to be personal embodiments not only of sanctity but also of legitimate authority. They had been given an elevated position in the church, with a connection to God they could share with those of lesser rank. By virtue of their ordination, theirs was a "dignity," as Margaret Gallant said, a nobility that even she, a laywoman, had been made to feel some responsibility to help preserve. More specifically, priests were the ones who had been "trained to make judgments in moral matters," and ordinary believers were supposed to have confidence in them in that capacity. This confidence was now shown, over and over, to have been tragically unwarranted.

Should Catholics submit themselves to such men for the moral instruction and correction that came in confession? What would absolution from such a person even mean? Catholic theology could insist all it wanted that the sacrament had an objective quality, one that did not depend on the character of the priest involved; absolution was understood to be valid so long as the penitent was not the "accomplice" in the abuse. But that was too fine a point. Priests who used the confessional for their offenses had clearly lost whatever standing they may once have had to judge the actions of others. Even worse, confessors who were not abusers were diminished because many of their colleagues had been. All were tarnished. Catholic clergy spoke often of their "brother priests," and their patterns of friendship, primarily with each other, reinforced the sense of fraternity. In addition to their other offenses, abusers were thus damaging their otherwise innocent "brothers." Penitents, for their part, could never know for sure who or what was on the other side of the grille. A parishioner who confessed to Paul Shanley in Boston or Lawrence Murphy in Milwaukee (both of them "so nice and understanding") and who had not been molested by them could nonetheless be excused for thinking that the sacrament was tainted. Better, perhaps, not to take a chance at all, not for oneself and certainly not for one's children.

At the same time, those who sought to address some troubling aspect of life had other options that were readily available and likely safer than confession. Not every sin had to

be redefined as a form of mental illness, as Karl Menninger
had warned, but the relief from inner burdens that confession alone had once seemed to offer could now be sought
elsewhere. American society had accepted modern psychological concepts, and gaining access to help was less daunting than going to confession. Consulting with psychologists
or counselors of all kinds had been largely normalized, in
part because such specialists had well-defined and hard-
earned credentials: the "training my psychiatrist has," as
one woman called it, a level of training that her parish priest
lacked. Practitioners also had professional oversight, and
there were sanctions should there be inappropriate behavior, as of course there sometimes was. The earlier hostility
between psychology and religion had given way to "peaceful
coexistence." And if a troubled Catholic did, for whatever
reason, want to seek help specifically from "a good Catholic
psychiatrist," few would disagree that "the emphasis should
be on the 'good' rather than on the 'Catholic.'" More generally, there were twelve-step and other self-help programs,
which had amply demonstrated their usefulness in counter-
ing destructive habits. As substitutes for and alternatives to
confession, such possibilities were well established, and they
seemed all the more obvious choices after the exposure of
clerical sexual abuse.

The two seismic shifts in thinking and practice rendered
efforts to revive confession, starting in the 1980s, doomed
from the beginning. A high-level theological commission at
the Vatican, a synod of church leaders from around the world,
a strong papal statement, a new comprehensive instructional
text to replace the Baltimore Catechism—all were undertaken in the hope that the long decline could be reversed.
The premise of these efforts (true enough on its own terms)
was that parishioners had lost their traditional "sense of sin,"
a sense that had to be recovered through "more effective"

preaching and teaching. Laypeople, the argument seemed to run, just didn't understand sin and their need for confession; they had to be told again—only better, somehow, this time. Individual bishops periodically mounted "come back to confession" campaigns in their dioceses, often timed during Lent, the penitential season of the church year in the weeks before Easter. Few, however, made any systematic attempt to measure the success of such programs; any increases in the number of confessions were usually temporary. There were other strategies too. With the proliferation of diocesan websites and internet postings, examinations of conscience could be published online, and many such sites are available. (Google "back to confession" and count the number of links that appear.) There are phone apps with examinations of conscience. Though dressed up in new technological garb, almost all of these are essentially unchanged in content from their predecessors. Many suggest, for example, that a penitent begin by reviewing the Ten Commandments, the very approach recommended by pamphlets published in 1920 or, for that matter, prayer books from 1820. Laypeople were unlikely to recover a "sense of sin" simply by being told that they really ought to do so. One survey of these multiple restoration efforts by a theologian (himself a layperson) concluded in 2018 that they were "not enormously successful."[3] Surely an understatement.

Questions about the past often raise questions about the future. With confession gone, practiced today by only a tiny minority of Catholics, what, if anything, will take its place? The loss is more than merely that of a once-familiar ritual. At risk of loss, too, is a larger framework for thinking about how we behave with one another, both personally and collectively. How are we to live out our ideals, and how come to terms with those times when we don't? It cannot be, as my interlocutor had joked, that everyone is better now than they used to

be, that they never have a need to say "I'm sorry," a need to be
sorry. Leaving that moral and ethical space empty has many
hazards and, while the duty to fill it does not rest with Catholics alone, learning from their traditions may prove helpful.
Though the comparison is imperfect, the Catholic church is
now in much the same position it was in during an earlier
epoch of its history. By the sixth century, more or less, the
means that the church had long been using to address the
sins and wrongful actions of its members were losing their
potency. The system of public penance had reached "a dead
end," the foremost historian of the sacrament concluded, and
Christians were shrinking from its "odious" demands. One
can imagine bishops and preachers of that era telling their
followers that they had lost their sense of sin and that they
really should come back to the traditional penitential rites.
In fact, we do not have to imagine: various synods of bishops tried to encourage a return to public penance, at least for
notorious public sins.[4] But such arguments failed to persuade;
new ways of expressing the central moral and ethical insights
of the church were needed. It would take centuries for those
newer forms to be broadly accepted and to coalesce into the
practice of private, auricular confession. So today, The older
form no longer speaks to the great majority of Catholic laypeople; a new form is needed. What that will be is unknown,
and it is certainly not the historian's job to prescribe it. But
church leaders and theologians neglect their duties if they do
not begin the long work of articulating it.

   If we are honest with ourselves, as noted in the Introduction to this book, few of us are as good as we want to be or
as good as we sometimes think (and even pretend) we are.
Absent the mental tools for thinking about our behavior and
our attitudes—a necessary step in changing the things we
want or need to change—how are we to go about individual
and collective improvement? Catholics once had a clear way

too American-centric to make such a universal claim

too bold a claim

to understand and to express their ideals, even as they were acknowledging failures to live up to them. How they and anyone else — everyone else — will accomplish that work are questions for the future, questions that history can illuminate even if it cannot, by itself, answer them.

ignores recent data on confession going up

main weakness of book is lack of emphasis on the role of priests' views in the decline of confession (radicalism of the post-60s generation) which is now being reversed by the overwhelming conservatism of seminarians and recently ordained priests

Abbreviations

AABo   Archives, Archdiocese of Boston, Braintree, Massachusetts

ACUA   American Catholic History Research Center and University Archives, Catholic University of America, Washington, DC

AGU   Archives, Georgetown University, Washington, DC

AUND   Archives, University of Notre Dame, South Bend, Indiana

BA   Bishop Accountability, https://www.bishop-account ability.org/

BHL   Bentley Historical Library, University of Michigan, Ann Arbor, Michigan

BLBC   Burns Library, Boston College, Chestnut Hill, Massachusetts

HPR   *Homiletic and Pastoral Review*

JARC   Jesuit Archives and Research Center, St. Louis, Missouri

JCP   *John Carroll Papers*, ed. Thomas O'Brien Hanley (Notre Dame, IN: University of Notre Dame Press, 1976), 3 vols.

JFP   John C. Ford Papers, New England Province Archives, JARC

MSH   *Messenger of the Sacred Heart* (Renamed *Sacred Heart Messenger* in 1962)

PFA   Paulist Fathers Archives, New York, New York

Notes

1. Habit

1. "Epistle or Diary of the Reverend Joseph Durand," *Records of the American Catholic Historical Society of Philadelphia* 26 (December 1915): 333, 341, and 344–345. A subsequent issue of the *Records* corrected the priest's name to Dunand.

2. "Ministeria Spiritualia," *Woodstock Letters* 27 (March 1898): insert, unpaginated. Both parishes had schools, which probably inflated the number of confessions. For an overview of the vitality of churches in New York, see Jon Butler, *God in Gotham: The Miracle of Religion in Modern Manhattan* (Cambridge, MA: Belknap Press of Harvard University Press, 2020).

3. Patrick Healy Diaries, AGU: "Yearly Statement of Confessions, July 96–June 97"; see also May 30 and June 11, 1896; April 3, 1897; February 3, 1898; and December 31, 1903.

4. Data compiled from the Parish Financial and Statistical Reports, Archives, Archdiocese of Milwaukee, Milwaukee, WI.

5. Joseph H. Fichter, *Dynamics of a City Church* (Chicago: University of Chicago Press, 1951); see especially tables 3–6. For his account of the disagreement with the pastor which caused suppression of the rest of the project, see Joseph H. Fichter, "The Dynamics of Suppression," chap. 2 in *One-Man Research: Reminiscences of a Catholic Sociologist* (New York: Wiley, 1973).

6. Fichter's discussion of confession is in chapter 5 of *Dynamics of a City Church*.

7. Fichter, *Dynamics of a City Church*, 48.

8. The best general survey of the history of the origins and practices of forgiveness is still Bernard Poschmann, *Penance and the Anointing of the Sick*, trans. Francis Courtney (New York: Herder and Herder, 1964). On the practices of the very early church, see also Wayne A. Meeks, *The Origins of Christian Morality* (New Haven, CT: Yale University Press, 1993), esp. chap. 7; and James F. Keenan, *A History of Catholic Theological Ethics* (New York: Paulist Press, 2022).

9. It is of course impossible to summarize the history of the sacrament in a paragraph or two. For a useful overview, see James Dallen, "Reconciliation," in *New Dictionary of Sacramental Worship*, ed. Peter E. Fink (Collegeville, MN: Liturgical Press, 1990), 1052–1064. See also Poschmann, *Penance and the Anointing of the Sick*, 122–131. As we see in Chapter 5, the nineteenth century classic by Henry Charles Lea, *A History of Auricular Confession and Indulgences in the Latin Church*, 3 vols. (Philadelphia: Lea Bros., 1896) contains much useful material, even if it is presented in an overtly hostile, anti-Catholic tone.

10. For the theological background of these developments, see Thomas N. Tentler, *Sin and Confession on the Eve of the Reformation* (Princeton, NJ: Princeton University Press, 1977), esp. chap. 1. For the legislation of Trent, see John W. O'Malley, *Trent: What Happened at the Council* (Cambridge, MA: Belknap Press of Harvard University Press, 2013), 152–154.

11. For examples, see James A. Sandos, *Converting California: Indians and Franciscans in the Missions* (New Haven, CT: Yale University Press, 2003), 96–98, 108; and Leslie Woodcock Tentler, *American Catholics: A History* (New Haven, CT: Yale University Press, 2020), 26–27, 35, 70. The later example from Wisconsin is in F. X. Weninger, "Autobiography," 74, typescript in Missouri Province Archives, JARC.

12. Mosley's letters are in *American Jesuit Spirituality: The Maryland Tradition, 1634–1900*, ed. Robert Emmett Curran (New York: Paulist Press, 1988), 103, 106. On the distinctive characteristics of Maryland Catholicism, see Michael D. Breidenbach, *Our Dear-Bought Liberty: Catholics and Religious Toleration in Early America* (Cambridge, MA: Harvard University Press, 2021).

13. John Carroll to Leonardo Antonelli, March 1, 1785, *JCP*, 1:182.

14. Joseph Greaton, "Method of Confessing," *American Jesuit Spirituality*, 88–92; *Manual of Catholic Prayers* (Philadelphia: Robert Bell,

1774), 106–110. The original manuscript of Greaton's sermon is in the American Catholic Sermon Collection in the Lauinger Library of Georgetown University.

15. Carroll to Charles Plowden, February 28, 1779, *JCP*, 1:53; Carroll to Plowden, June 29, 1785, *JCP*, 1:192; Carroll to Antonelli, March 1, 1785, *JCP*, 1:181.

16. Carroll to Plowden, June 4, 1787, *JCP*, 1:253.

17. Carroll to John Rivet, no date but probably 1796, *JCP*, 2:164; Carroll to Edward Fenwick, April 14, 1807, *JCP*, 3:17. The complaint about being "pestered" is quoted in Patrick W. Carey, *Confession: Catholics, Repentance, and Forgiveness in America* (New York: Oxford University Press, 2018), 110.

18. Anne Hartfield, "Profile of a Pluralistic Parish: Saint Peter's Roman Catholic Church, New York City, 1785–1815," *Journal of American Ethnic History* 12, no. 3 (Spring 1993): 30–59; James M. O'Toole, "From Advent to Easter: Catholic Preaching in New York City, 1808–1809," *Church History* 63 (September 1994): 365–377.

19. O'Toole, "From Advent to Easter," 369–370. The original manuscripts of Kohlmann's sermons are in AABo.

20. The fullest statement of rules regarding confession came at the Second Plenary Council of Baltimore, held in 1866. See *Concilii Plenarii Baltimorensis . . . Acta et Decreta* (Baltimore: John Murphy, 1867), 145–158 (no. 270–296). Still useful for understanding the growth of church infrastructure in the United States is Peter Guilday, *A History of the Councils of Baltimore, 1791–1884* (New York: Macmillan, 1932).

21. Mission Chronicle, April 6–20, 1851, PFA.

22. James A. Walsh Diary, February 18, 1899, AABo; Cathedral of the Madeleine, Spiritual and Canonical Report, 1952, Archives, Archdiocese of Salt Lake City, Salt Lake City, UT.

23. See *The Hour*, a newsletter for Blessed Sacrament parish in Detroit, July 24, 1921, in the Birney Family Papers, BHL, box 4; Pulpit Announcement Books, St. Jean Parish Newton, MA, AABo, entry of December 18, 1927; Pulpit Announcement Books, Sacred Heart parish, Newton, MA, AABo, entries of June 17, 1900, January 3, 1920, and February 17, 1920.

24. Vincent Hankerd to "Snippies," May 10, 1905, Birney Family Papers, BHL, box 2.

25. James A. Walsh Diary, April 29 and May 4, 1899, AABo; Patrick Healy Diary, February 3, 1898, AGU; Fichter, *Dynamics of a City Church*, tables 3, 4, and 5.

26. Pulpit Announcement Books, Sacred Heart Parish, AABo, June 17, 1900; James A. Walsh Diary, AABo, December 1, 1899.

27. The classic study of this phenomenon is Jay P. Dolan, *Catholic Revivalism: The American Experience, 1830–1900* (Notre Dame, IN: University of Notre Dame Press, 1978).

28. The experience in Louisiana is described in the Louis Gergaud Diary, April 13, 1869, and April 24, 1870, Archives, Diocese of Shreveport, LA. The volumes of Mission Chronicles in PFA provide statistics and other documentation for the missions conducted by that order, identified by city and dates.

29. For the pastor who announced the coming of unknown priests, see Pulpit Announcement Books, St. Jean Parish, Newton, MA, November 17, 1912, AABo. The quotations are from the Mission Chronicles, PFA, for "Lent 1894," March 18–25, 1894, February 21–March 3, 1894, and November 11–25, 1894.

2. Sin

1. For the context of Catholic publishing and reading habits, see Una M. Cadegan, *All Good Books Are Catholic Books: Print Culture, Censorship, and Modernity in Twentieth-Century America* (Ithaca, NY: Cornell University Press, 2013); see also Robert A. Orsi, "Printed Presence," chap. 4 in *History and Presence* (Cambridge, MA: Belknap Press of Harvard University Press, 2016).

2. "Sign Post," *Sign* 34, no. 1 (August 1954): 58; "Our Question Box," *MSH* 78, no. 2 (February 1943): 80; "Our Question Box," *MSH* 70, no. 9 (September 1935): 79; "Our Question Box," *MSH* 70, no. 5 (May 1935): 79.

3. "Our Question Box," *MSH* 82, no. 11 (November 1947): 71; "Our Question Box," *MSH* 78, no. 9 (September 1943): 63; "Sign Post," *Sign* 43, no. 10 (May 1964): 53.

4. Charles R. Morris, *American Catholic: The Saints and Sinners Who Built America's Most Powerful Church* (New York: Times Books, 1997),

175–176; quotations from *Father McGuire's New Baltimore Catechism, No. 1* (New York: Benziger Brothers, 1942), questions 1 and 2.

5. Thomas F. Kinkead, *An Explanation of the Baltimore Catechism of Christian Doctrine, For the Use of Sunday-School Teachers and Advanced Classes*, 6ᵗʰ ed. (New York: Benziger Brothers, 1891), no. 45–49 and 152.

6. Kinkead, *Explanation of the Catechism*, no. 51–55 and 57–58. On the "geography of the other world," see Jacques LeGoff, *The Birth of Purgatory*, trans. Arthur Goldhammer (Chicago: University of Chicago Press, 1984), quotation at 2.

7. Kinkead, *Explanation of the Catechism*, no.56.

8. *A Short Abridgement of the Christian Doctrine; Newly Revised and Augmented for the Use of the Catholic Church in the Diocese of Boston* (Boston: Thomas B. Noonan, 1872), 47; Joseph Greaton, "Method of Confessing," *American Jesuit Spirituality*, 89; Knights of Columbus, *Yes, A Priest Can Forgive Your Sins!* (St. Louis: Knights of Columbus, 1954), 9.

9. Mother Bolton, *The Spiritual Way, Book Four* (Yonkers-on-Hudson, NY: World Book Co., 1930), 88.

10. For a comprehensive study, see Joseph M. White, *The Diocesan Seminary in the United States: A History from the 1780s to the Present* (Notre Dame, IN: University of Notre Dame Press, 1989). For sample curricula, see pages 239 and 365.

11. Carroll to Grassi, November 30, 1813, *JCP*, 3:243–244, quoted in White, *Diocesan Seminary*, 124; John B. Hogan, *Clerical Studies* (Boston: Marlier, Callanan, and Co., 1898), 204. For a summary of some of the most important manuals, see James F. Keenan, "From Teaching Confessors to Guiding Lay People: The Development of Catholic Moral Theologians from 1900–1965," *Journal of the Society of Christian Ethics* 28 (Fall/Winter 2008): 141–157. Noldin was used in American seminaries into the 1960s; see Charles E. Curran, *Catholic Moral Theology in the United States: A History* (Washington, DC: Georgetown University Press, 2008), 38. For a review of the English edition of Jone, see *Franciscan Studies* 6 (March 1946): 118–119. For the breakdown of class time, see "Seminary Survey on Re-Evaluation and Examination of the Curriculum," National Catholic Educational Association, Seminary Division Files, ACUA, box 78.

12. This copy of the third volume of Jerome Noldin, *Summa Theologiae Moralis*, 30th ed., ed. Gottfried Heinzel (Innsbruck: F. Rauch, 1952), is in the Liturgy and Life Collection (BX1758.N6/1952), BLBC. The book seems to have been owned by Joseph Gaudet, a student of Saint John's Seminary, Brighton, MA. The notes on the blank pages are written in three different hands, however, suggesting that the book may have been owned or used by other seminarians as well, practicing the same method of annotation. The professor is identified as "L.J.R."—Lawrence J. Riley, later an auxiliary bishop of Boston.

13. "Preface," in *The Casuist: A Collection of Cases in Moral and Pastoral Theology* (New York: Joseph F. Wagner, 1917), iii. For a useful overview of this entire subject, see Albert R. Jonsen and Stephen Toulmin, *The Abuse of Casuistry: A History of Moral Reasoning* (Berkeley: University of California Press, 1988).

14. Examples from *The Casuist*, 1:i; 1:31–35; 1:71–72; 1:73–74; 2:192–194; 5:33–35; and 5:71–72.

15. On Liguori and his influence, see White, *Diocesan Seminary*, 21–22 and 139; Curran *Catholic Moral Theology*, 4–6; and Patrick W. Carey, *Confession: Catholics, Repentance, and Forgiveness in America* (New York: Oxford University Press, 2018), 127–128. The perjury case is in *The Casuist*, 3:288–291.

16. Knights of Columbus, *These Are Our Seven Deadly Enemies* (St. Louis: Knights of Columbus, 1952), 13, 16, 17, 24, 28, 32.

17. *The Catholic Encyclopedia: An International Work of Reference on the Constitution, Doctrine, and History of the Catholic Church*, ed. Charles George Herbermann, special ed. (New York: Encyclopedia Press, 1913), s.v. "sin."

18. Henry Frank, *A Guide for Confession* (Huntington, IN: Our Sunday Visitor, 1941), 7; "Questions of the Month," *MSH* 87, no. 2 (December 1952): 70. There is no indication whether the person asking about disobedience was a parent or a child.

19. Bernard A. Sause, *I Have Sinned: Helps for Adult Lay Persons to Confess Worthily* (St. Meinrad, IN: Grail Publications, 1952), 53; *Father McGuire's New Baltimore Catechism. No. 1*, no. 113 and 123.

20. Gerald Kelly, *Modern Youth and Chastity* (St. Louis; Queen's Work, 1941), 89; Lincoln J. Walsh, "The Campus Corner," *MSH* 98,

no. 6 (June 1963): 42; J. D. Conway, *What They Ask About Modesty, Chastity, and Morals* (Notre Dame, IN: Ave Maria Press, 1960), 3.

21. Kinkead, *Explanation of the Catechism*, 197; "Questions of the Month," *MSH* 97, no. 6 (June 1962): 60; Frederic Schultze, *Manual of Pastoral Theology: A Practical Guide for Ecclesiastical Students and Newly Ordained Priests* (Milwaukee: Wilzius, 1899), 174–175; M. A. Feit, *Whirlpools of Destruction: The Occasions of Sin* (Liguori, MO: Liguorian Pamphlets, 1962), 15; D. F. Miller, *How to Stop Committing Sin* (Liguori, MO: Liguorian Pamphlets, n.d., ca. 1951), no pagination.

22. Feit, *Whirlpools of Destruction*, 1–14; Schultze, *Pastoral Theology*, 175.

23. The definitive treatment of this entire subject is Leslie Woodcock Tentler, *Catholics and Contraception: An American History* (Ithaca, NY: Cornell University Press, 2004); the papal encyclical, *Casti Conubii*, is quoted in Curran, *Catholic Moral Theology*, 47; Joseph A. Breig, *A Father Talks to Anti-Lifers* (Oconomowoc, WI: Liguorian Pamphlet Office, 1944), 7; "Our Question Box," *MSH* 78, no. 9 (September 1943): 63.

24. Frederick E. Klueg, "Marriage and Rhythm," *Integrity* 7, no. 11 (August 1953): 11; J. D. Conway, *What They Ask About Birth Control* (Notre Dame, IN: Ave Maria Press, 1955), 11–12; Lawrence J. Riley, "Moral Aspects of the Practice of Periodic Continence," *HPR* 57 (June 1957): 825; student notes in Noldin, *Summa Theologiae Moralis*, no. 374, BLBC.

25. Heribert Jone, *Moral Theology*, trans. Urban Adelman (Westminster, MD: Newman Press, 1962), no. 212, emphasis in original; radio ad quoted in Tentler, *Catholics and Contraception*, 170; "Sign Post," *Sign* 29, no. 12 (July 1950): 58.

26. *Father McGuire's New Baltimore Catechism, No. 1*, 64; "Our Question Box," *MSH* 81, no. 1 (January 1946): 62; "Questions of the Month," *MSH* 97, no. 12 (December 1962): 60; Francis F. Brown, *Scandal: The Sin Nobody Knows* (Notre Dame, IN: Ave Maria Press, 1960), 16; "Our Question Box," *MSH* 81, no.10 (October 1946): 76. For earlier attempts to specify a time limit on servile work, see *MSH* 69, no. 7 (July 1934): 73, and *MSH* 81, no. 1 (January 1946): 62. For general background, see Alexis McCrossen, *Holy Day, Holiday: The American Sunday* (Ithaca, NY: Cornell University Press, 2000).

27. *Father McGuire's New Baltimore Catechism, No. 1*, 127; chaps. 35–36 of Kinkead, *Explanation of the Catechism*, suggest a number of ways the often complicated requirements of these commandments can be presented to students.

28. Patrick J. Cullinane, "Memoirs," typescript in BHL; Kinkead, *Explanation of the Catechism*, 337; "Questions of the Month," *MSH* 97, no. 12 (December 1962): 60.

3. Confessing

1. On the cathedral and its construction, see James M. O'Toole, "Portrait of a Parish: Race, Ethnicity, and Class in Boston's Cathedral of the Holy Cross, 1865–1880," in *Boston's Histories: Essays in Honor of Thomas H. O'Connor*, ed. James M. O'Toole and David Quigley (Boston: Northeastern University Press, 2004), 92–112; quotation at 94.

2. John Welch to John Williams, February 5, 1884, and "Specifications for the Black Walnut Furniture required for the Cathedral of the Holy Cross," both in Cathedral Construction Correspondence, 1872–1884, AABo. Welch's "Calumet" finish was apparently a brand name.

3. Francis X. Reuss, "St. Peter's Church, Columbia, Lancaster Co., Pa.," *Records of the American Catholic Historical Society of Philadelphia* 4 (June 1893): 90–124.

4. Greaton sermon on confession, *American Jesuit Spirituality: The Maryland Tradition, 1634–1900*, ed. Robet Emmett Curran (New York: Paulist Press, 1988), 89; John C. Ford, SJ, class lecture notes, JFP, box 19, folder 9.

5. George T. Schmidt, *The Principal Catholic Practices* (New York: Benziger Brothers, 1920), 33.

6. Bernard A. Sause, *I Have Sinned: Helps for Lay Persons to Confess Worthily* (St. Meinrad, IN: Grail Publications, 1952), 3; *Saint Joseph Daily Missal: The Official Prayers of the Catholic Church for the Celebration of Daily Mass*, completely rev. ed. (New York: Catholic Book Publishing Co., 1959), 1299; Joseph Safiejko, *Five Steps to Pardon* (St. Paul, MN: Catechetical Guild Educational Society, 1961), 17; June Verbillion, *The Sign of Renewal: Confession* (St. Louis, MO: Cross and Crown, 1964), 6; *Father McGuire's New Baltimore Catechism, No. 1* (New York:

Benziger Brothers, 1942), 174. For an alternative approach, see Donald F. Miller, *Examination of Conscience for Adults: A Comprehensive Examination of Conscience Based on Twelve Virtues for Twelve Months of the Year* (Liguori, MO: Liguorian Pamphlets, 1942), and Sause, *I Have Sinned*, 22–25.

7. "Our Question Box," *MSH* 82, no. 8 (August 1947): 73–74; "Sign Post," *Sign* 37, no. 4 (November 1957): 63; Miller, *Examination of Conscience for Adults*, no pagination; student notes in Noldin, *Summa Theologiae Moralis*, no. 277, BLBC. Schmidt, *The Principal Catholic Practices*, 33–34, was another source recommending a time limit of fifteen minutes. The special problems of "dull children" are considered in M. Gatterer and F. Krus, *The Theory and Practice of the Catechism*, trans. J. B. Culemans (New York: Pustet, 1914), 369–370.

8. Sause, *I Have Sinned*, 39; Urban S. Wagner, *Self Scrutiny: An Examination of Conscience for Catholics Before Receiving the Sacrament of Penance* (Chaska, MN: Conventual Franciscan Fathers, 1960), 3 and 6; A. J. Wilwerding, *Examination of Conscience for Boys and Girls* (St. Louis, MO: Queen's Work, 1927), 3.

9. Class lecture notes on examination of conscience, JFP, box 15, folder 1.

10. "Our Question Box," *MSH* 69, no. 7 (July 1934): 73; "Sign Post," *Sign* 42, no. 6 (January 1963): 52; Miller, *Examination of Conscience for Adults*, 63; Father Dooley, *I Accuse Myself: A Modern Examination of Conscience* (Techny, IL: Mission Press, 1939), 20.

11. Joseph DeHarbe, *A Catechism of the Catholic Religion*, new ed. (London: Burns & Oates, 1886), 233, 235; "Varia," *Woodstock Letters* 38 (1909): 317–318. The DeHarbe catechism was published and distributed in America by Benziger Brothers of New York, a major Catholic publisher at the turn of the twentieth century. It was often used in secondary schools and colleges.

12. *Father Maguire's New Baltimore Catechism No. 1*, 176; Wilwerding, *Examination of Conscience*, 9; Bernard Häring, *The Law of Christ: Moral Theology for Priests and Laity*, trans. Edwin G. Kaiser, vol. 1, *General Moral Theology* (Paramus, NJ: Newman Press, 1966), 439–440. On the influence of Häring and his students, see Curran, *Catholic Moral Theology in the United States*, 94–97.

13. Häring, *Law of Christ*, 1:436; John B. Sheerin, *Confession: Peace of Mind* (New York: Paulist Press, 1951), 12–13; "Our Question Box," *MSH* 71, no. 1 (January 1936): 77.

14. Parish annual reports, Archives, Archdiocese of Detroit, Detroit, MI. I have sampled the forms for Saint Alphonsus Parish in Dearborn for 1880, 1917, and 1940.

15. Examples of different styles of confessionals can be seen in the advertising sections of the annual *Official Catholic Directory* (New York: P. J. Kenedy). On priests' reading while in the confessional, see Patrick Healy Diary, AGU, February 26, 1898.

16. Mother Bolton, *The Spiritual Way, Book Four* (Yonkers on Hudson, NY: World Book, 1930), 88–89. A companion text for the Baltimore Catechism, this is one of many presentations of the proper form for confession.

17. John Ford class lecture notes, undated but 1950s, JFP, box 17, folder 11; Walsh Diary, AABo, January 7 and February 25, 1899; Healy Diary, AGU, May 30, 1896; Joseph H. Fichter, *Dynamics of a City Church* (Chicago: University of Chicago Press, 1951), 47; "How It Looks: A Word of Comment on the 'Speedkings,'" *The Priest* 6 (July 1950): 509–510.

18. Gerald Kelly, *Modern Youth and Chastity* (St. Louis: Queen's Work, 1946), 89; John Ford class lecture notes: for Boston College students, 1948, JFP, box 19, folder 9; for Jesuit seminarians, JFP, box 17, folder 11. Kelly's pamphlet had appeared in several earlier printings (1941ff.) with slightly varying titles.

19. Frederic Schulze, *Manual of Pastoral Theology: A Practical Guide for Ecclesiastical Students and Newly Ordained Priests* (Milwaukee: Wiltzius, 1899), 136; Gerald Kelly, *The Good Confessor* (New York: Sentinel Press, 1951), chapter 5; William Stang, *Pastoral Theology*, second, revised, and enlarged ed. (New York: Benziger Brothers, 1897), 184; student notes in Noldin, no. 387, BLBC.

20. Thomas F. Casey, *Pastoral Manual for New Priests* (Milwaukee: Bruce, 1962), 45–46; "Fervorinos for Confession," *The Priest* 1 (January 1945): 56. Intended as a recurring monthly feature, the "fervorinos" appeared only sporadically and ceased altogether by June of 1946.

21. On the theology of how absolution was actually conveyed, see Thomas N. Tentler, *Sin and Confession on the Eve of the Reformation*

(Princeton, NJ: Princeton University Press, 1977), 22–27. The essential parts of the absolution are described in Henry Davis, *Moral and Pastoral Theology: A Summary* (New York: Sheed and Ward, 1952), 287. The requirement that the priest say the words clearly enough so that he himself could hear them, even if the penitent could not, is stressed in student notes in Noldin no. 237, BLBC.

22. "Our Question Box," *MSH* 80, no. 4 (April 1945): 52; Henry Davis, *Moral and Pastoral Theology*, 8th ed., vol. 3 (New York: Sheed and Ward, 1959), 262; Thomas J. P. Brady, *Is Confession a Delusion?* (New York: Paulist Press, 1938), 12–13. For the long history of viewing sin as a debt, see Gary B. Anderson, *Sin: A History* (New Haven, CT: Yale University Press, 2009). On temporal punishment, see DeHarbe, *Catechism of the Catholic Religion*, 251.

23. Spiridion Grech, *The Neo-Confessor: A Concise Outline for Confessional Practice and Sick-Calls* (Philadelphia: Dolphin Press, 1940), 19; Kelly, *The Good Confessor*, 73 and 74; Davis, *Moral and Pastoral Theology*, 292.

24. Student notes in Noldin, no. 303, BLBC; Grech, *Neo-Confessor*, 19 and 22; Davis, *Moral and Pastoral Theology*, 265; Stang, *Pastoral Theology*, 190–192. On the advisability of performing the penance before leaving the church after confession, see "Our Question Box," *MSH* 74, no. 3 (March 1939): 78.

25. Mission Chronicles, January 23–February 6, 1853, and February 7–15, 1855, PFA.

26. Sheerin, *Confession: Peace of Mind*, 12–13; "Sign Post," *Sign* 29, no. 12 (July 1950): 58; class lecture notes, JFP, box 16, folder 8.

27. "Casti Conubii," no. 57, *The Papal Encyclicals, 1903–1939*, ed. by Claudia Carlen (Wilmington, NC: McGrath 1981), 400. The unspoken division of labor between diocesan priests and those who preached parish missions is discussed in Leslie Woodcock Tentler, *Catholics and Contraception: An American History* (Ithaca, NY: Cornell University Press, 2004), 23 and 60; the quotation from Joseph Turner, a Redemptorist preacher, is at 60.

28. "Sign Post," *Sign* 43, no. 10 (May 1964): 53. Ford's opinions are expressed in two undated lectures from the 1950s: "Prudent Questions When Marital Abuses Are Vaguely Confessed," JFP, box 50, folder 19, and "Pastoral Remarks on Erroneous Conscience," box 14, folder 1.

29. Kelly, *Good Confessor*, 39–40; Mundelein's effort at strict enforcement is discussed in Tentler, *Catholics and Contraception*, 81–83; Tentler cites one priest, a seminarian in the early 1940s, who recalled being told to inquire particularly of penitents who had been away from the sacrament for at least six months. See also the generally pastoral approach adopted by many priests, 145–149.

30. "Sign Post," *Sign* 38, no. 1 (August 1959): 53.

4. Experience

1. Lucille Halsey, "Feelings Don't Count," *The Priest* 6 (1950): 912–917; Quentin Donoghue and Linda Shapiro, *Bless Me, Father, For I Have Sinned: Catholics Speak Out About Confession* (New York: Primus, 1984), 92–93 and 166; anonymous respondent, *U.S. Catholic* Surveys, AUND, 24/16.

2. Donoghue and Shapiro, *Bless Me, Father*, 95 and 224; Halsey, "Feelings Don't Count," 916.

3. Two women in *U.S. Catholic* Surveys, AUND, 3/08 and 24/16; Gerald Kelly, *The Good Confessor* (New York: Sentinel Press, 1951), 45; Donald F. Miller, *I Hear Confessions* (Liguori, MO: Liguorian Pamphlet Office, 1957), no pagination.

4. "Father Robert Fulton: A Sketch," *Woodstock Letters* 25 (1896): 105; James A. Walsh Diary, AABo, January 7, 1899. See the statistics for Paulist missions, PFA: Dubuque (October 20–November 16, 1901); McKeesport (January 25–February 8, 1903); Worcester (February 19–March 4, 1888); and New Brunswick (October 15–29, 1905).

5. Frederic Schultze, *Manual of Pastoral Theology: A Practical Guide for Ecclesiastical Students and Newly Ordained Priests* (Milwaukee: Wiltzius, 1899), 147; William Stang, *Pastoral Theology*, second, revised, and enlarged ed. (New York: Benziger Brothers, 1897), 177–178; "How Can Men Be Induced to Frequent Communion?" in *The Casuist: A Collection of Cases in Moral and Pastoral Theology* (New York: Joseph F. Wagner, 1917), 2:266.

6. Thomas J. P. Brady, *Is Confession a Delusion?* (New York: Paulist Press, 1938), 10; John B. Sheerin, *Confession: Peace of Mind* (New York: Paulist Press, 1951), 18; *To Sin is To Die* (St. Louis: Knights of Columbus

Religious Information Bureau, 1967), 7; Donoghue and Shapiro, *Bless Me, Father*, 94; Paul F. Flynn, *Examination of Conscience for Teen-Age and Up* (New York: Paulist Fathers, 1949), 18. For heroic virtue, see *The Catholic Encyclopedia: An International Work of Reference on the Constitution, Doctrine, and History of the Catholic Church*, ed. Charles George Herbermann, special ed. (New York: Encyclopedia Press, 1913), s.v. "heroic virtue."

7. Herbert Raterman, *Charity and Sex and the Young Man* (Cincinnati: St. Xavier High School, 1967), 38–42. Raterman's title page says "Charity," but from the content of the pamphlet that seems a misprint, with "Chastity" probably intended instead.

8. *In His Name: Official Holy Name Manual* (New York: National Headquarters of the Holy Name Society, 1941), 25; *Holy Name Spiritual Director's Handbook* (New York: National Headquarters of the Holy Name Society, 1941), 28; James A. Walsh Diary, AABo, April 9, 1899; Pulpit Announcement Books, Sacred Heart, Newton Centre, AABo, March 25, 1900. On the extent and influence of the Holy Name Society, see James M. O'Toole, *The Faithful: A History of Catholics in America* (Cambridge, MA: Belknap Press of Harvard University Press, 2008), 149–153.

9. "Spiritual Drive in Los Angeles Diocese," *Woodstock Letters* 58 (June 1929): 478; Patrick Healy Diaries, AGU, January 12, 1899, and May 18, 1898; James A. Walsh Diary, AABo, May 18 and 19, 1899.

10. Stang, *Pastoral Theology*, 178 and 179; Schultze, *Manual of Pastoral Theology*, 147 and 148; "Misuse of General Confession by Penitents of the Female Sex," *The Casuist*, 3:211.

11. Stang, *Pastoral Theology*, 179; Spiridion Grech, *The Neo-Confessor: A Concise Outline for Confessional Practice and Sick-Calls* (Philadelphia: Dolphin Press, 1940), 15; the sermons that show changing attitudes about questioning men and women on birth control are quoted in Leslie Woodcock Tentler, *Catholics and Contraception: An American History* (Ithaca, NY: Cornell University Press, 2004), 29–30 and 94.

12. "Our Question Box," *MSH* 73, no. 3 (March 1940): 75; Winfrid Herbst, *How to Make a Good Confession* (St. Paul, MN: Catechetical Guild Educational Society, 1954), 53. On devotional confessions generally, see Suso Mayer, "Devotional Confession," *Orate Fratres* 18, no.

Notes to Pages 118–122

4 and 5 (February and March 1944): 159–165 and 206–213, and Patrick W. Carey, *Confession: Catholics, Repentance, and Forgiveness in America* (New York: Oxford University Press, 2018), 169–173.

13. For different recommendations on the frequency of confession, see "Our Question Box," *MSH* 68, no. 10 (October 1933): 79, and *MHS* 70, no. 11 (November 1935): 79; Paul A. Stauder, *The Other Side of the Confessional* (St. Louis: Queen's Work, 1962), 14; and Benedict J. Fenwick, *A Short Abridgement of the Christian Doctrine* (Boston: T. B. Noonan, 1842), 67. For an explanation of the confession of sins already forgiven, see Bernard A. Sause, *I Have Sinned: Helps for Adult Lay Persons to Confess Worthily* (St. Meinrad, IN: Grail Publications, 1952), 79–80; and Vincent Fecher, *When a Boy Goes to Confession* (Techny, IL: Divine Word Publications, 1960), 4.

14. The prayer of unworthiness is quoted in O'Toole, *The Faithful*, 121. For instances of infrequent communion, see William Leonard, *The Letter Carrier* (Kansas City, MO: Sheed and Ward, 1993), 9; and James A. Walsh Diary, AABo, May 21, 1899. The link between confession and communion is in Joseph H. Fichter, *Dynamics of a City Church* (Chicago: University of Chicago Press, 1951), 57. On changing practice regarding communion, see Margaret M. McGuinness, "Let Us Go to the Altar: American Catholics and the Eucharist, 1926–1976," in *Habits of Devotion: Catholic Religious Practice in Twentieth-Century America*, ed. James M. O'Toole (Ithaca, NY: Cornell University Press, 2004), 187–235.

15. "Our Question Box," *MSH* 68, no. 10 (October 1933): 79; and *MSH* 70, no. 11 (November 1935): 79. On the practice in Philadelphia, see "Obituary: Father Charles Lyons, 1868–1939," *Woodstock Letters* 68, no. 3 (1939): 350.

16. Jim Conniff, "The Church of 1,000 Confessions a Day," *U.S. Catholic* 39, no. 11 (November 1974): 30–34.

17. J. H. Schutz, *A Little Book of Church Etiquette, or How to Behave before Our Lord in the Blessed Sacrament and at Devotional Exercises in General* (St. Louis: B. Herder, 1929), 81; Jesuit House Diary, AGU, March 19, 1876; "Our Question Box," *MSH* 71, no. 1 (January 1936): 78–79; *Sex in Marriage, Love-Giving, Life-Giving: Questions Asked since the Encyclical "Humanae Vitae"* (Washington, DC: Archdiocese of Washington, 1968), 23.

18. Stang, *Pastoral Theology*, 180. On the impact of the papal lowering of the age, see Carrie T. Schulz, "Do This in Memory of Me: American Catholicism and First Communion Practices in the Era of Quam Singulari," *American Catholic Studies* 115, no. 2 (Summer 2004): 45–66.

19. Daniel M. Dougherty, *Confession Prayers for Children* (New York: Paulist Press, 1934), 19–20; Ernest F. Miller, *Examination of Conscience for Grade School Children* (Liguori, MO: Liguorian Pamphlets, 1959), 16 and 20; Ernest F. Miller, *Examination of Conscience for Teen-Agers* (Liguori, MO: Liguorian-Queen's Work Pamphlets, 1964), 25–26; Roderick McEachen, *MacEachen's Course in Religion, First Manual* (New York: Macmillan, 1912), 286.

20. Donoghue and Shapiro, *Bless Me, Father*, 204; Thomas F. Casey, *Pastoral Manual for New Priests* (Milwaukee: Bruce, 1962), 45; Hugh Calkins, *How to Make a Good Confession* (Chicago: Claretian Publications, 1966), 17; unidentified man in *U.S. Catholic* surveys, AUND, 24/16; Michael Scanlan, *The Power in Penance: Confession and the Holy Spirit* (Notre Dame, IN: Ave Maria Press, 1972), 27.

21. The classic study of religious developments in Ireland and their impact is Emmett Larkin, "The Devotional Revolution in Ireland, 1850–1875," *American Historical Review* (June 1972): 625–652. For an overview of the principal Catholic ethnicities, see Jay P. Dolan, *The American Catholic Experience: A History from Colonial Times to the Present* (Garden City, NY: Doubleday, 1985), esp. chaps. 5 and 6. On the experience of the Black penitent in Detroit, see John T. McGreevy, *Parish Boundaries: The Catholic Encounter with Race in the Twentieth-Century Urban North* (Chicago: University of Chicago Press, 1996), 101.

22. For an overview of the American priesthood, see E. Brooks Holifield, *God's Ambassadors: A History of the Christian Clergy in America* (Grand Rapids, MI: Eerdman's, 2007), esp. chaps. 6 and 9. On the Irish missionary in Virginia, see Mission Chronicles, undated but 1853, PFA.

23. Parish Financial and Statistical Reports, Archives, Archdiocese of Milwaukee; Mission Chronicle, Bound Brook, New Jersey, May 6–13, 1894, PFA.

24. Grech, *The Neo-Confessor*, 27.

25. Joseph McSorley, *Italian Confessions: How to Hear Them; An Easy Method for Busy Priests* (New York: Paulist Press, 1916); John B.

Sheerin, *Spanish Confessions: How to Hear Them* (St. Louis: B. Herder, 1942); J. C van der Loos, *Methodus Excipiendi Confessiones Ordinarias Variis in Linguis* (Amsterdam: G. Borg, 1911).

26. William Wolkovich-Valkavicius, *Lithuanian Religious Life in America*, 3 vols. (Norwood, MA: privately printed, 1991), 1:373. On the remote origins of the practice, see Wietse DeBoer, *The Conquest of the Soul: Confession, Discipline, and Public Order in Counter-Reformation Milan* (London: Brill, 2001), 187–188.

27. Wolkovich-Valkavicius, *Lithuanian Religious Life in America*, 1:273 and 1:456; student notes in Noldin, *Summa Theologiae Moralis*, no. 418, BLBC; Henry Davis, *Moral and Pastoral Theology: A Summary*, (New York: Sheed and Ward, 1952), 300; Mission Chronicle, Evansville, Indiana, February 22–March 2, 1880, PFA.

28. "Sign Post," *Sign* 40, no. 4 (November 1960): 61; "Code and Cult," *The Priest* 6 (May 1950): 353; student notes in Noldin, no. 273, BLBC. For a general account of the difficulties in this matter, see Florence A. Waters, "The Deaf Penitent," *The Priest* 12 (May 1956): 412–415; Waters was herself deaf.

29. *Official Catholic Directory, 1950* (New York: P. J. Kenedy, 1950), advertising page 13f; *Official Catholic Directory, 1960* (New York: P.J. Kenedy, 1960), advertising page 16f.

30. The fullest (though, at 24 pages, still brief) treatment of this subject is Gerard Breitenbeck, *Confession for the Retarded* (Liguori, MO: Liguorian-Queen's Work Pamphlets, 1965); student notes in Noldin, no. 273, BLBC.

31. Mission Chronicle, Sing Sing Prison, January 27–February 8, 1889, PFA; Casey, *Pastoral Manual for New Priests*, 117; Joseph B. Schuyler, *Northern Parish: A Sociological and Pastoral Study* (Chicago: Loyola University Press, 1960), 211–214. On the confessions and anointing of the sick, see James M. O'Toole, "Reinventing the Sacrament: American Catholics and Extreme Unction," *Josephinum Journal of Theology* 16, no. 1 (Winter/Spring 2009): 72–85.

32. "A Year with the Army of the Potomac: Diary of the Reverend Father [Peter] Tissot, S.J., Military Chaplain," *Historical Records and Studies* 3 (January 1903): 46, 51, and 65; *For God and Country: The War Diary of Lieutenant Commander John P. Foley, S.J., Navy Chaplain, 1943–1945*

(e-book, 2021; available at www.bc.edu/bc-web/bcnews/faith-religion/jesuit-catholic/for-god-and-country.html), entry of January 8, 1944; Donald F. Crosby, *Battlefield Chaplains: Catholic Priests in World War II* (Lawrence: University Press of Kansas, 1994), 155.

33. *For God and Country*, entries of February 7, 1943; May 8, 1943; and March 23, 1943; Crosby, *Battlefield Chaplains*, 124. Departures from the normal rules that were acceptable in wartime are outlined in Henry Davis, *Moral and Pastoral Theology: A Summary* (New York: Sheed and Ward, 1952), 287–288.

34. Kelly, *Good Confessor*, 8; M. Eugene Boylan, *The Spiritual Life of the Priest* (Westminster, MD: Newman Press, 1949), 101; Casey, *Pastoral Manual for New Priests*, 46. Boylan's work was originally published in Ireland.

35. Boylan, *Spiritual Life of the Priest*, 100; Casey, *Pastoral Manual for New Priests*, 45; Miller, *Examination of Conscience for Teen-Agers*, 4 and 14.

36. "From an Ordinand to His First Pastor," *The Priest* 8 (April 1952): 267–268.

37. Schultze, *Manual of Pastoral Theology*, 5; Stauder, *Other Side of the Confessional*, 8–9.

38. On Ford, see Eric Marcelo Genilo, *John Cuthbert Ford, S.J.: Moral Theologian at the End of the Manualist Era* (Washington, DC: Georgetown University Press, 2007), and Peter Cajka, "'Each Individual Catholic Can and Does Form His Own Conscience on This and Every Other Subject': John Ford, S.J., and the Theology of Conscience, 1941–69," in *Crossings and Dwellings: Restored Jesuits, Women Religious, American Experience, 1814–2014*, ed. Kyle B. Roberts and Stephen R. Schloesser (Leiden and Boston: Brill, 2017), 567–602. Ford's papers are full of letters from priests, otherwise unknown to him, asking for his advice.

39. "Some Notes on the Exam 'Ad Audiendas Confessiones,'" undated but 1950s, JFP, box 8, folder 9; see also the class handout, "Specimen Confessions on Chastity," box 50, folder 9, and "De Confessione," box 14, folder 5. Ford's papers (box 8, folders 8–13) contain cases he used in class and in examinations.

40. These two cases, both from the 1960s, are in JFP, box 8, folder 11 and folder 10, respectively. See also "Some Notes on the Exam," box 8, folder 9.

41. Casey, *Pastoral Manual for New Priests*, 3; Davis, *Moral and Pastoral Theology*, 265; "Our Question Box," *Messenger of the Sacred Heart* 76, no. 11 (November 1941): 74.

5. Secrecy

1. This account and all the quotations from it are taken from William Sampson, *Catholic Question in America: Whether a Roman Catholic Clergyman Be in Any Case Compellable To Disclose the Secrets of Auricular Confession* (New York: Edward Gillespy, 1813).

2. Kohlmann's refusal is in Sampson, *Catholic Question*, 8–12; the petition from the parishioners at 52–54. It is likely that Kohlmann prompted, or at least approved of, the parishioners' petition.

3. Clinton's decision is in Sampson, *Catholic Question*, 95–114. For a general summary of the trial, see Vincent Hopkins, "Kohlmann's Case: Religious Liberty in Question," *Historical Records and Studies* 50 (1964): 53–82; Jason K. Duncan, *Citizens or Papists?: The Politics of Anti-Catholicism in New York* (New York: Fordham University Press, 2005), 167–172; and Patrick W. Carey, "The Confessional Seal: Legal and Apologetic Dimensions of the Sacrament of Penance," chap. 2 in *Confession: Catholics, Repentance, and Forgiveness in America* (New York: Oxford University Press, 2018).

4. For an overview, see Jacob M. Yellin, "The History and Current Status of the Clergy-Penitent Privilege," *Santa Clara Law Review* 23, no. 1 (1983): 95–156.

5. Henry Charles Lea, *A History of Auricular Confession and Indulgences in the Latin Church*, 3 vols. (Philadelphia: Lea Brothers, 1896), quotations at 1:v, 415, and 431.

6. Heribert Jone, *Moral Theology*, trans. Urban Adelman (Westminster, MD: Newman Press, 1962), no. 612–621; Henry Davis, *Moral and Pastoral Theology: A Summary* (New York: Sheed and Ward, 1952), 298–299; this work is a one-volume abridgement of Davis's four-volume original text.

7. Student notes in Noldin, *Summa Theologiae Moralis*, no. 408, BLBC; Michael O'Callaghan, "The Seal of Confession," *The Priest* 12, no. 9 (September 1956): 743–748; Thomas F. Casey, *Pastoral Manual for New Priests* (Milwaukee: Bruce, 1962), 47.

8. Quentin Donoghue and Linda Shapiro, *Bless Me, Father, For I Have Sinned: Catholics Speak Out About Confession,* (New York: Primus, 1984), 199; "Ten Years a Priest," *The Priest* 15, no. 6 (June 1956): 482; "Our Question Box," *MSH* 76, no. 11 (November 1941): 74; Ford lecture notes, JFP, box 17 folder 1; Heribert Jone, *Moral Theology,* trans. Urban Adelman (Westminster, MD: Newman Press, 1962), no. 613 and 614.

9. "Weekly Calendar of Feast Days," May 4, 1931, Catholic News Service; "Bravery of Faulhabers Is Not New Thing in Germany," *St. Louis Register,* March 19, 1943; "Priest Refuses to Break Seal of Confession, Gets Prison Term," *St. Louis Register,* March 4, 1949; "Father Gill's Imprisonment," *Catholic Telegraph,* March 26, 1896; and "Priest Sustained," *Catholic Telegraph,* July 16, 1896; all available at Catholic News Archive, https://thecatholicnewsarchive.org. See also "Passports to Paradise," *Treasure Chest of Fun and Fact,* January 3, 1957, 17–22, available from the ACUA, https://cuislandora.wrlc.org.

10. "Our Question Box," *HPR* 65 (October 1964): 84–85; student notes in Noldin no. 387, BLBC.

11. Mission at Lenox and Lee, Massachusetts, October 9–23, 1887, PFA.

12. Walsh Diary, AABo, January 6, 1899.

13. Woman from Louisiana in *U. S. Catholic* surveys, AUND, 3/08; Dorothy Dohen, "An Inquiry on Confession and Spiritual Direction," *Integrity* 9, no. 1 (October 1954): 27.

14. *The Catholic Encyclopedia: An International Work of Reference on the Constitution, Doctrine, and History of the Catholic Church,* ed. Charles George Herbermann, special ed. (New York: Encyclopedia Press, 1913), s.v. "solicitation." See also student notes in Noldin, no. 379, BLBC, and Jone, *Moral Theology,* no. 587–599.

15. Lea's discussion of solicitation is in *History of Auricular Confession,* 1:382–393; see also Lea's *History of Sacerdotal Celibacy in the Christian Church,* 3rd. ed. (New York: Macmillan, 1907), 2:251–295; and his *History of the Inquisition of Spain* (New York: Macmillan, 1907), 4:95–139. For the investigation of concubinage in late medieval Spain, see Stephen Haliczer, *Sexuality in the Confessional: A Sacrament Profaned* (New York: Oxford University Press, 1996); the role and jurisdiction of the Inquisition is described 5–62.

16. Patrick Cullinane, "Memoirs," BHL, 17–18, 77; "Father Sharp on the Chapel Car," *Woodstock Letters* 58 (October 1929): 700–702.

17. On the religious expressions, both Protestant and Catholic, of this cult of domesticity, see Colleen McDannell, *The Christian Home in Victorian America, 1840–1900* (Bloomington: Indiana University Press, 1986).

18. The fullest discussion of this entire literary genre is Cassandra L. Yacovazzi, *Escaped Nuns: True Womanhood and the Campaign Against Convents in Antebellum America* (New York: Oxford University Press, 2018); see also chapters 6 and 7 in Jenny Franchot, *Roads to Rome: The Antebellum Protestant Encounter with Catholicism* (Berkeley: University of California Press, 1994).

19. *Six Months in a Convent, or, The Narrative of Rebecca Theresa Reed* (Boston: Russell, Odiorne, and Metcalf, 1835); *Awful Disclosures by Maria Monk of the Hotel Dieu Nunnery of Montreal* (New York: Maria Monk, 1836). Both works are still in print in modern editions. An accessible edition of Monk was published by Arno Press in 1977, part of its "Anti-Movements in America" series. Franchot, *Roads to Rome*, 159, reproduces the floor plan.

20. *Awful Disclosures* (Arno edition), 19, 21, 109.

21. The fullest account of his life is Paul LaVerdure, "Charles Chiniquy: The Making of an Anti-Catholic Crusader," Canadian Catholic Historical Association, *Historical Studies* 54 (1987): 39–56.

22. *The Priest, The Woman, and The Confessional, by Father Chiniquy*, 43rd ed. (New York: Fleming H. Revell Company, 1880), 21, 22, 63, 77.

23. "The Question Box, Fr. Hurley," *San Francisco Monitor*, February 3, 1961; "Old and New Ex-Priests," *Our Sunday Visitor*, November 12, 1922. See also Lea, *History of the Inquisition*, 4:106, 139.

24. On Hitchcock's Catholicism and its enduring impact on his work, see Richard A. Blake, *Afterimage: The Indelible Catholic Imagination of Six American Filmmakers* (Chicago: Loyola Press, 2000), chap. 3; and Edward White, *The Twelve Lives of Alfred Hitchcock: An Anatomy of the Master of Suspense* (New York: Norton, 2021), chap.12. Patricia Hitchcock married Joseph O'Connell, grandnephew of Cardinal William O'Connell, the archbishop of Boston from 1907 to 1944. On the many forms of cinematic presentation of Catholic characters, see

Anthony Burke Smith, *The Look of Catholics: Portrayals in Popular Culture from the Great Depression to the Cold War* (Lawrence: University Press of Kansas, 2010).

25. A detailed summary of the plot is available in Blake, *Afterimage*, 54–68.

26. "Our Question Box," *HPR* 65 (October 1964): 84–85. On the application of general Catholic sacramental theology to confession, see Peter E. Fink, ed., *New Dictionary of Sacramental Worship* (Collegeville, MN: Liturgical Press, 1900), 1052–1064. See also Davis, *Moral and Pastoral Theology: A Summary*, 287, 307.

27. *Law & Order*, season 8, episode 1, "Thrill," aired September 24, 1997, on NBC; *Law & Order*, season 12, episode 11, "The Collar," aired January 9, 2002, on NBC.

28. This case may be followed in reports in the *New York Times*. See in particular "Gigante Holds Firm to Cleric's Privilege," August 30, 1977; "Councilman Gigante's Privilege to Silence as a Priest is Upheld," August 31, 1977; "Court Says Priest's Confidentiality is Limited to Talks with Penitent," May 9, 1979; "Father Gigante Starts Serving 10-Day Contempt Term," October 20,1979; and "The City: Gigante Is Released," October 26, 1979. The priest died in 2022: "Louis Gigante, Priest Who Led South Bronx Revival, Dies at 90," *New York Times*, October 23, 2022.

6. Psychology

1. On Luce and his influence, see Alan Brinkley, *The Publisher: Henry Luce and His American Century* (New York: Knopf, 2010); and David A. Hollinger, *Protestants Abroad: How Missionaries Tried to Change the World but Changed America* (Princeton, NJ: Princeton University Press, 2017), esp. 24–33.

2. *Life*: "The Age of Psychology," January 7, 1957, 68–82; "The Tools Psychologists Invented," January 14, 1957, 106–120; "The Psychologist's Service in Solving Daily Problems," January 21,1957, 84–102; "Unlocking the Mind in Psychoanalysis," January 28, 1957, 118–132; and "Where Does Psychology Go From Here?" February 4, 1957, 68–88. The series, revised and slightly expanded, was

subsequently compiled into a single volume by Ernest Havemann, *The Age of Psychology* (New York: Simon and Schuster, 1957).

3. Havemann, "The Age of Psychology," *Life*, January 7, 1957, 80, 82; and Havemann, "Unlocking the Mind in Psychoanalysis," *Life*, January 28, 1957, 120. On Menninger, see "Are You Always Worrying?" *Time*, October 25, 1948, 69–70. On the rapid adoption of psychology among Protestant clergy, see E. Brooks Holifield, *A History of Pastoral Care in America: From Salvation to Self-Care* (Nashville, TN: Abingdon Press, 1983), esp. chaps. 6 and 7.

4. "Sheen Denounces Psychoanalysis," *New York Times*, March 10, 1947. See also Thomas C. Reeves, *America's Bishop: The Life and Times of Fulton J. Sheen* (San Francisco: Encounter Books, 2001), 197–203.

5. "Treatment of Sin Lies Outside Psychiatry, CU Cleric Says," *Washington Post*, November 7, 1950.

6. William J. McGarry, "Freud Has Passed On and Freudianism Also Dies," *America*, October 7, 1939, 607; John C. Ford and Gerald Kelly, *Contemporary Moral Theology* (Westminster, MD: Newman Press, 1958), 1:203. The fullest history of Catholic responses, positive and negative, to modern psychology is Robert Kugelmann, *Psychology and Catholicism: Contested Boundaries* (New York: Cambridge University Press, 2011). On the Catholic understanding of the role of conscience, see Peter Cajka, *Follow Your Conscience: The Catholic Church and the Spirit of the Sixties* (Chicago: University of Chicago Press, 2021).

7. Charles Menig, "The Priest's Attitude Toward Psycho-analysis: Its Theory and Practice," *Ecclesiastical Review* 75 (August 1926): 120 and 121; untitled limerick in *Integrity* 1. no. 4 (January 1947): 13; *The Catholic Encyclopedia: An International Work of Reference on the Constitution, Doctrine, and History of the Catholic Church*, ed. Charles George Herbermann, special ed. (New York: Encyclopedia Press, 1913), s.v. "psychotherapy." The author of the encyclopedia entry was James J. Walsh, a New York physician, who also published a book on the subject (*Psychotherapy* [New York: Appleton, 1912]), which stressed the connections between mental and physical health.

8. Menig, "The Priest's Attitude Toward Psycho-analysis," 113; Richard Galen, "'Mental Health' v. Religion," *The Priest* 16 (July 1960): 611.

9. "Sheen Denounces Psychoanalysis"; Ernest Miller, *The Why and How of Catholic Confession* (Liguori, MO: Liguorian Pamphlets, 1957), 7; "Ode to a Psychiatrist," *Integrity* 1, no. 4 (January 1947): 43.

10. On Pace and Moore, see C. Kevin Gillespie, *Psychology and American Catholicism: From Confession to Therapy?* (New York: Crossroad, 2001), 32–45; and Kugelmann, *Psychology and Catholicism*, 79–82, 92–97; on Walters, see Gillespie, *Psychology and American Catholicism*, 69–81. For another, somewhat mercurial pioneer in this period, see Paula M. Kane, "Confessional and Couch: E. Boyd Barrett, Priest-Psychoanalyst," in *Crossings and Dwellings: Restored Jesuits, Women Religious, American Experience, 1814–2014*, ed. Kyle B. Roberts and Stephen R. Schloesser (Leiden: Brill, 2017), 409–453.

11. Kugelmann, *Psychology and Catholicism*, 271–274; and Robert Kugelmann, "Out of the Ghetto: Integrating Catholics in Mainstream Psychology in the United States After World War II," *History of Psychology* 12 (August 2009): 201–226. See also Gillespie, *Psychology and American Catholicism*, 64–68. On Bier, see "William C. Bier, S.J.: A Testimonial," *Catholic Psychological Record* 1, no. 1 (Spring 1963): 3–5; the *Record* was published from 1963 to 1968.

12. William C. Bier, "Psychological Testing of Candidates and the Theology of Vocation," *Review for Religious* 12 (1953): 291–304; and Bier, "Practical Requirements of a Program for the Psychological Screening of Candidates," *Review for Religious* 13 (1954): 13–27.

13. "Directory of U.S. Roman Catholic Seminaries and Religious Houses of Formation with a Summary of Statistics, September 1, 1963," Records of the National Catholic Educational Association, Seminary Division, ACUA, box 79; Bier, "Practical Requirements," 16; John C. Ford, "Religious Superiors, Subjects and Psychiatrists," Catholic Theological Society, *Proceedings of the Seventeenth Annual Convention* (June 25–28, 1962), 65–129. Ford's essay, with the same title, was subsequently published and distributed as a pamphlet. The observation that Catholic analysts and theologians "tended to shy away" from sexuality is in Gillespie, *Psychology and American Catholicism*, 106.

14. Walter J. Coville, "Basic Issues in the Development and Administration of a Psychological Assessment Program for the Religious Life," in *Assessment of Candidates for the Religious Life: Basic Psychological*

Issues and Procedures, eds. Walter J. Coville, et al. (Washington, DC: Center for Applied Research in the Apostolate, 1968), 7 and 33–34; John F. Muldoon, "The Role of the Psychologist as a Consultant to Religious Communities," *Catholic Psychological Record* 3, no. 1 (Spring 1965): 39; Richard P. Vaughan, "A Psychological Assessment Program for Candidates to the Religious Life: Validation Study," *Catholic Psychological Record* 1, no. 1 (Spring 1963): 69–70; Paul VI, "Sacerdotalis caelibatus," no. 63, in Claudia Carlen, ed., *The Papal Encyclicals, 1958–1981* (Wilmington, NC: McGrath, 1981), 203–221.

15. See the sample evaluation reports in *Assessment of Candidates for the Religious Life*, appendices C and D.

16. The fullest account is Edward E. Thornton, *Professional Education for Ministry: A History of Clinical Pastoral Education* (Nashville, TN: Abingdon Press, 1970); see also Stephanie Muravchik, *American Protestantism in the Age of Psychology* (New York: Cambridge University Press, 2011), esp. part one; and E. Brooks Holifield, *God's Ambassadors: A History of the Christian Clergy in America* (Grand Rapids, MI: Eerdman's, 2007), 241–242, 247–248, and 283–284. For the experience of a CPE pioneer, see Porter French, "Innocents Abroad: Clinical Training in the Early Days," *Journal of Pastoral Care* 29 (March 1975): 7–10.

17. For the Catholic adoption of CPE, see Gerald G. Daily, "Toward a Pastoral Theology Program," *Review for Religious* 25 (1966): 836–852; James Michael Lee, "Overview of Educational Problems in Seminaries: II—Administration," in *Seminary Education in a Time of Change*, ed. by James Michael Lee and Louis J. Putz, (Notre Dame, IN: Fides Publishers, 1965), 124–127; and Brian Francis Kelly, "The Minister of the Sacrament of Penance and the Pastoral Skills of Clinical Pastoral Education" (MTS thesis, St. John's Seminary, Boston, 1977). Kelly's thesis includes the transcript of a verbatim on pages 9–13.

18. Menig, "The Priest's Attitude Toward Psycho-analysis," 121; Galen, "'Mental Health' v. Religion," 604–612; John J. O'Rourke, "Collaboration of Priest and Psychotherapist," *American Ecclesiastical Review* 149 (October 1963): 217–228; Walter J. Smith "Psychoanalysis and Pastoral Counseling," *American Ecclesiastical Review* 153 (August 1965): 82–95; Richard Vaughan, "The Neurotic Religious," *Review for Religious* 17 (1958): 271–278; Richard Vaughan, "Severe Mental Illness

Among Religious," *Review for Religious* 18 (1959): 25–36; Thomas Hennessy, "A 'Do It Yourself' Course in Counseling," *Jesuit Educational Quarterly* 26 (March 1964): 230–233.

19. On the coursework and majors in psychology in Newton and Boston, see *Newton College of the Sacred Heart Catalog, 1960–1961*, 30, and *Boston College Fact Book, 1975*, 49, both available at libguides.bc.edu /universityarchives/primary. For the development of professional psychology at Boston College, see James F. Moynihan, "Reflections of a Departmental Chairman: Retrospect and Prospect," *Catholic Psychological Record* 1, no. 2 (Fall 1963): 43–45; and John R. McCall, "Philosophy and Psychology at Boston College," *Catholic Psychological Record* 1, no. 2 (Fall 1963): 47–51.

20. The comparisons of priests and psychologists are in Quentin Donoghue and Linda Shapiro, *Bless Me, Father, For I Have Sinned: American Catholics Speak Out About Confession* (New York: Primus, 1984), 232; and *U.S. Catholic* Surveys, AUND, 3/09.

21. "Our Question Box," *MSH* 68, no. 3 (March 1933): 77; "Our Question Box," *MSH* 74, no. 9 (September 1939): 73; "Sign Post," *Sign* 37, no. 4 (November 1957): 63; "Sign Post," *Sign* 33, no. 3 (October 1953): 48.

22. Student notes in Noldin, no. 427, BLBC; "Sign Post," *Sign* 37, no. 4 (November 1957): 63; "St. Paul's College, Class Notes, 1963–1967," PFA; "Our Question Box," *MSH* 81, no. 1 (January 1946): 63; Dermot Casey, *The Nature and Treatment of Scruples: A Guide for Directors of Souls* (Westminster, MD: Newman Press, 1948), 7; "Questions of the Month," *MSH* 86, no. 11 (November 1951): 67. On general confession, more likely to be practiced by priests and religious than by the laity, see Henry Davis, *Moral and Pastoral Theology: A Summary* (New York: Sheed and Ward, 1952), 317–318.

23. James H. Murphy, *When You Go to Confession* (Paterson, NJ: St. Anthony's Guild, 1941), 7; William Schaefers, "Our Tie-Up With Purgatory," *The Priest* 7 (November 1951): 838; *Confession: Its Fruitful Practice* (Clyde, MO: Benedictine Convent of Perpetual Adoration, 1953), 9–10; unidentified newspaper clipping in JFP, box 14, folder 5; and Bernard A. Sause, *I Have Sinned: Helps for Adult Lay Persons to Confess Worthily* (St. Meinrad, IN: Grail Publications, 1952), 26.

24. Thomas Verner Moore, *Personal Mental Hygiene* (New York: Grune and Stratton, 1949), 35–36, 40; Charles A. Curran, "The Personality Dynamics of Scrupulosity," *Catholic Psychological Record* 1, no. 2 (Fall 1963): 33; George Hagmaier and Robert W. Gleason, *Counselling the Catholic: Modern Techniques and Emotional Conflicts* (New York: Sheed and Ward, 1959), 151, 161–162; their endorsement of Alcoholics Anonymous is in chapter 6. See also Smith, "Psychoanalysis and Pastoral Counseling," 95.

25. Thomas Tobin, "The Tangled Torment of Scrupulosity," *Liguorian* 51 (October 1963): 14–20.

26. *Scrupulous Anonymous*: "Our Motto" (March 1964); "Like Yourself" (June 1964); "How to Keep Your Children from Becoming Scrupulous" (July 1964); untitled survey report (March 1965); "Ten Commandments for the Scrupulous" (January 1975). The magazine, always four pages, was not paginated.

27. Victor White, "The Analyst and the Confessor," *Commonweal* 48, no. 15 (July 23, 1948): 347; John B. Sheerin, *Confession: Peace of Mind* (New York: Paulist Press, 1951), 9; "Sign Post," *Sign* 41, no. 8 (April 1962): 49.

28. White, "The Analyst and the Confessor," 349; Marc Oraison, "The Psychoanalyst and the Confessor," trans. by James Greene, *Cross Currents* 8 (1958): 374; James H. VanderVeldt and Robert P. Odenwald, *Psychiatry and Catholicism*, 1st ed. (New York: McGraw-Hill, 1957), 237; Erik Berggren, *The Psychology of Confession* (London: Brill, 1975), 196 and 113; Hagmaier and Gleason, *Counseling the Catholic*, 53 and 175.

29. Karl Menninger, *Whatever Became of Sin?* (New York: Hawthorn Books, 1973), 46, 188, 228. See also Philip Rieff, *The Triumph of the Therapeutic: Uses of Faith after Freud* (New York: Harper and Row, 1966), 245; and Christopher Lasch, *The Culture of Narcissism: American Life in an Age of Diminishing Expectations* (New York: Norton, 1979), 13.

7. Collapse

1. For an overview of Highland Park in its heyday, see Works Progress Administration, *Michigan: A Guide to the Wolverine State* (New York: Oxford University Press, 1941), 289–295.

2. The weekly schedule and other activities are taken from the parish newspaper, the *St. Benedict Weekly*, December 18, 1949, copy in Birney Family Papers, BHL, box 4. Basic statistics on the parish are available throughout the period from the *Official Catholic Directory* (New York: P. J. Kenedy).

3. For St. Moses, see https://www.aodfinder.org/parishes/7735. On the resistance to African Americans among Catholics in Detroit and elsewhere, see John T. McGreevy, *Parish Boundaries: The Catholic Encounter with Race in the Twentieth-Century Urban North* (Chicago: University of Chicago Press, 1996). On the closure of parishes, see Leslie Woodcock Tentler, *Seasons of Grace: A History of the Catholic Archdiocese of Detroit* (Detroit: Wayne State University Press, 1990), 520–521.

4. Shirley Saldahna et al., "American Catholics—Ten Years Later," *Critic* 33, no. 2 (January-February 1975): 14–21; Jim Castelli and Joseph Gremillion, *The Emerging Parish: The Notre Dame Study of Catholic Life Since Vatican II* (San Francisco: Harper and Row, 1987), table 16 on 145, 148. William V. D'Antonio et al., *American Catholic Laity in a Changing Church* (Kansas City, MO: Sheed and Ward, 1989), table 3.1; William V. D'Antonio et al., *American Catholics: Gender, Generation, and Commitment* (Walnut Creek, CA: Alta Mira Press, 2001), fig. 3.2; Federation of Diocesan Liturgical Commissions (FDLC), Executive Committee Report (1977), FDLC Records, ACUA, box 1.

5. Julester Shrady Post, "Confessors," *Sign* 14, no. 2 (September 1934): 106; Paul A. Stauder, *The Other Side of the Confessional* (St. Louis: The Queen's Work, 1962), 19; Dorothy Dohen, "An Inquiry on Confession and Spiritual Direction," *Integrity* 9, no. 1 (October 1954): 26; Quentin Donoghue and Linda Shapiro, *Bless Me, Father, For I Have Sinned: American Catholics Speak Out About Confession* (New York: Primus, 1984), 224.

6. "Sign Post," *Sign* 46, no. 4 (November 1966): 62; "Communications from Our Readers," *HPR* 65, no. 9 (June 1965): 718–720; Frank Quinliven, "Decline of Confession," *The Priest* 28, no. 2 (March 1972): 54.

7. Sally Cunneen, *Sex: Female; Religion: Catholic* (New York: Holt, Rinehart and Winston, 1968), 58–59, 64, and table 4 on 65; Donoghue and Shapiro, *Bless Me, Father*, 236; unidentified woman in *U.S.*

Catholic Surveys, AUND, 24/16; unidentified man, *U.S. Catholic* Surveys, AUND, 24/16.

8. Hugh Calkins, *Youth and Confession* (Chicago: Claretian Publications, 1967), 17–18; *U.S. Catholic* Surveys, AUND, 3/08, 24/16, and 9/15.

9. *New Saint Joseph's Daily Missal and Hymnal* (New York: Catholic Book Publishing Co., 1966), 1382; "Sign Post," *Sign* 47, no. 10 (May 1968): 45; Doris Donnelly, "The Problem with Penance," *America* 128, no. 14 (April 14, 1973): 324; man from Iowa, *U.S. Catholic* Surveys, AUND, 24/16; Michael Scanlan, *The Power of Penance: Confession and the Holy Spirit* (Notre Dame, IN: Ave Maria Press, 1972), 27; Hugh Calkins, *How to Make a Good Confession* (Chicago: Claretian Publications, 1966), 17.

10. J. B. Gremillion, "Thinking Parishioners," *Social Order* 6 (June 1956): 253; "Sign Post," *Sign* 48 no. 6 (January 1969): 33; unidentified man in *U.S. Catholic* Surveys, AUND, 24/16.

11. The historical scholarship on the council is vast. The best overviews of its work and impact are John W. O'Malley, *What Happened at Vatican II* (Cambridge, MA: Belknap Press of Harvard University Press, 2008), and Joseph P. Chinnici, *American Catholicism Transformed: From the Cold War Through the Council* (New York: Oxford University Press, 2021). For the council's texts, see Walter M. Abbott, ed., *The Documents of Vatican II*, (New York: Guild Press, 1966), the quotation from the statement on liturgy is at 143.

12. The best account of this new spirit within the church as it played out among Catholic lay people is Colleen McDannell, *The Spirit of Vatican II: A History of Catholic Reform in America* (New York: Basic Books, 2011), for the "little parishes," see 166–168. For the broad "pedagogy of participation" that came to characterize the church in this period, see Joseph P. Chinnici, "The Catholic Community at Prayer, 1926–1976," in *Habits of Devotion: Catholic Religious Practice in Twentieth-Century America*, ed. James M. O'Toole (Ithaca, NY: Cornell University Press, 2004), 9–87.

13. Hugh J. O'Connell, *Putting Vatican II into Practice* (Liguori, MO: Liguorian Pamphlets, 1966), 70; McDannell, *Spirit of Vatican II*, 115–116, 198, 230, chap. 7. On the outsized role of Friday abstinence and its

place in the larger penitential system of the church, see Maria C. Morrow, *Sin in the Sixties: Catholics and Confession, 1955–1975* (Washington, DC: Catholic University of America Press, 2016), esp. chap. 5.

14. For a useful summary of some of these findings regarding Catholics, see Robert D. Putnam and David E. Campbell, *American Grace: How Religion Divides and Unites Us* (New York: Simon and Schuster, 2010), 137–141; see also Michele Dillon, *Catholic Identity: Balancing Reason, Faith, and Power* (New York: Cambridge University Press, 1999).

15. For the minimal references to confession during the council, see *Documents of Vatican II*, 161, 418–419. For the idea of "defecting in place," see David Gibson, *The Coming Catholic Church: How the Faithful are Shaping a New American Catholicism* (New York: HarperCollins, 2004), 65–66.

16. Bernard A. Sause, *I Have Sinned: Helps for Lay Persons to Confess Worthily* (St. Meinrad, IN: Grail Publications, 1952), 34.

17. John C. Ford and Gerald Kelly, *Contemporary Moral Theology*, vol. 2 (Westminster, MD: Newman Press, 1963), 277; Francis Lee, *The Priest's Side of the Confessional* (Liguori, MO: Liguorian Pamphlets, 1960), 7; *These Are Our Seven Deadly Sins* (St. Louis: Knights of Columbus, 1964), 18; Henry Frank, *A Guide to Confession* (Huntington, IN: Our Sunday Visitor, 1941), 27–28; Dominic Pruemmer, *Birth Control* (New York: Paulist Press, 1933), 17–18.

18. For these societal shifts in attitude, see Leslie Woodcock Tentler, *Catholics and Contraception: An American History* (Ithaca, NY: Cornell University Press, 2004), 78, 134–136; for the changing Catholic view of rhythm in particular, see 174–189. See also John T. Noonan, *Contraception: A History of Its Treatment by the Catholic Theologians and Canonists* (Cambridge, MA: Belknap Press of Harvard University Press, 1965) and, for a general history of the subject, Linda Gordon, *Woman's Body, Woman's Right: A Social History of Birth Control in America* (New York: Grossman, 1976).

19. Sally Cunneen, *Sex: Female; Religion: Catholic* (New York: Holt, Rinehart and Winston, 1968), 120–121, 67; "Sign Post," *Sign* 48, no. 6 (January 1969): 52; unidentified woman in *U.S. Catholic* Surveys, AUND, 3/08.

20. This striking dialogue is in Tentler, *Catholics and Contraception*, 243; for the Chicago priest's views, see Michael P. Cahill, *Catholic Watershed: The Chicago Ordination Class of 1969 and How They Helped Change the Church* (Chicago: In Extenso Press, 2014), 305. On the formation of conscience by lay people, see Peter Cajka, *Follow Your Conscience: The Catholic Church and the Spirit of the Sixties* (Chicago: University of Chicago Press, 2021), esp. chap. 4.

21. Woman from Massachusetts in *U.S. Catholic* Surveys, AUND, 3/08. See also the responses to a 1965 survey of married couples in Robert McClory, *Turning Point: The Inside Story of the Papal Birth Control Commission and How Humanae Vitae Changed the Life of Patty Crowley and the Future of the Church* (New York: Crossroad, 1997), chap. 10.

22. Albert H. Dolan, *All the Answers about Marriage and Birth Control* (Englewood, NJ: Carmelite Press, 1937), 4–5; "Answers to Questions," *American Ecclesiastical Review* 152 (February 1965): 141–142; J. D. Conway, *What They Ask About Birth Control* (Notre Dame, IN: Ave Maria Press, 1955), 13; "Sign Post," *Sign* 48, no. 3 (October 1968): 22.

23. The story of the commission, the draft reports, and the encyclical has been told in many places. See particularly, McCrory, *Turning Point*, esp. chap. 12–13, and Tentler, *Catholics and Contraception*, 225–228, 264–265. On Ford's role, see Eric Marcelo O. Genilo, *John Cuthbert Ford: Moral Theologian at the End of the Manualist Era* (Washington, DC: Georgetown University Press, 2007), 139–149.

24. Mrs. Jeanne-Marie Vecsey to Lawrence Shehan, October 20, 1968; Mr. and Mrs. W. F. Jones to Shehan, November 4, 1968; Annette Armetta to "Dear Sirs," July 31, 1968; and Sister Margaret Robert Farrell to Shehan, [November 1968]: all in Lawrence Shehan Papers, Humanae Vitae, Archives, Archdiocese of Baltimore.

25. Rev. F. R. Podgorski to Shehan, November 4, 1968, and O'Boyle's "Pastoral Instruction . . . in Regard to Humanae Vitae," August 31, 1968: both in Shehan Papers, Humanae Vitae, Archives, Archdiocese of Baltimore. The story of the dissenting Washington priests is told in detail in Cajka, *Follow Your Conscience*, chap. 4. See also James Patrick Shannon, *Reluctant Dissenter: An Autobiography* (New York: Crossroad, 1998).

26. Copy of letter, Karl Meister to O'Boyle, October 10, 1968, and James Laubacher to Shehan, [November 1968]: both in Shehan

Papers, Humanae Vitae, Archives, Archdiocese of Baltimore; National Opinion Research Center, *The Catholic Priest in the United States: Sociological Investigations* (Washington, DC: U. S. Catholic Conference, 1972), table 6.20.

27. Bernard Häring, *The Law of Christ: Moral Theology for Priests and Laity*, trans. Edwin G. Kaiser, vol. 1 (Paramus, NJ: Newman Press, 1966), ix,370; Michael Scanlan, *The Power of Penance: Confession and the Holy Spirit* (Notre Dame, IN: Ave Maria Press, 1972), 22; Felix Funke, "Survey of Published Writings on Confession over the Past Ten Years," in *Sacramental Reconciliation*, ed. Edward Schillebeeckx (New York: Herder and Herder, 1971), 120. On Häring and his influence, see Charles E. Curran, *Catholic Moral Theology in the United States: A History* (Washington, DC: Georgetown University Press, 2008), 93–99. For the parallel shift among Protestant theologians from sins (plural) to sin (singular), see Andrew S. Finstuen, *Original Sin and Everyday Protestants: The Theology of Reinhold Niebuhr, Billy Graham, and Paul Tillich in an Age of Anxiety* (Chapel Hill: University of North Carolina Press, 2009), chap. 1.

28. William F. Allen, "Second Thoughts on Sin," *The Priest* 28, no. 5 (June 1972): 49; John Carmody, "Modern Sin: God and Man From a New Perspective," *The Priest* 24, no. 11 (November 1968): 843; John Gallen to Thomas Gumbleton, [1972], Thomas Gumbleton Papers, AUND, 11/02; *HPR* 70 (April 1970): 553–554.

29. Susan M. Mountin, "What Readers Think about the New Confession, *U.S. Catholic* 42, no. 5 (May 1977): 24–27; man from Philadelphia in *U.S. Catholic* Surveys, AUND, 3/08; Cunneen, *Sex: Female; Religion: Catholic*, 61; "Sign Post," *Sign* 47, no. 1 (August 1967): 48–49; "Questions of the Month," *MSH* 98, no. 11 (November 1963): 51–52.

30. Doris Donnelly, "The New Rite of Penance: A Place to Meet God and Neighbor," *Sign* 55, no. 7 (April 1976): 22; Robert R. Earl, *Confession: Christ's Power Declares Peace* (Liguori, MO: Liguorian Pamphlets, 1970), 10; John Gallen comments on draft statement on penance, 1972, Thomas Gumbleton Papers, AUND, 11/02; John R. Reedy, "Sin—Personal and Social," Federation of Diocesan Liturgical Commissions, *The New Rite of Penance: Background Catechesis* (Pevely, MO: FDLC, 1975), 12; *Manual for the Penitent* (New York: Pueblo, 1976), 16–17.

31. Joseph T. Nolan, *Confession: A New Look and a New Service* (Chicago: Claretian Publications, [1968]), 3–4; Hugh Calkins, *How to Make a Good Confession* (Chicago: Claretian Publications, 1976), 16; "The New Penance," *Commonweal* 99, no. 2 (March 1, 1974); man from Wisconsin in *U.S. Catholic* Surveys, AUND, 24/16.

32. Karl Menninger, *Whatever Became of Sin?* (New York: Hawthorn Books, 1973), 224; Engelbert Schwartzbauer, *Forgiveness of Sins in Current Catholic Practice*, trans. Gregory J. Rottger (Collegeville, MN: Liturgical Press, 1976), 9–10; Eamon Tobin, *How to Forgive Yourself and Others: Steps to Reconciliation* (Liguori, MO: Liguorian Publications, 1983), 13–14; W. F. McKee, *Am I Being Punished for Past Sins?* (Liguori, MO: Liguorian Pamphlets, 1962), 15.

33. Florence Wedge, *God and Your Sins* (Pulaski, WI: Franciscan Publishers, 1959), 12.

34. The schedule for Immaculate Conception parish in Everett, Massachusetts, given in the collection of parish bulletins in AABo, shows the typical overlap of Mass and confession on Saturdays. For the Confiteor prayer and the expression of forgiveness, see *New Saint Joseph Daily Missal and Hymnal* (New York: Catholic Book Publishing, 1966), 647; the precise wording of these prayers changed over time, but the essence remained the same. On changing attitudes toward the Eucharist, see "Sign Post," *Sign* 48, no. 2 (May 1969): 25; John Gallen comments on draft statement on penance, 1972, Gumbleton Papers, AUND, 11/02; nun quoted in Donoghue and Shapiro, *Bless Me, Father*, 286; and man from Tennessee in *U.S. Catholic* Surveys, AUND, 9/15.

35. Robert P. O'Neill and Michael A. Donovan, *Psychological Development and the Concept of Mortal Sin* (Chicago: Franciscan Herald Press, 1965), 14, 31–32; Archdiocese of Detroit, Religious Education Office, "Questionnaire for Evaluation of First Communion/First Confession Practice" [1972], copy in Thomas Gumbleton Papers, AUND, 11/02; St. Columban's parish, Birmingham, Michigan, "Survey, Opinions of Parents," copy in Gumbleton Papers; Nolan, *Confession: A New Look*, 7. The entire controversy over the age for first confession is reviewed in Patrick W. Carey, *Confession: Catholics, Repentance, and Forgiveness in American* (New York: Oxford University Press, 2018), 235–241.

36. "A Letter from the Vatican: First Penance/First Communion," *Origins* 7, no. 2 (June 2, 1977): 17–20; letter from Cardinal Augustin Mayer to Archbishop John May, December 20, 1986, copy in Dearden Papers, AUND, 12/08.

37. F. Sottocornola, *A Look at the New Rite of Penance*, trans. Thomas A. Krosnicki (Washington, DC: United States Catholic Conference, 1975) provides a timeline of the revision process; see p. 5 for the "happier" assessment. For other contemporaneous discussions, see Joseph M. Champlin, *Preparing for the New Rite of Penance: A Homily and Teaching Guide* (Notre Dame, IN: Ave Maria Press, 1975), and *The Sacrament of Reconciliation: An Invitation to Peace* (Pittsburgh: Archconfraternity of Christian Mothers, 1975). For the hopeful assessment of the rite's possible impact, see Joseph T. Nolan, "An Ordinary Sinner's Guide to the New Confession," *U.S. Catholic* 42, no. 3 (March 1977): 11, and for disappointment over the slow approval of the document, see George McCauley, "The Next New Rite of Penance," *America* 134, no. 13 (April 3, 1976): 280–283. The official texts, together with explanatory notes are in *The Rite of Penance* (New York: Pueblo Publishing Company, 1975).

38. Woman from Maine in *U.S. Catholic* Surveys, AUND, 24/16; *HPR* 70 (August 1970): 878–880; Charles E. Miller, *Love in the Language of Penance: A Simple Guide to the New Rite of Penance* (New York: Alba House, 1976), 14; Christopher Farrell, *What You Should Know About the Sacrament of Penance* (Liguori, MO: Liguori Publications, 1976), 12; "Is the New Confession Working?" *U.S. Catholic* 42, no. 11 (November 1977): 27–33; man from New York, *U.S. Catholic* Surveys, AUND, 9/14.

39. John Gallen, "Penance as Ritual," in *The New Rite of Penance: Background Catechesis* (Pevely, MO: Federation of Diocesan Liturgical Commissions, 1975), 43–44; "Is the New Confession Working?" *U.S. Catholic*; Nolan, "An Ordinary Sinner's Guide to the New Confession," 6; Castelli and Gremillion, *Emerging Parish*, 147.

40. A full description and the texts of the services, together with some of the preparatory documentation, is in Carroll Dozier, *A Call to Reconciliation* (Memphis, TN: Diocese of Memphis, 1976).

41. The Vatican letter and Dozier's response are in "General Absolution: Were the Norms Followed in Memphis?" *Origins* 7, no. 1 (May

26, 1977): 1–4; see also Salvatore J. Adamo, "Inquisition by Any Other Name," *National Catholic Reporter*, June 3, 1977, and *The Rite of Penance* (New York: Pueblo Publishing Company, 1975), xxii. The hesitancy to promote general absolution services more widely is seen in Federation of Diocesan Liturgical Commissions (FDLC), Executive Committee Minutes, May 9, 1977, and Board of Directors Minutes, June 6–9, 1977, FDLC Records, ACUA, boxes 3 and 1, respectively. For a useful summary of this entire case, see Carey, *Confession*, 241–246.

42. D'Antonio et al., *American Catholics: Gender, Generation, and Commitment*, table 4.4; Dean R. Hoge et al., *Young Adult Catholics: Religion in a Culture of Choice* (Notre Dame, IN: University of Notre Dame Press, 2001), table 9.1. See also Brian T. Joyce, *Penance: Parent and Child* (New York: Sadlier, 1974), 39.

8. Revelations

1. The long history of the church's awareness of this problem is sketched in Thomas P. Doyle, A. W. Richard Sipe, and Patrick J. Wall, *Sex, Priests, and Secret Codes: The Catholic Church's 2000-Year Paper Trail of Sexual Abuse* (Los Angeles: Volt Press, 2006). See also James A. Brundage, *Medieval Canon Law* (New York: Longman, 1995), esp. 90–93; and Stephen Haliczer, *Sexuality in the Confessional: A Sacrament Profaned* (New York: Oxford University Press, 1996).

2. Documentation for the case of Father Theodore Metcalf consists of a single ten-line notation, in the hand of Archbishop John Williams, dated November 20, 1889, in the file of Clergy Disciplinary Cases, 1880–1907 (RG III.A.03), AABo; see also "Changes Among Boston Priests," *Boston Pilot*, June 7, 1890.

3. A very useful chronology of the exposure of abuse is given in James T. O'Reilly and Margaret S. P. Chalmers, *The Clergy Sex Abuse Crisis and the Legal Responses* (New York: Oxford University Press, 2014), 411–422. The early, unenforced policy recommendations to the bishops are contained in Doyle, Sipe, and Wall, *Sex, Priests, and Secret Codes*, 99–174.

4. National Review Board for the Protection of Children and Young People, *A Report on the Crisis in the Catholic Church in the United*

States (Washington, DC: United States Conference of Catholic Bishops, 2004). O'Reilly and Chalmers, *Clergy Sex Abuse Crisis*, considers the legal issues surrounding statutes of limitations (61–69, 101–102) and mandatory reporting (96–98, 113–119). For the work of survivors, see Brian J. Clites, "Breaking the Silence: The Catholic Sexual Abuse Survivor Movement in Chicago" (PhD diss., Northwestern University, 2015).

5. All data are taken from *The Nature and Scope of Sexual Abuse of Minors by Catholic Priests and Deacons in the United States, 1950–2002* (Washington, DC: United States Conference of Catholic Bishops, 2004); see especially the executive summary, 3–7. On the abuse of girls and young women, see Doris Reisinger, "Reproductive Abuse in the Context of Clergy Sexual Abuse in the Catholic Church," *Religions* 13 (2022): 198–218; see also Kathleen M. Sands, "Clergy Sexual Abuse: Where Are the Women?" *Journal of Feminist Studies in Religion* 19, no. 2 (Fall 2003): 79–83.

6. *Nature and Scope of Sexual Abuse*, tables 3.5.7, 4.4.1, 4.5.3. Reisinger, "Reproductive Abuse," describes the procuring of abortions in cases of pregnancy.

7. Julie Zauzmer, Michelle Bornstein, and Dana Hogpeth, "Cardinal Theodore McCarrick, Former Archbishop of Washington, Accused of Sexual Abuse and Removed from Ministry," *Washington Post*, June 20, 2018; Ruth Graham, "Former Cardinal McCarrick Found Unfit for Trial Over Sexual Abuse," *New York Times*, August 30, 2023.

8. Kathleen L. McChesney, "The Charter Report Card: Have the Bishops Lived Up to the Promises Made in Dallas?" in *Sexual Abuse in the Catholic Church: A Decade of Crisis, 2002–2012*, ed. by Thomas G. Plante and Kathleen L. McChesney (Santa Barbara, CA: Praeger, 2011), 65–78. See also the chapter by Karen J. Terry, Katarina Schuth, and Margaret Leland Smith, "Incidence of Clerical Sexual Abuse Over Time: Changes in Behavior and Seminary Training Between 1950 and 2002," 17–30.

9. Bishop Accountability (https://www.bishop-accountability.org) is a searchable public website. The following examination of abuse in confession would have been impossible without it. Citations from these files, all of them accessed between 2020 and 2022, will be identified as

BA, followed by the priest's name. I am particularly grateful to Terry McKiernan, who maintains the site and who is himself preparing a more detailed study of confession and abuse.

10. Mrs. Robert Burns to Richard Cushing, April 14, 1970, BA: Shanley; see also "Catholic Gays Claim Diocese Ignores Them," *Boston Globe*, August 29, 1982; and "Priest's Transfer Indicates Strife on Homosexuality," *New York Times*, April 25, 1979. On Murphy, see "Vatican Declined to Defrock U.S. Priest Who Abused Boys," *New York Times*, March 20, 2010.

11. "Roman Catholic Clergy Sexual Abuse of Children in Colorado from 1950 to 2019: Special Master's Report," October 22, 2019, pp. 223–224, BA: Sciose; John McCormack memo to file, March 18, 1991, BA: Burns. See also "Archdiocese Faces Suit over Alleged Abuse," *Boston Globe*, September 11, 1998. For examples of abuse in confession in England, Ireland, and elsewhere, see John Cornwell, *The Dark Box: The Secret History of Confession* (New York: Basic Books, 2014), chap. 10.

12. On Cotter, see "Forensic Psychological Consultation, December 23, 1993," BA: Cotter-2. On Haynes, see "Priest, 55, already facing child porn and molestation charges forced a teenage girl to perform oral sex on him while in the confessional,'" London *Daily Mail*, March 4, 2015, copy in BA: Haynes. On O'Friel, see Pennsylvania Attorney General, "A Report of the Thirty-Seventh Statewide Investigatory Grand Jury," 2016, pp. 87–88, BA: OFriel. See also *Awful Disclosures by Maria Monk of the Hotel Dieu Nunnery of Montreal* (New York: Maria Monk, 1836), 21.

13. On Cudemo, see "Philadelphia Investigating Grand Jury Report into Allegations of Clergy Sexual Abuse in the Archdiocese of Philadelphia," September 21, 2005, p. 130, copy in BA: Cudemo. On Gondek, see "Catholic Leaders in Charlotte, Raleigh Allowed Priests to Continue Ministry Despite Abuse Reports," WBTV (Charlotte, NC) report, September 6, 2018, transcript in BA: Gondek. See also Heribert Jone, *Moral Theology*, trans. Urban Adelman (Westminster, MD: Newman Press, 1962), no. 431, 587.

14. On Lambert, see "Abuse Testimony Made Public," *Sioux Falls Argus-Leader*, February 27, 1993, copy in BA: Lambert; on Feely, see "Man Sues over Alleged 1969 Rape by Priest," *Chicago Tribune*,

February 24, 2006, copy in BA: Feely; on Grear, see "Lawsuit Accuses Diocese of Lafayette of Covering Up Clergy Abuse," WIBC radio (Indianapolis) report, September 27, 2018, transcript in BA: Grear.

15. On Nassar, see "Maroney, Describing Abuse, Calls Doctor a 'Monster of a Human Being,'" *New York Times*, January 19, 2008; on Hastert, see "J. Dennis Hastert Is Sorry for Past 'Transgressions,' Lawyer Says," *New York Times*, April 6, 2016.

16. For these and other facile explanations, see Thomas G. Plante, "Clergy Sexual Abuse in the Roman Catholic Church: Dispelling Eleven Myths and Separating Facts from Fiction," *Spirituality in Clinical Practice* 7, no. 4 (December 2020): 220–229.

17. Undated statement (signed "Prisoner of Love") in BA: Robert Meffan; Pius XI, "Ad Catholici Sacerdotii," *The Papal Encyclicals, 1903–1939*, ed. Claudia Carlen (Wilmington, NC: McGrath Publishing, 1981), paragraphs no. 16 and no. 22; Archdiocese of Boston, *A Guide: Ordination to the Priesthood* (Brighton, MA: St. John's Seminary, 1962), 33; Julie Hanlon Rubio and Paul J. Schutz, *Beyond "Bad Apples": Understanding Clergy Perpetrated Sexual Abuse as a Structural Problem and Cultivating Strategies for Change* (Santa Clara, CA: University of Santa Clara, 2022). The language of reduction is in Jone, *Moral Theology*, no. 638.

18. The fullest description and analysis of priestly training is Joseph M. White, *The Diocesan Seminary in the United States: A History from the 1780s to the Present* (Notre Dame, IN: University of Notre Dame Press, 1989).

19. For the seal/wax analogy, see Robert E. Sullivan, "Beneficial Relations: Toward a Social History of the Diocesan Priests of Boston, 1875–1944," in *Catholic Boston: Studies in Religion and Community, 1870–1970*, ed. Robert E. Sullivan and James M. O'Toole (Boston: Archdiocese of Boston, 1985), esp. 217–219. The behavioral expectations of seminarians are outlined in *The Common Rule of St. John's Seminary, Brighton* (Boston: St. John's Seminary, 1946), 4 and 5; and in *The Common Rule of St. John's Seminary* (Boston: St. John's Seminary, 1964), 6. Acceptance of the enduring apartness of the clergy is described in National Opinion Research Center, *The Catholic Priest in the United States: Sociological Investigations* (Washington, DC: United States Catholic Conference, 1972), table 6.1. See also Donn J. Drucker, "An

'Aristocracy of Virtue': Cultural Development of the American Catholic Priesthood, 1884–1920s," *Religion and American Culture* 21, no. 2 (Summer 2011): 227–258.

20. Servants of the Paraclete assessment report, July 17, 1984, and [name redacted] to Thomas Daily, May 12, 1984, BA: Forry; Margaret Gallant to Humberto Medeiros, August 10, 1982, and Medeiros to Gallant, August 20, 1982, BA: Geoghan Addendum. For the "invisible backdrop," see Rubio and Schutz, *Beyond "Bad Apples,"* 2.

21. "Questions of the Month," *MSH* 86, no. 11 (November 1951): 67. On the priest's authority with the scrupulous, see Chapter 7.

Conclusion

1. Andrew Greeley, *The Catholic Imagination* (Berkeley, CA: University of California Press, 2000); Robert A. Orsi, *History and Presence* (Cambridge, MA: Belknap Press of Harvard University Press, 2016).

2. Quoted in Robert McClory, *Turning Point: The Inside Story of the Papal Birth Control Commission, and How Humanae Vitae Changed the Lives of Patty Crowley and the Future of the Church* (New York: Crossroad, 1997), 122.

3. For a summary of these efforts, see Patrick W. Carey, *Confession: Catholics, Repentance, and Forgiveness in America* (New York: Oxford University Press, 2018), 247–269.

4. Bernhard Poschmann, *Penance and the Anointing of the Sick* (New York: Herder and Herder, 1964), 123, 135–136.

Acknowledgments

A book this long in the making leaves its author with many debts, not all of which can be properly acknowledged and some of which, irresponsibly enough, cannot now be remembered. The idea had its origins more than two decades ago, and a start was even made on a couple of chapters before other projects intruded. I am well pleased with both of the books those interruptions produced and am happy, too, that retirement from teaching—together, providentially, with the enforced isolation of pandemic—brought me back to confession, so to speak. It had all begun with the "Catholicism in Twentieth-Century America" project, sponsored by the Cushwa Center for the Study of American Catholicism at the University of Notre Dame. The smart and congenial colleagues in my working group at that time—Scott Appleby; Joseph Chinnici, OFM; Paula Kane; Margaret McGuinness; Leslie Woodcock Tentler—helped to convince me that it was indeed possible to study the practice of confession. More recently, the Cushwa Center's "Gender, Sex, and Power" project helped me grapple with the difficult matter of clergy sexual abuse. In those discussions, the participation and the wisdom of Terry McKiernan of Bishop Accountability were crucial, bringing to light evidence long and carefully hidden from public view but essential in engaging that sad subject. What is here represents only a beginning of what will necessarily be the long task of coming to terms with those tragic cases historically.

As is usual in an effort like this, archivists and librarians have quite literally made it all possible. "No archives, no history," some wise scholar (Leopold von Ranke?) is supposed to have said, a truth no less true in a digital age than it was when we were all hopelessly analog. The rich holdings that provided the evidence for this work include especially the Burns Library of Boston College, whose Liturgy and Life Collection (particularly its trove of pamphlets) documents the thick religious culture of American Catholics; the library of the School of Theology and Ministry of Boston College; archives at the Catholic University of America, at Georgetown University, and at the University of Notre Dame; the Archives of the Archdiocese of Boston and those of other American sees; the Bentley Historical Library of the University of Michigan. Two archives have moved since I first used them, but their resources are happily still available. The archives of the New England Province of the Society of Jesus (containing the highly informative papers of the moral theologian John Ford) were expertly cared for by the College of Holy Cross; they are now in the Jesuit Archives and Research Center in St. Louis. The detailed mission chronicles of the Paulist Fathers (the Missionary Society of St. Paul the Apostle) were in Washington, DC, and are now in New York City. This book could not have been written without the generous assistance and the genuine friendship of the people in all these repositories, and I am grateful for both.

The staff at Harvard University Press are responsible for bringing the actual book into existence. At the beginning of our conversations, Andrew Kinney expressed his enthusiasm for the idea, and that enthusiasm has been more than matched by Emily Silk, who has offered keen insights and has overseen the review and production process. Kathi Drummy guided me through the difficulties of assembling the accompanying photographs, no small task since there are few photos of people going to confession. Stephanie Vyce offered sage counsel about the uncertain terrain of copyright and fair use. Every effort has been made to identify copyright holders and to obtain their permission for the use of copyright material. Notification of any additions or corrections that should be incorporated in future reprints or editions of this book would be greatly appreciated. Thanks, too, for the skilled copyediting of Katrina Vassallo, and for the very helpful comments of the Press's two anonymous readers.

It is the fate of a writer's friends to be dragooned into reading drafts and listening to extended monologues, and I have rounded up the usual suspects for those purposes here. Lynn and Richard Cox read the entire manuscript in pieces, and our conversations—often conducted as we sat and watched the tide come in and out in Maine—helped me think through more carefully what I wanted to say. Tim Meagher was full of ideas, as always, reminding me to look for connections between the ethereal world of religious belief and the real lives of real people. Two readers of first attempts at understanding confession and what it meant are unfortunately no longer here to see the final product, but their early encouragement helped sustain and reassure me that I was on the right track: RIP, John O'Malley, SJ, and Thomas Tentler. Finally, there must be (or ought to be) a rule that a history major always make friends with an English major and hang on for life. Paul Ginnetty has read and improved virtually everything I have ever written. The dedication of this book to him scarcely begins to express my gratitude for the length and depth of our friendship.

Index